The Social Context of Learning and Development

The Social Context of Learning and Development

Edited by

John C. Glidewell

THE UNIVERSITY OF CHICAGO

GARDNER PRESS, Inc., New York

Distributed by HALSTED PRESS

A Division of JOHN WILEY & SONS, Inc.

New York · Toronto · London · Sydney

GARDNER PRESS, INC.
32 Washington Square West
New York, New York 10011

Distributed solely by the HALSTED PRESS Division of
John Wiley & Sons, Inc., New York

Library of Congress Cataloging in Publication Data
Main entry under title:

The Social context of learning and development.

1. Educational sociology—Addresses, essays,
lectures. I. Glidewell, John C.
LC191.S654 370.19'3 76-8867
ISBN 0-470-15078-5

1 2 3 4 5 6 7 8 9

Book Design by Raymond Solomon

Printed in the U.S.A. by
NOBLE OFFSET PRINTERS INC.
New York, N. Y. 10003

Contributors

Bruno Bettelheim Former director, Sonia Shankman Orthogenic School, and Stella M. Rowley Professor Emeritus of Educational Psychology and Professor Emeritus of Psychology and Psychiatry, The University of Chicago.

Bertram J. Kohler Associate professor of Education and Human Development, The University of Chicago.

David H. Gallant Assistant professor, Department of Psychiatry, Tufts Medical School.

Enid Gamer Graduate student, Department of Psychology, Boston University.

J. W. Getzels Wendell Harrison Distinguished Service Professor of Education and Behavioral Sciences, The University of Chicago.

John C. Glidewell Professor of Education and Social Psychology, The University of Chicago.

Henry V. Grunebaum Associate clinical professor of Psychiatry, Harvard Medical School.

Philip W. Jackson David Lee Shillinglaw Distinguished Service Professor of Education and Behavioral Sciences, and Chairman of the Department of Education, The University of Chicago.

Kenneth Kaye Assistant professor of Education, The University of Chicago.

Frederick F. Lighthall Associate professor of Education and Chairman of the Educational Psychology Faculty, The University of Chicago.

Jacquelyn Sanders Director, Sonia Shankman Orthogenic School and Lecturer in Education, The University of Chicago.

Diana T. Slaughter Assistant professor of Education and Human Development, The University of Chicago.

Justin L. Weiss Assistant clinical professor of psychology, Harvard Medical School, and Chief, Clinical Psychology Service, Massachusetts Mental Health Center.

Joseph M. Wepman Professor of Education, Cognition and Communication, and Surgery, The University of Chicago.

Acknowledgements

This work is the outcome of the combined efforts of such a number of people that full acknowledgement is simply impossible. The efforts of Allison Clarke-Stewart were especially enabling. Dorothea Meroz bore the brunt of typing.

Acknowledgement is made of the generous permission of the *School Review* to reprint the chapters by Bettelheim and by Getzels; the permission of the Meredith Corporation and Stuart Golann to reprint the chapter by Glidewell; the permission of G. S. Lesser and Scott Foresman to reprint the chapter by Jackson.

Contents

The Social Context of Learning and Development

CHAPTER ONE

On the Analysis of Learning in a Social Context

John C. Glidewell

Most animals learn. However it is that learning proceeds—whether by imitation, by reinforcement, by association, or by cognitive reorganization,—most animals show stable behavior changes parallel to their interaction with their environment. In addition, the human animal is particularly adept at transferring learning from one generation to the next. Humans teach, thus accumulating a culture over many generations. The process of transfer of learning across generations is fundamentally a social process, requiring communication and interaction:—an *exchange* of ideas, feelings, and skills.

Social institutions, as the teacher-pupil role set in schools, have evolved to enable and enhance the transfer of learning across generations. Educational institutions also limit, to varying degrees, the social power of educators to exploit the young or to endanger the core beliefs of the culture. The institutions are considered the influencing agents; the children are the influenced learners. But that consideration overlooks some of the realities of social life. Social interaction is necessarily a two-way process. Each participant has some influence on the others. The pupil has some influence on the teacher, the child on the parent, the family on the school, the school on the family. The social power process is rarely symmetrical in amount of influence actually exerted, but it is equally rarely just a one-way process.

If the institutionalized transmission of culture is a circular, mutually influencing process, how is it to be analyzed? Where on the circle does one begin? What is antecedent and what is consequence? The chapters that follow represent attempts to find answers to these questions, and each in its search raises new, more revealing questions.

The classroom has been the salient unit of analysis for most educational researchers. In the next chapter Getzels looks at classrooms with an informed perspective, and he explicates clearly how classrooms are both consequences and antecedents of evolving beliefs about learners and learning.

> The images of habitation that people envision are expressions of their visions of themselves. Churches are expressions not only of man's vision of God but of man's vision of man. They represent not only conceptions of places for worshipping but also conceptions of the worshipper. The classrooms we envision for our children represent not only conceptions of spaces for learning but also our conceptions of the learner.
>
> And the dwellings, churches, and classrooms we create also create us. The classrooms we build for our children are not only places where lessons intended by the teacher are taught. These classrooms teach lessons of their own; they tell the child who he is supposed to be (or at least who we think he is) and how he is supposed to learn.

Following Getzel's analysis of classrooms, Jackson delves into the way teachers think. Clearly, the classroom is the teacher's domain. Self-contained, isolated, its boundaries carefully protected, the classroom has been created by and for teachers. The professional life of the teacher is almost totally contained by the walls of this isolated, active, fast-moving, arena in which the teacher *must* make one professional decision after another, and in a few seconds. With speed often far surpassing that of computers, teachers draw from their experience and intuition particular actions aimed to teach a particular child. Learning experiences are created in classrooms, often for one child with other children all around. But all of them also respond in some way, each child with a different kind and degree of involvement.

In such classrooms teachers usually avoid rigorous intellectual analysis of what they do. They must act on fragments of knowledge, experience, and intuition. They must focus on individuals within a group; they must value intuition; they must maintain an unflagging optimism; and they must cope with their doubts about the true impact of their work. Jackson explains just why they must think as they do, and he presents his explanations with the empathy and understanding of his many years as a teacher watcher.

Sanders adds a psychoanalytic dimension to classrooms. In preschool classrooms she observed "unnoticed details" that were giving messages to children about how they should behave: (1) single-file lines, distances prescribed at rest time, one-at-a-time in speaking and receiving snacks—all signal the utility of individual isolation; (2) the teacher's white skirt, the emphasis on cleanliness and neatness—all signal the unacceptability of impulses. At another level of the educational institution Sanders records her experiences in seminars of student teachers. The recurrent themes were: (1) the novice in the role of the authority, a juxtaposition with its accompanying expectation of both precise professional action and awareness of pervading uncertainty; (2) the shock to the teacher of her own anger in response to aggression by children, and (3) the ambivalence underlying professed objectives, such as spontaneity in group participation. Sanders then turns to the insight that understanding one's self is a necessary condition for understanding children and their stages of development. Thus, she opens another view of the circular, mutually influencing cycle of teacher-child-environment interaction.

As Sanders shows, classrooms exist in schools and are constantly influenced, as subtly as may be, by the schools they comprise. Lighthall and Zientek address the school as a unit of analysis and explore a role for a psychologist in a school. They give an analytic account of their experiences in a girls' parochial high school. Lighthall was the external consultant, Zientek the internal social-psychological specialist. They recorded and analyzed the issues addressed by the school's administrative council and found a dramatic discrepancy between the importance assigned to issues by the council and the amount of time spent discussing the issues. Least important issues tended to be discussed most. They present as a model their approach to reporting these data to the council, the council's search for the explanation of the discrepancy, and the role of the consultant in the interchange. Their model sets out a new role for social psychologists who focus on the whole school as the salient unit of the educational institution.

"Wouldn't it be nice if all children could begin their learning in school in a relaxed mood that a good meal in good company creates?" With that question Bruno Bettelheim begins his characteristically adroit and discerning analysis of the psychological connections between food for the body and food for the mind.

On the Analysis of Learning

> School is the first great encounter of the child with society. It represents to him society and what it stands for — Thus, it is even more important that we convince . . . children from the moment they come into contact with society that it both gives and demands, and gives first before it demands. And there is no more obvious giving to the child than the giving of food.

The learner, the teacher, the classroom, the school—all in their roles but all in a community of families. Diana Slaughter focusses on yet another point of mutual influence: the family, the child, the school, and back through the child to the family. She followed 56 children and 40 of their mothers from a summer Head Start program in 1965 to their school experiences in 1971, generally in fourth grade. From a broad and complex set of data Slaughter shows how families are affected by a child's schooling and how a child's schooling is affected by a child's family. She concludes that "We need programs that simultaneously emphasize the ecology of home and school contexts, if they are to influence patterns of achievement socialization. We need to consider the reciprocal interactions between the child and all his significant others."

Taking a similar but more specialized view, Cohler and his colleagues look especially at attention dysfunctions of children of mentally ill mothers and children of well mothers. They focus on dramatic disturbances in a most significant other, the child's mother. Their findings lead them to highlight a mother's differentiating her own needs from those of her child and fostering a sense of separateness in children. Both factors appear to enhance both a child's cognitive field independence and a child's social-psychological differentiation.

Still focusing on cognitive activity, Wepman presents a hypothetical model of levels of functioning in the central nervous system. His model explicates the modality-bound nature of the inputs and outputs in the process of transmission of culture, especially its mode of communication. Some children develop vision first, others audition, others the tactile mode. An approach to children is most effective if it is in their most developed modality, but a distinct lag in the development of a modality requires a flexibility of approach to all modalities.

Kaye reports an intriguing analysis of mother-infant dyads in which mothers tried to teach their six-month-old infants to reach around a transparent barrier to get a toy. By attention to subtle cues and an astute analysis of sequences of actions, Kaye shows that the infants controlled the timing of the alternations in the mothers' approaches to teaching. In addition, the basic strategy of each mother was seen to grow out of her observations of the child's approach to the problem prior to her teaching. Even at six months of age, an infant's influence on a mother's actions are considerably more extensive than the stereotype of the helpless infant would allow.

In the final chapter is an analysis of the helping subsystems created by educational institutions and societies to cope with individuals who do not accept the transmission of culture, who are hard to teach, who behave badly or strangely. Here, as in the foregoing, the analysis is systemic: the explications of cycles of mutually influencing actions, each interdependent with the others. Such is the morphogenesis of learning in a social context.

CHAPTER TWO

Images of the Classroom and Visions of the Learner

J. W. Getzels

Almost within sight of my office are four school buildings. In one, dating from the turn of the century, the spaces called classrooms are rectangular in shape, the pupils' chairs are firmly bolted to the floor in straight rows, and the teacher's desk is front and center. In the second building, dating from the 1930s, the classrooms are square, the pupils' chairs are movable into various patterns around the room, and the teacher's desk is out of the way in a corner. In the third building, dating from the 1950s, the classrooms are also square, but the pupils' movable desks are now trapezoidal in shape, so that when they are placed next to each other they make a circle, and the teacher's desk has vanished! In the fourth building, there is a classroom, constructed a year or so ago, that is four times the size of the ordinary classroom. It has no teacher's or pupils' desks at all but is filled instead with odds and ends, from fish bowls and birds' nests to drawing boards and Cuisinaire rods. If one were not told it was a classroom, this space might be mistaken for an overgrown playroom or a warehouse full of children's paraphernalia.

I am grateful to Professor Benjamin D. Wright, who contributed valuable comments on an earlier draft of the paper.

Reprinted with permission from the *School Review*, 1974, *82*, 527–540.

Images of the Classroom

I shall refer to the spaces in the first building as the "rectangular" classroom, in the second as the "square" classroom, in the third as the "circular" classroom, and in the fourth as the "open" classroom.

Since architectural space or form presumably follows from the function for which it is intended, and since the function—teaching and learning—is presumably the same for all four classrooms, why are there these obvious differences among them? More specifically, is there some reason for the succession of rectangular, square, circular, and open classroom forms, or was this succession accidental? Indeed, there is the more fundamental question: Why does any classroom have a *particular* architectural form?

If one looks into the classrooms in operation, the differences often seem to disappear. The movable chairs are placed in straight rows and the trapezoidal desks are lined up behind one another rather than joined in the circle for which they were designed. In one renovated classroom I visited the movable chairs were placed exactly on the bolt marks left by the fixed chairs they had supplanted. But that is not my problem. Despite the usage, the design of the altered classroom had obviously been *not* to have straight rows. The problem is how to account for the standard straight-row classroom symbolized by the original bolted school chair and for the images (if not always actualities) of the altered classrooms symbolized by the changing school chair.

The form of the standard straight-row American classroom is usually attributed to three sources. One was the nineteenth-century tradition of building and architecture; since the typical shape of a building was rectangular, the simplest layout of rooms in the building was also rectangular. A second source was the physical requirements for lighting, ventilation, and ease of entry and egress of 30 or so children in a restricted space. As Sommer states, "The typical long, narrow shape resulted from the desire to get light across the room."[1] The third source was the curricular and pedagogical philosophy that emphasized discipline and the teacher's gaining the attention of the pupils. "The straight rows tell the students to look ahead and ignore everyone except the teacher."[2]

The alterations in the subsequent forms are attributed to transformations in these factors. As traditions in building and architecture changed, so did the structure of the classroom.[3] Modifications in the physical requirements for lighting, ventilation, and safety of access and departure were also reflected in the architecture of the classroom.[4] And, of course, changes in educational programs and philosophies and in methods and materials—the introduction of team teaching, television, computer-aided instruction—required alterations in the size and contours of the classroom. "The most radical departures from straight-row layout are found in schools utilizing open-plan architecture for team teaching."[5]

The role of physical and pedagogical factors in establishing the original image of the classroom and in contributing to changes in that image cannot be minimized, nor is it my intention to do so. But there is another factor, albeit a less manifest one, that may ultimately be a more decisive determinant of the images of the classroom. This is the vision, the conception, that is held of the learner.

Just as it is impossible to understand differences between the Catholic cathedral and the Congregational prayer house or between the Lutheran church and the Quaker meeting room as spaces for worship by looking only at the traditions of building and architecture or the physical requirements for habitation, or even the materials and methods of the litanies, without considering also the different visions they reflect of man as worshipper, so it is impossible to understand the rectangular, square, circular, and open classroom as spaces for learning without considering the different beliefs and conceptions—the visions—of the child as learner.

RECTANGULAR CLASSROOM: EMPTY LEARNER

At the turn of the century a dominant conception of the child as learner was that he was cognitively an "empty organism" responding more or less randomly to stimulation, and characteristically learning when specific responses were connected with specific stimuli through the mediation of pleasure or pain.[6] The organism itself, it was believed, would do nothing to learn or think if it were not impelled to such activity by primary drives like hunger or thirst or by externally applied motives like reward and punishment. Experimenters in the laboratory were connecting correct responses of animals to puzzle boxes by giving or withholding food, and teachers in the classroom were connecting correct responses of children to problem cards by giving or withholding approval.

In pointing to this aspect of the turn-of-the century view of the learner, I do not mean to derogate the historic achievement of the connectionist formulation of learning. But the essential point remains: a conception of the learner as an ideationally empty organism associating discrete stimuli and responses through the operation of rewards and punishments under the control of the teacher. Both the stimulus—what was supposed to be learned—and the response—what was actually learned—were believed to be determined by the teacher.

It was no accident that the materials and methods of instruction and the form of the classroom were teacher-centered. The teacher was necessarily placed in front of the classroom—sometimes on a dais or platform—and the pupils in chairs rigidly fastened to the floor in straight rows facing forward so they would not turn away from the only source of the learning experience: the teacher. Given this contemporary vision of the learner, what could be a more eminently practical and sensible image of the ideal learning environment? Indeed, there is a letter by John Dewey dating from this period in which he complains that when he was trying to equip his new school according to his different conception of child as learner, he was unable to find any other kind of classroom furniture.[7]

SQUARE CLASSROOM: ACTIVE LEARNER

How then did we evolve from the apparently sensible and practical rectangular classroom with the teacher's desk up front and the pupils' chairs bolted to the floor in straight rows (and all that this symbolizes) to the apparently equally sensible and practical but almost opposite classroom with no teacher's desk and the pupils' chairs movable all over the place (and all that *this* symbolizes)?

This transformation did not occur because someone suddenly happened to have a bright idea that a change in the physical appearance of the classroom might be a good thing, or that rooms with movable chairs might assure better lighting and ventilation, or that children might be easier to discipline in movable chairs than in fixed chairs (if anything, the reverse is true). Nor was it demonstrable that children in the new movable chairs learned better than in the old rigid chairs. Unquestionably, a multitude of factors contributed to the transformation—those that have already been mentioned as well as others, especially the general progressive movement in political and social thought.[8] But another factor that is too often overlooked was fundamental, namely, a modification in the conception of the child, and more specifically of the child as learner.

It became evident that the earlier vision of learners did not account for a large proportion of the behavior observed in the learning situation. Learners did not seem to experience what they were to learn as discrete stimuli; instead, they often insisted on seeing discrete stimuli as "belonging together," as making a configuration, or Gestalt. They saw three discrete dots placed in a certain relation to each other as a single triangle, two open brackets facing each other as one rectangle. Two pieces of information given separately by the teacher were brought together by the learners into a single idea not given by the teacher in the separate pieces.[9]

Moreover, personality theory was postulating that human beings were not psychologically empty organisms. On the contrary, they were tumultuous bundles of needs, values, persuasions, projections, repressions, and conscious, preconscious, and unconscious psychic forces that determined behavior. What learners would and would not respond to, what they would and would not learn, were seen as determined by these forces. When individuals with different values were required to respond to words some of which were consonant with their values and others not, they responded more rapidly to the former than to the latter,[10] and when they were required to learn material favorable and unfavorable to their persuasions, they recalled what was favorable and forgot what was unfavorable.[11]

The vision of the learner as an empty organism was transformed into a vision of the learner as an *active* organism. Learning was conceived of not only as a connective process but as a dynamic cognitive and affective process as well. From this point of view the learner—not the teacher—became the center of the learning process. It was the learner rather than the teacher who determined both the stimulus—what was to be learned—and the response—what was learned. Experimenters in the learning laboratory became concerned with the relation between the learner's personality and his learning, and the teacher in the classroom with the learner's needs and his adjustment in the learning situation.

It was no accident that the image of the ideal classroom took on a new conformation. The teacher-centered classroom became the pupil-centered classroom. The teacher's desk was moved from the front of the room to the side, and the pupils' rigid chairs in straight rows, which had seemed so sensible and practical from the older point of view, became quaint if not primitive objects and were replaced by movable chairs that could be shifted at will, according not only to the requirements of the teacher but, even more important, to the needs of the pupil.

CIRCULAR CLASSROOM: SOCIAL LEARNER

If the vision of the learner in the initial period was predominantly as an empty organism and in the next as an active organism, in the period that followed it was as a social organism. The beliefs regarding the nature of the learner in the first period drew heavily from the associationist view of the human being, in the second from the Gestalt and personalistic views; later they also drew from the emerging social psychological and group dynamics views.

The child as learner was envisioned as a social organism, and learning was perceived as occurring through interpersonal actions and reactions, each person in the classroom serving as a stimulus for every other person. It is hard to overemphasize the impact on the classroom of the "group climate" concepts and studies by Lewin and his associates beginning in the late 1930s, which were given added cogency by the ideological issues of World War II.[12] Innumerable treatises, textbooks, and programs applied these ideas and findings to the classroom, and such terms as "authoritarian," "democratic," and "laissez-faire" became, for good or ill, integral parts of the educational vocabulary. Experimenters in the learning laboratory became concerned with such previously unheard-of matters as "interpersonal cohesion" and "small group processes," and teachers in the classroom with "sociometric structure" and "group dynamics."

Concomitant changes in the image of the ideal classroom could again be observed. If the child is primarily a social organism, then the objectives of his education should be primarily social in character. And if learning is a social or group process, then a circular or group-centered classroom where everyone faces everyone else (as once they had been forced to face only the teacher) is the most sensible and practical, even necessary, learning environment. And this indeed became a favorite image of the classroom.[13]

OPEN CLASSROOM: STIMULUS-SEEKING LEARNER

We come now to the present. I have been stressing the dissimilarities among the preceding conceptions of the learner. There was, however, a critical similarity among them that is in retrospect even more significant. The preceding visions of the learner had this basic *paradigm* in common: they were founded on a combination of the homeostatic model of self-maintenance and the drive- or tension-reduction theory of behavior.[14]

According to this paradigm, the organism's natural state is conceived to be equilibrium, and the organism always acts in such a way as to return to this optimum natural state. Hunger produces tensions driving the organism to seek food, and when it has eaten it ceases to seek food; fear produces tensions driving the organism to seek cover or to flee, and when the danger is over it ceases to seek cover or to flee; lack of cognitive closure produces tensions driving the organism to seek closure, and when the gap is filled it ceases to seek closure; conscious or unconscious conflict produces tensions driving the organism to seek resolution, and when the conflict is resolved it ceases to seek resolution. With respect specifically to learning (or thinking, problem solving, and other forms of intellectual activity), the organism is similarly said to be driven (we call it "motivated" in education). As Hilgard describes this position, "Without drives the organism does not behave and hence does not learn."[15] Learning always involves the reduction of a drive, a decrease in tension and stimulation.

There has been a growing discontent with this paradigm of behavior, at least as it is applied to learning and other forms of intellectual activity. To be sure, learning, thinking, problem solving, and intellectual exploration may be means for reducing certain drives. Yet they may also be ends in themselves, as the organism seeks to *increase* as well as to decrease stimulation.

It is surprising that we have come to this altered view of the learning organism only so recently. One of the most obvious features of animal behavior, as Robert White points out, is the tendency to explore the environment. In his words, "Cats are reputedly killed by curiosity, dogs characteristically make a thorough search of their surroundings, and monkeys and chimpanzees have always impressed observers as ceaseless investigators."[16] In a series of illuminating experiments, Harlow and his co-workers have shown that monkeys who are viscerogenically sated—that is, not hungry, thirsty, or otherwise driven by any recognizable primary drive—will tend to unassemble a puzzle of some complexity for no other apparent motive than the "privilege of unassembling it."[17] The behavior of the animals in learning to solve the puzzles reduced no drives, decreased no identifiable tension or stimulation. Far from trying to reduce tension or stimulation, the animals seemed to seek stimulation; once they had learned to solve one puzzle, they seemed to become bored and turned spontaneously to solving a different puzzle.

Images of the Classroom

Conceptions of the human learner based on experiments with animals are a dubious enterprise, and using the hungry animal in a maze as the analogue of the child in a classroom has already proved misleading. But the recent discontent with the drive-reduction paradigm has not been restricted to animal behavior. Piaget, Hunt, and White among others point out that the central fact in the growth and development of children is not hunger satisfaction or thirst satisfaction or some other so-called primary drive satisfaction but the opportunity for effective interaction with the environment, as manifested in the child's curiosity and exploratory activity.[18] A child whose bodily needs have been satisfied does not, as the homeostatic model would suggest, remain at rest. On the contrary, it is just then that the child's play is most vigorous and constructive. Moreover, a conspicuous portion of adult life is devoted to activities that can be classified only as "fine art," "basic science," "pure adventure"—activities which by no stretch of the imagination can be said to contribute to bodily maintenance through satisfying primary drives and attaining states of rest.[19]

Donald Hebb points to the significance not only of art, science, and adventure but of more common activities such as working at riddles, reading mystery stories, traveling to strange places, or exploring the unfamiliar, all of which also provide pleasure not by reducing some bodily drive but by raising the level of excitement.[20] The normal person, he argues, needs sensory stimulation for his well-being just as he needs food and shelter and will seek out such stimulation if it is not readily available.

Bexton, Heron, and Scott put this observation to experimental test.[21] They paid subjects handsomely "to do nothing." The subjects were well fed and comfortably housed. But there was one experimental condition: stimulation was minimized. Subjects could not see, hear, touch, or communicate with anyone. At first nothing happened; the subjects merely rested or slept. Soon, however, they became restless, could not sleep, and exhibited random behavior as if looking for something to do, problems to work on. The situation became so unbearable that it was impossible to keep the subjects in the experiment for more than two or three days despite the satisfaction of all their bodily needs and the pay for presumably doing nothing. On leaving, they reported feelings of intellectual disorganization, nausea, and fatigue. In short, normal, intelligent, adaptive behavior requires sensory input to cope with, an opportunity to seek out problems for solution.

Put most briefly, what seems to be at the core of our changing paradigm of the human being as learner is this: in addition to the familiar viscerogenic drives like hunger and thirst (on which many assumptions about the learner are based) that are satisfied by satiation, there seem to be as yet ill-defined neurogenic needs that are gratified by stimulation—needs for excitement, novelty, sensory variation, and perhaps above all for the challenge of the problematic.[22] From this point of view the human being as learner is not like a mechanical calculating or information-processing device that lies idle until it is sparked by some drive, stimulus, conflict, problem, or teacher goad; rather, the human being as learner is a vital entity perpetually in motion (even when apparently at rest) that must be given an effective opportunity to remain in motion if it is to function and continue to live. Human beings need not be driven to explore, to think, to learn, to dream, to seek out problems for solution; they are intrinsically constituted to do just this. The learner is not only a problem-solving and stimulus-reducing organism but also a *problem-finding* and *stimulus-seeking* organism.

The image of the open classroom is isomorphic with this vision of the learner.[23] Barth writes of his attempt to institute such a classroom in a traditional school and gives as the first assumption underlying the open classroom, "Children are innately curious and will explore without adult intervention";[24] and as the second assumption, "Exploratory behavior is self-perpetuating."[25]

The appropriate spatial organization of the classroom follows from this conception of the learner. In Barth's words:

> The teacher in the open classroom organizes his classroom not to produce optimal conditions for transmission of knowledge but to extend the range of possibilities children can explore. Children's desks are often removed from the room, and only chairs and tables are left. . . . Space within the classroom is divided, often by movable screens or furniture, into an "interest area." . . . While in the traditional classroom the child learns at his desk, in the open school *the locus of learning is where something of particular interest to the child happens to be.* [Italics in original][26]

This does not mean that all that needs to be done is to fill a space with odds and ends that *might* be interesting to children and let nature take its course. On the contrary, as Taylor points out in *Organizing the Open Classroom,* the arrangements and instruction in the new classroom require more rather than less teacher skill and attention.

Initially I characterized the new classroom in the fourth building as appearing haphazard and looking like a playroom or warehouse but not like a classroom. This is so only when I regard the arrangements in the light of the traditional visions of the learner. If I now regard these arrangements with a vision of the learner as a stimulus-seeking organism, what did not look like a classroom looks very much like an appropriate place for children to learn, appropriate for permitting them to seek out the stimulation they need for thinking and learning. Now it is the more familiar traditional classroom of sterile spaces and bare walls, straight rows and rigid chairs, that does not look like a classroom and seems an inappropriate place for learning.

The images of habitation that people envision are expressions of their visions of themselves. Churches are expressions not only of man's vision of God but of man's vision of man. They represent not only conceptions of places for worshipping but also conceptions of the worshipper. The classrooms we envision for our children represent not only conceptions of spaces for learning but also our conceptions of the learner.

And the dwellings, churches, and classrooms we create also create us. The classrooms we build for our children are not only places where the lessons intended by the teacher are taught. These classrooms teach lessons of their own; they tell the child who he is supposed to be (or at least who we think he is) and how he is supposed to learn. One classroom tells the child he is an empty organism learning through the operation of rewards and punishments at the command of the teacher; a second classroom tells him he is an active organism learning through the solution of problems that satisfy his needs; a third classroom tells the child he is a social organism learning through interactions with others; the fourth classroom tells him he is a stimulus-seeking organism learning because he intrinsically has to.

Our visions of human nature find expression in the buildings we construct, and these constructions in turn do their silent yet irresistible work of telling us who we are and what we must do. Our habits impel our habitations and the habitations impel our lives. Winston Churchill's observation during the debate on rebuilding the House of Commons after the war holds for the common school as well: "We shape our buildings and afterwards our buildings shape us."

Notes

1. R. Sommer, *Personal Space: The Behavioral Basis of Design* (Englewood Cliffs, N. J.: Prentice-Hall, Inc., 1969), p. 98.

2. *Ibid.*, p. 99.
3. Educational Facilities Laboratories, Inc., *The Cost of the Schoolhouse* (New York: Educational Facilities Laboratories, 1960), p. 38.
4. *Ibid.*, p. 34.
5. Sommer, p. 104.
6. Portions of this and succeeding analyses of the conception of the learner have appeared in J. W. Getzels, "Theory and practice in educational administration," in R. F. Campbell and J. M. Lipham (Eds.), *Administrative Theory as a Guide to Action*, (Chicago: Midwest Administration Center, 1960), pp. 37-58. See also J. W. Getzels, J. M. Lipham, and R. F. Campbell, *Educational Administration as a Social Process: Theory, Research, and Practice.* (New York: Harper, 1968).
7. Personal communication from Professor R. L. McCaul, Department of Education, University of Chicago.
8. See L. Cremin, *The Transformation of the School* (New York: Alfred A. Knopf, 1961). Also C. Bereiter, Moral alternatives to education, *Interchange* (1972), pp. 25–41, this argues that the recent changes in the school are due to the circumstance that "the march of freedom has caught up with education" (p. 27).
9. For a discussion of changes in views of the learner and of learning generally, see E. M. Segal and R. Lockman, Complex behavior or higher mental processes: Is there a paradigm shift? *American Psychologist* (1972),pp. 46-55. For a comparison of the connectionist and the Gestalt conceptions of the learner and of learning specifically, and their effects on the classroom from a Gestalt perspective, see M. Wertheimer, *Productive Thinking, Enlarged Edition* (New York: Harper, 1959).
10. L. Postman, J. S. Bruner, and E. McGinnies, Personal values as selective factors in perception, *Journal of Abnormal and Social Psychology* (1948), pp. 142–54.
11. A. L. Edwards, "Political frames of reference as a factor influencing recognition, *Journal of Abnormal and Social Psychology* (1944), pp. 34-50. See also J. M. Levine and G. Murphy, The learning and forgetting of controversial material, *Journal of Abnormal and Social Psychology* (1943), pp. 507–517.
12. K. Lewin, R. Lippitt, and R. K. White, Patterns of aggressive behavior in experimentally created "Social Climates," *Journal of Social Psychology* (1939), pp. 271–300.
13. The catch-words "empty organism," "active organism," and "social organism" for the learner, and "teacher-centered," "pupil-centered," and "group-centered" for the classroom are, of course, only shorthand designations to be used with utmost caution. The periods so demarcated were by no means so sharply defined as the necessarily schematic account unavoidably implies; at any given time it was a question of relative emphasis rather than the all-or-none presence or absence of a particular point of view. There is no implication of a one-to-one relation between the periodic modifications in the visions of the learner and the images of the classroom. Nonetheless, I cannot help observing that schools with rectangular, square, and circular classrooms were not constructed haphazardly but by and large appeared successively in the indicated periods.
14. See J. McV. Hunt, Experience and development of motivation: Some reinterpretations, *Child Development* (1960), pp. 489–504; R. W. White, "Motivation reconsidered: The concept of competence, *Psychological Review* (1949), pp. 297–333. See also J. W. Getzels, Creative thinking, problem-

solving, and instruction, in E. R. Hilgard, (Ed.), *Theories of Learning and Instruction,* 63d Yearbook of the National Society for the Study of Education, Part I (Chicago: University of Chicago Press, 1964), pp. 240–267, "The problem of interests: A reconsideration," in H. A. Robinson (Ed.), *Reading: Seventy-five Years of Progress* (Chicago: University of Chicago Press, 1966), pp. 97–106.

15. E. R. Hilgard, *Theories of Learning* (New York: Appleton-Century Crofts, 1948), p. 78.

16. White (n. 14 above), p. 298.

17. H. F. Harlow, Motivational forces underlying behavior, in Kentucky Symposium, *Learning Theory, Personality Theory, and Clinical Research* (New York: Wiley, 1954), pp. 36–53.

18. See J. Piaget, *The Origins of Intelligence* (New York: International Universities Press, 1952); *The Construction of Reality in the Child* (New York: Ballantine Books, 1954); also Hunt (n. 14 above); White (n. 14 above).

19. D. E. Berlyne, Curiosity and exploration, *Science* 153 (1966),: pp. 25–33.

20. D. O. Hebb and W. R. Thompson, The significance of animal studies, in G. Lindzey (Ed.), *Handbook of Social Psychology* (Reading, Mass.: Addison-Wesley, 1954), 1:227–234; D. O. Hebb, *The Organization of Behavior* (New York: Wiley, 1949), pp. 227–234.

21. W. H. Bexton, W. Heron, and T. H. Scott, Effects of decreased variation in sensory environment, *Canadian Journal of Psychology* (1954), pp. 70–76.

22. J. W. Getzels, Creative administration and organizational change: An essay in theory, in L. J. Rubin (Ed.), *Frontiers in School Leadership* (Chicago: Rand-McNally & Co., 1970), pp. 69–85.

23. See R. S. Barth, *Open Education and the American School* (New York: Agathon Press, 1972); also J. Taylor, *Organizing the Open Classroom* (New York: Schocken Books, 1972).

24. Barth, p. 18.

25. *Ibid.,* p. 19.

26. *Ibid.,* p. 74.

CHAPTER THREE

The Way Teachers Think

Philip W. Jackson

INTRODUCTION

Any attempt to describe the psychological attributes of such a large and diverse group of people as those who answer to the title "teacher" is almost doomed to failure from the start. This is so for at least two reasons. First, the sheer facts of size and diversity make it inevitable that whatever might be said about the "typical" member of such a group will prove to be untrue for a sizeable number of others within the same classification. Teachers are of many sorts—college instructors and nursery-school assistants, "good" teachers and "poor" teachers, novices and veterans. The variability among these subcategories would seem, at the outset, to defy all efforts to arrive at generalizations. Second, the goal of saying something about the *psychological* characteristics of such a group—its habits of thought and customary mental posture—makes the task doubly difficult. Cognition is a private affair, mirrored darkly, if at all, in what people say and do. Though it may be relatively easy to compute the average age of teachers or the range of their annual income, the task of describing their ways of thinking is infinitely more difficult—so difficult, in fact,

Reprinted with permission from G. S. Lesser (Ed.), *Psychology and Educational Practice*, New York: Scott Foresman, 1971, pp. 10-34.

that it seems the better part of wisdom to admit defeat before we begin.

Yet the importance of the topic eggs us on. Teaching, in the most fundamental sense, is a cognitive affair. It is the translation of thoughts and intentions into actions and words. Though we may study the teacher's movements and catalogue the fragments of his speech, the order to be found in these behavioral effects seems to have its source not in the behavior itself but in the mental events that accompany or precede it. Thus, to the extent that we wish to understand teaching, we are led inevitably to make some conjectures about the psychology of its practitioners, recognizing that obscurity and the danger of misinterpretation will dog us along the way.

In order to limit the scope of our inquiry, this essay will focus chiefly on the thinking habits of teachers of younger children—those who work in the elementary and primary grades. In addition to ensuring a more manageable task (though still one of awesome proportions), this limitation is prompted by both personal and theoretical considerations.

On the personal side, the author's experience in both research and practice (e.g., Jackson, 1968) has been concentrated at these lower levels of education, and these are the teachers and the classroom settings he knows best. But personal experience is by no means the only reason for choosing to concentrate on this level of education. From a more theoretical point of view there is much to be said for studying teachers of young children. In addition to being more numerous than their colleagues at other levels of schooling they are also likely to wield an unusually powerful influence over the lives of their pupils. This is so not only because the young child is more impressionable than his older brothers and sisters, but also because of the institutional arrangements that characterize our lower schools. The self-contained classroom, a form of organization typical in primary and elementary grades, ensures that the child's contact with his teacher will be sustained (approximately 1,000 hours a year) and often quite intimate. While it is not denied that high school teachers and college instructors often have a profound impact upon their students, children are first exposed to a pedagogical perspective through their relations with teachers in the lower grades. The timing and quality of this exposure heightens our interest in the adults involved in it.

In order to reduce the likelihood of misunderstanding, the speculative nature of much that will be said must be emphasized in advance. Though most of this speculation is based on interviews with many teachers and observations in their classrooms, it lacks the empirical exactitude which many readers might justifiably desire. The only excuse for this tentativeness is the lack of comprehensive and detailed studies on which more confident pronouncements will ultimately be based. The reader is advised to keep this *caveat* in mind as he proceeds.

The body of this chapter is divided into two main sections. In the first an attempt is made to identify some of the more salient characteristics of what has already been referred to as *the pedagogical perspective*. The second section focuses on the sources of this perspective, including, in particular, the ways in which it is supported and sustained (and sometimes threatened) by the facts of classroom life. The chapter concludes with some comments on the nature of the teacher's work and the efforts of those who would assist him in performing it.

THE PEDAGOGICAL PERSPECTIVE

Educational ideas command a respected position in the history of human thought. No account of our intellectual and social progress would be complete without them. Accordingly, as we consider how today's teachers view their work, it is appropriate to begin with some mention, though necessarily brief, of the heritage of competing beliefs and opinion with which some form of intellectual allegiance or ideological linkage might be established.

The Dichotomy of Educational Thought

Though there is a seemingly endless variety of viewpoints from which to examine educational purposes and procedures, much of this variability can be subsumed under a dual classification marking off two large and loosely organized families of educational thought.

The halves of this dichotomy have been crowned with a wide variety of descriptive labels, including *child-centered vs. teacher-centered, progressive vs. traditional, activity-oriented vs. subject-matter-oriented, and democratic vs. authoritarian,* to mention but a few. Doubtless there are important shades of meaning unique to each of these pairs of descriptive terms, but there is also considerable overlap among their separate meanings. We can, however, speak of them as representing two distinguishable, if not discrete, universes of educational discourse.

On the one side are ranked those goals and procedures in which the differences between education and other spheres of human activity are minimized. Educational experiences that are "meaningful" and "real" and closely linked to the pupils' needs and natural interests are emphasized. On the other side are ranked those goals and procedures in which the uniqueness of the school experience, particularly its intellectual character and its preparatory function, is the focus of concern. Concepts such as training, discipline, and mastery are central to this view.

The development and defense of the child-centered half of this dichotomy is associated with the writings of several prominent educational theorists, from Froebel, Pestalozzi, and Rousseau to Dewey, Kilpatrick, and Rudolph Steiner. Contemporary spokesmen whose writings lend support to variants of this perspective include A. S. Neill, Edgar Friedenberg, John Holt, and others of the so-called *romantic critics* of education, as well as several psychologists who have stressed the importance of the concept of *self* in human development. The works of Carl Rogers, Arthur T. Jersild, Arthur Coombs, and Abraham Maslow are prominent among the latter group. More popular treatments of the educational ideas connected with this view can be found in many contemporary novels, whose authors include John Hersey, Sylvia Ashton-Warner, and "Miss Read," as well as in several recent films, such as *Blackboard Jungle, Up the Down Staircase,* and *To Sir, with Love.*

Writings that lend support to the more traditional half of this dichotomy are relatively few in number and are not as salient as are those written in defense of the child-centered view. Often they are to be found embedded in larger philosophical works, such as the *Dialogues* of Plato and the treatises of some of the British empiricists, notably John Locke. Herbart is sometimes identified as one of the most prominent educational advocates of this position, though his work receives scant attention from modern educators.

Contemporary apologists for the traditional view tend to emerge from outside the ranks of practicing educators. Typically their arguments take the form of attacks against the alleged evils of progressive doctrines and methods as contrasted with more positive statements of a countervailing position. The critical writings of Rickover, Kerner, Barzun, Rafferty, Bestor, and others fall within this camp. In a somewhat more positive vein are the views of those psychologists who are particularly interested in the techniques of behavioral change. B. F. Skinner is clearly the most prominent member of the latter group, which would also include many of the proponents of behavioral objectives and programed materials in education, as well as some of the more recent advocates of formal training for the very young child—among them Carl Bereiter and Sigfried Englemann.

Such a rough-and-ready classification obviously does violence to the subtleties of the arguments and controversies marking the history of educational thought. Surely a serious student of this subject would be vexed by the distortions created by such a dichotomy. Yet this crude division, with all its defects, is a useful conceptual tool in the analysis of teachers' thinking, for it calls attention to several important characteristics of the intellectual climate within which teachers work.

An interesting empirical question is whether the two views are really in opposition to each other—i.e., whether they occupy *bipolar* positions on a single continuum. The conventional use of *versus* as a linking term might lead us to believe they are, but recent factor-analytic studies of educational attitudes indicate that the two families of ideas may be correlationally independent of one another (*orthogonal* in factor-analytic terms) rather than negatively related. Thus, the extent to which a person agrees or disagrees with a statement such as "Intellectual mastery is the chief goal of education" might be useful in predicting how he would respond to another statement from within the same family of ideas (e.g., "Discipline is at the root of all human achievement") but it might not be of much help in determining how he would respond to a statement from the other set of attitudes (e.g., "Children respond to love like fish to water"). The most definitive work on this topic has been done by F. N. Kerlinger (1967). It is well to remember, however, that even though these two constellations of attitudes might be shown to be empirically independent under certain conditions, they are commonly discussed *as though* they were bipolar, and it is tacitly assumed that the proponent of one view will be the enemy of the other.

When the alternatives are cast in dichotomous terms, there is little doubt on which side of the argument the bulk of today's teachers, especially those who work with young children, cast their lot. Though the child-centered view may have its critics (even among primary teachers!), and though certain extreme forms of progressive practice may suffer abuse from friend and foe alike, this broad family of ideas continues to be dominant in the public utterances of educators, as it has been for several decades running. Anyone who doubts this contention need only attend a few educational conferences, read a scattering of articles in teachers' trade journals, or examine the outpourings of the local curriculum committee to be convinced. Why this should be so is far from clear, but it seems evident that these child-centered doctrines exert some kind of a natural attraction among teachers. Moreover, this appeal is by no means limited to teachers alone but extends to many others, particularly persons of so-called artistic temperament. Here, then, is one of the first "facts" to be reckoned with as we begin to understand the pedagogical perspective. Its significance will mount as we continue.

The dichotomization of educational thought, with all its inaccuracy, has another redeeming virtue. Its simplicity is in keeping with the actual level of theoretical sophistication revealed in the everyday conversations of teachers as they talk about their work. Teachers do not seem to delight in the joys of doctrinal hairsplitting. Or, to put the matter differently, they are more interested in the conclusions or practical implications of an educational argument than in the argument itself. This preference for conceptual simplicity and the avoidance of—one might almost say, distaste for—rigorous intellectual analysis is yet another characteristic of teachers' thought to which we will be giving continued attention. Critics of education have often attacked teachers for their apparent failure to become deeply engrossed in a rational analysis of what they were doing. The traditional mode of teachers' thinking, so the critics imply, is sluggish and intellectually naive. But this form of castigation misses the point. If teachers often make do with crude dichotomies and simple ideas rather than seeking a more highly differentiated and complicated conceptualization of their work, we must ask why this is so. To label such a condition a moral or intellectual failing before considering its possible cause and functional significance is to jump to a premature conclusion.

Though there may be some advantage in beginning a study of teachers' thinking with an overview of the two competing camps of educational thought, that advantage is quickly lost if such an overview creates the impression that teachers, as a group, are serious students of *any* ideological doctrine. Almost all will know something about John Dewey and will at least recognize the names of the more famous educational theorists, but the number who have read the actual writings of any of these men (apart from brief quotations in textbooks) is probably quite small. Not only have teachers not read or studied the founding fathers, as it were, or the ideas to which they subscribe, but neither do they seem to be intimately acquainted with the writings of modern descendents of these educational pioneers. In fact, it is often charged that the bulk of today's teachers rarely read *any* professional literature aside from occasional magazine articles, once their formal training is finished.

Thus the question of ideological allegiance, though useful as a starting point, does not take us too far in understanding the pedagogical perspective. After we have said that teachers seem to be more sympathetic toward child-centered and progressive ideas than toward a more traditional point of view, there does not seem to be too much more to add. The appeal of these doctrines does pose an interesting problem, but even more interesting perhaps are the limits of that appeal in intellectual terms. Why aren't teachers as involved in these matters as their critics would like them to be? Why is a journal entitled *Educational Theory* almost unknown among practicing teachers? Why don't more teachers pore over the works of Dewey and Rousseau? Is laziness the only answer?

Fragmentation and Dissonance in Teachers' Thinking

Newcomers to teaching, and those who view the profession solely from the outside, are apt to be a bit puzzled, if not annoyed, by several aspects of educational thought and its relation to practice. There is, first, a peculiar faddishness, almost a journalistic fervor, that seems to grip the educational scene. Ideas come and go swiftly as the spotlight of national attention moves with almost seasonal regularity from one set of pedagogical problems to another. Now the plight of the *culturally deprived* child is the focus of concern, a few years ago it was the *gifted* child, next year it will be who knows what? New and revolutionary practices—I.T.A., team teaching, programmed instruction, family grouping—capture the headlines for a few months and then are pushed aside to make room for the next innovation. Within this climate of rapid change superficiality is inevitable. The result is that ideas and practices are adopted and abandoned without a fair test or a thorough understanding of their strengths and weaknesses. Like last year's fashions, they are discarded before they are outworn, sometimes before they are even tried on.

But the fashion show spirit engendered by the search for the new is tempered by the persistence of several ideas and concepts that have been around long enough to have hardened into educational cliches. These occur with the regularity of punctuation marks or unconscious genuflections in the public shoptalk of educators. Expressions such as *the whole child, meeting the needs of children,* and *individualizing instruction* have issued so often from the lips of convention speakers, school administrators, and teachers themselves that they have begun to acquire the sonorous ring of old temple bells to all whose work is connected with schools. Though these clichés and hackneyed expressions may be embarrassing to the newcomer and a source of amusement to the outsider, such evaluative reactions fail to explain their persistence. In particular, they overlook the possibility that these customary speech habits, though perhaps lamentable, contain important information about the thought processes lying behind them.

The recurrence of stock phrases and other evidence of stereotypy in the language of educators reflect, in part, the fragmentary nature of the ideas that enjoy wide currency within the profession. These ideas are not joined together by an elaborate system of thought but exist, instead, as isolated bits and pieces, shards of ideation, that can be summed up in a catchword and inserted with ease into almost any educational discussion. Their emotive function in these contexts is often greater than their informational value.

At no time is this quality of fragmentation more evident than when teachers are called upon or volunteer to explicate their "philosophy of education." In fact, the very use of the word *philosophy* in such a context is often enough to rankle the sensibilities of professional philosophers. As one of them (O'Connor, 1957) puts it, ". . . if we look critically at the use of phrases like 'the philosophy of education' . . . it becomes clear that they (often) are no more than vague though high-sounding titles for miscellaneous talk about the aims and methods of teaching." When a teacher says that his philosophy is to treat all children equally or to consider the needs of the individual child he may be saying something that is personally meaningful, and meaningful to other teachers, but there remains something disconnected about his statement. It does not seem to have roots in any larger perspective of his task.

The ceremonial use of slogans and catchwords in educational discussions raises the suspicion of a tenuous linkage between thought and action. As stock phrases multiply and the talk begins to take on an idealistic ring, the wary listener might well begin to wonder whether the lip service paid to these concepts is connected with what actually goes on in classrooms. It is difficult in this day and age to be opposed to democracy, creativity, and innovation in education, but how are these attractive words related to the more mundane business of teaching practice? The answer, of course, is that the two are often not related—a fact that accounts for one of the most frequently recurring complaints among today's educators: the all-too-obvious gap between theory (i.e., educational talk) on the one hand and practice on the other.

The dissonance between what teachers say, or at least what their leaders say, and what they do takes many forms and has several important consequences. For some it lays the groundwork for the development of a cynical outlook toward the admonitions of idealists and the advocates of new and supposedly revolutionary practices. This cynicism, which grows out of a prior sense of disillusionment, strikes many young teachers as they begin to appreciate the unrealistic quality of several of the expectations aroused during the period of their professional training. Teaching as actually experienced and as described in textbooks and college courses often turns out to be two quite different states of affairs. The result is that college instructors of education and other outsiders begin to be looked upon with suspicion by many practitioners. Even the testimony of fellow teachers may be viewed suspiciously when it conflicts with the listener's own experience in the classroom.

The mixture of hope and suspicion with which teachers view the work of educational researchers is but a variant of the feelings generated by the schism between theory and practice. Though researchers may avoid the pompous and high-sounding phrases of the convention speaker, they are often no less guilty than he of raising unrealistic expectations in what William James once called "many a really innocent pedagogic breast." Teachers soon learn, if they did not already know it before they became teachers, that what works in the laboratory does not necessarily work in the classroom. The tough-minded researcher, it turns out, is just as far removed from reality in his own way as is the tender-minded idealist upon whom he looks with such scorn.

Fortunately, cynicism and mistrust are not the only ways of coping with the discrepancy between the real and the ideal. Another strategy is to distort one's perception of reality until it approximates the image of what one would like it to be. This blindness to reality may be bought at a high cost, but anyone who has spent much time in the company of teachers cannot fail to conclude that many are willing to pay it. The tenacity with which many teachers cling to an idealistic perspective, despite the rude assaults of contradictory experience, seems to have little to do with the intellectual merits of the ideals themselves but is, instead, the expression of a much more primordial set of tendencies. It is these to which we now turn.

The Romantic Temperament in Teaching

Although teachers' affinity for child-centered and progressive doctrines is based in part upon a rational appraisal of the educational practicality of these positions, it seems to have a deeper source in the unverbalized frame of reference that characterizes the world view of many who teach. Because of its tacit quality this aspect of teachers' thinking is extremely difficult to describe. Not only does any attempt to do so run the risk of creating a psychological fiction, but in the very process of trying to lift the fog of vagueness in which these qualities are usually shrouded there is the danger of causing them to appear more rational and well defined than they are in reality. Yet despite all difficulties these hidden underpinnings of the pedagogical perspective are too important to ignore, for they are intimately related, as we shall see, to the demands of classroom life as experienced by teachers.

The term *romantic temperament* requires a word of explanation. It was chosen primarily because of a perceived similarity between the perspective of many of today's teachers and the view of life implicit in the works of the major Romantic poets: a view in which the innocence and inherent goodness of childhood are emphasized, the life of the imagination is celebrated, and the forces of rationality are distrusted and scorned (e.g., Bowra, 1961). Although too much can be made of this similarity, and the term *romantic temperament* may itself be a bit too romantic when applied to teachers, it does seem rather appropriate as an organizing concept for the qualities to be discussed.

When listening to the informal conversation of teachers or observing them in the classroom, the observer, especially if he is new to the task, is apt to be struck by the extent to which individuals stand out in the teacher's frame of reference. Teachers are constantly thinking and talking and acting in terms of people, not just people in the abstract, but particular people. Their problems as well as their rewards are connected with thoughts of specific students. The students themselves may leave school at three o'clock in the afternoon, but memories of them linger on long after they have gone and begin to crowd into the teacher's mind before he greets them again in the morning.

A recognition of this concern with individuals may seem to add very little to the abstract description of teaching as an interpersonal activity, but it implies much more than that. Selling shoes is also an interpersonal activity, but apart from his fellow salesmen and possibly his employer, the people with whom the salesman has contact never emerge in his perception as highly differentiated individuals in the same way as do pupils in the minds of their teachers. Indeed, there are few other social settings outside the family in which the personal identity of the participant is more sharply revealed and shared than it is in the classroom.

The teacher's awareness of the uniqueness of each student ("the whole child," as he might say) helps explain his impatience with generalizations that seek to obliterate that uniqueness. In the jargon of social science, his is an *idiographic* as contrasted with a *nomothetic* view. He is interested, as the old cliché reminds us, in what makes Johnny tick. Explanations of what makes boys in general tick are of limited usefulness to him in achieving that end. Somehow it is always the things that are left out of such accounts that prove to be of crucial importance in the case of Johnny. Between the specific and the general, the individual and the *average* individual, there yawns an unbridgeable gap.

The intensity of the teacher's involvement with specific students not only makes him a reluctant consumer of generalizations about large groups of people, but it also makes him hesitant about moving toward a more *molecular* level of analysis, one in which the individual is dissected into a number of smaller parts. If chi-square tables and factor-analytic studies tend to bore him, so too do reinforcement schedules and subscores on individual intelligence tests. The former seem to offer too little in the way of knowledge, the latter offer too much.

The distrust of any analysis, whether molar or molecular, that threatens to deny or obscure the reality of events as teachers see them is part of a broader distrust of rationality that is particularly evident in the role played by intuition in the teacher's work. Although teaching typically involves a fair amount of planning and preparation, much of it, if we can believe the testimony of experienced teachers, seems to call for doing what comes naturally and feeling one's way. The techniques that work well with one student fail with the next, the well-prepared lesson falls flat and the *ad lib* activity is an unqualified (and unexpected) success, the discussion that was dragging along for several minutes suddenly, for no apparent reason, comes to life. Experiences such as these (and they seem to be exceedingly common in most classrooms) serve to reinforce the intuitive basis of the teacher's actions and encourage him to think of teaching as far more of an art than a science.

In seeking a conceptual model that might be helpful in understanding the process of teaching, several investigators have likened the job of the teacher to that of a person engaged in making decisions, solving problems, or testing hypotheses. There is no doubt but that such rational processes do bear some resemblance to what happens in classrooms: As they go about their work, teachers do indeed make decisions, solve problems, and test hypotheses of a sort. But the resemblance between the teacher's actions and these formal models of rationality can be easily exaggerated. When the teacher's subjective experience is taken as a guide, such models seem to miss the mark by a wide margin.

A closer analogy might be drawn between the teaching situation and the problems facing the creative artist. As a painter, for example, goes about his work he is surely involved in making decisions—whether to add a dab of color here, alter a contour there, change this highlight or that, and so on. He may even be a hypothesis-tester in the sense of making a guess about what will work, trying it, and observing whether or not his guess was correct. Yet when we describe his work in these rational terms, we run the risk of making it appear to be more cerebral than it truly is. More important, the artist himself would probably not recognize our description. In all probability he would claim that he did not *feel* much like a decision maker as he went about his work. Indeed, if queried about a particular decision, he might well be completely at a loss to explain why he acted as he did. Instead of outlining for us the pros and cons that led him to choose from among many alternatives, he is more likely to refer in veiled terms to his intuitive powers by saying something like, "It just felt right to do it that way."

The analogy between the teacher and the artist can also be easily overdrawn. If teachers do not behave like well-programed automata—advancing hypotheses, gathering data, analyzing them, making inferences, and revising their original hypotheses—neither do they respond to their world with the emotional expressiveness and spontaneous freedom of the artist. Yet the unplanned and intuitive component of their work is very much in evidence in both their actions and their talk.

Parenthetically, the prominent role of intuition in the teacher's work may help explain the peculiar aversion many seem to have toward quantitative reasoning. Anyone who has ever taught mathematics or statistics to group of in-service teachers, particularly those who work with young children, cannot have failed to notice this aversion. Often it is explained by pointing to the poor background in mathematics from which many teachers suffer before they begin their work, but such an explanation is partial at best. Equal attention, it would seem, ought to be given to the irrational, if not antirational, component of the teacher's tacit approach to his world.

At this point, if not before, the discerning reader may detect a somewhat feminine theme in what is being said. When it is remembered that most teachers of young children are women, and that women are allegedly more intuitive in their approach to life than are men, it is natural to ask whether a description of the characteristics of teachers, at least of those who work in the early grades, involves anything more than a cataloging of so-called feminine traits. In other words, are female teachers simply women who happen also to be teachers, or is there something distinctve, in a psychological sense, about those who enter this profession? But such a question is not as reasonable as it might appear when it is recognized that many women do become doctors, lawyers, engineers, and bus drivers. Though the women in these presumably masculine occupations may appear to be less feminine than their sisters who work in classrooms, the important question is why the possession of a particular set of characteristics is associated with one occupational role and not another. As a group, women may find the job of teaching young children more compatible with their psychological makeup than is the case for men, but such a fact, even if true, leaves unexplained the peculiar fit between the characteristics in question and the role demands.

The intuitive qualities we have been discussing are part of a larger network of response biases that seem to underlie the teacher's approach to his (or perhaps now we should say *her*) work. This network reveals itself in many different ways. It is evident, for example, in the teacher's view of the causal forces at work in the classroom.

Teachers, as a group, seem to be less interested in questions of causality than one might be led to expect, given the highly instrumental nature of their task. Instead of tracing events back to their beginnings they seem unusually willing to accept things as they are, without probing too deeply into the whys and wherefores. This judgement does not imply that they are uninvolved with what is going on about them or that they do not care what happens to the pupils under their care. It means only that they seem not to be driven by an analytic interest in seeking causal explanations. Indeed, both the fact of their involvement and the extent of their caring—their immersion in the immediacy of the situation—often prevent them from adopting a more detached and analytic point of view.

Associated with the teacher's relative indifference to the causal nexus of the events he witnesses is a susceptibility to surprise and delight that at times can only be described as childlike in its manifestations. Many teachers, like the children with whom they work, seem to have a lingering belief in miracles, a belief that is sustained by the frequent occurrence of the unusual and the unexpected. The apathetic student suddenly comes to life, the nonreader arrives in class one morning with three words scrawled on a scrap of paper, the troublesome boy in the back row volunteers to stay after school to help with the new bulletin board, and the dazed teacher shakes his head in wonder and disbelief. He could, of course, ask why these changes have occurred, but he is more likely to cross his fingers and hope that they will not be undone when his back is turned. When good fortune strikes, the teacher seems to be saying, "It is best not to ask too many questions."

When teachers do ask causal questions, as they are bound to do from time to time, they seem to be satisfied with relatively simple answers. In so doing they share the common fallacy of believing that single events have single causes. Why is Billy doing so well in school? Because he has a high IQ. Why is Fred such a troublemaker? Because he comes from a broken home. Why are the pupils so noisy today? Because the Christmas holiday is approaching. When pressed, the teacher might admit that the situation is really more complicated than these simple explanations imply, but he reveals no strong urge to become more entangled in this complexity.

The teacher's belief in the possibility of miracles, though that may be too strong a way of expressing it, is linked to a spirit of faith and optimism characterizing the emotional tone, as it were, of his professional outlook. Although the unexpected may be either good or bad, pleasant or unpleasant, it is in the direction of the good and pleasant that the teacher's expectations are oriented. A critic might say that teachers are hopelessly naive and Pollyannish in their approach to the world. But the spirit of faith and optimism referred to here is of a very subtle variety and is not so easily caricatured. It is evident in the hopes teachers have for the success of their own efforts and those of their students. It is revealed in the teacher's frequent use of encouragement and in the positiveness of his response to the disobedient student who promises to reform. Even the time he spends trying to make the classroom look attractive and cheerful tells us something about this spirit.

In its extreme forms romanticism shades imperceptibly into sentimentality. Among teachers of young children a weakness for sentimental extravagance is clearly noticeable. Though not all may share this weakness, it is obvious that many do. It is no accident, for example, that writers of textbooks intended for elementary school teachers have a habit of including photographs and sketches of children in their works. Nor is it simply for aesthetic reasons that publishers of periodicals aimed at an audience of teachers often decorate the covers of their journals with pictures of smiling six-year-old children. These conventions say something about the tastes of teachers and are not, as some critics would have it, simply devices for sugar-coating or watering down the intellectual content of the material presented (though that may happen as well). Teachers, it would seem, have a well-known capacity for being aroused, sentimentally, by scenes that are sweet, adorable, and cute.

Another route to the teacher's sentimental sweet tooth is through messages that inspire and elevate. Convention speakers and planners of educational conferences understand this well. Speakers whose words are stirring or moving are more likely to be asked back than those whose message is simply instructive or informative.

These signs of sentimentality are, of course, not limited to teachers but are clearly evident in the popular tastes of the larger culture. Pretty children may indeed be plentiful on the covers of teachers' trade journals, but they are even more abundant in television commercials and billboard advertisements. The inspiring words at teachers' conventions often sound downright sober when compared with the effusive utterances of politicians. Yet why should teachers be closer to this aspect of popular taste than are the members of any other occupational group? Why don't legal journals feature pictures of happy-looking clients? Why is it that engineering societies rarely begin their meetings with a song or a prayer, whereas educational groups often do?

To say that one group is less intelligent or less well educated than the other fails to satisfy. The answer, at least in part, has to do with the functional utility of different psychological perspectives within different contexts. If teachers tend to be sentimental in their outlook, that tendency cannot be viewed in isolation but must be examined in relation to other features of their ways of thinking. These other features, several of which have been discussed in this section, will only begin to make sense when they, in turn, are seen in relation to the demands of the classroom situation.

Pedagogical Doubt and Defensiveness

Although teachers may exhibit a strong preference for child-centered ideologies and may appear to be firmly set in their opposition to contrary views, it would be incorrect to conclude that they therefore must possess a high degree of self-assurance and confidence in the correctness of their beliefs. Quite the opposite seems to be true. When attacked intellectually, teachers quite typically assume a defensive posture. By so doing they can often protect the views they cherish, but they are in no position to fight back.

Attitudes of doubt and defensiveness are not limited to the teacher's posture under fire but seem to comprise an integral part of the pedagogical perspective. William James, with characteristic charm, alluded to these same qualities in his famous *Talks to Teachers* (1899), in which he said, ". . . and I think that, if you teachers in the earlier grades have any defect—the slightest touch of a defect in the world—it is that you are a mite too docile. . ." (pp. 6-7).

The teacher's attitudes of doubt and defensiveness are revealed in several different ways and seem to spring from a wide variety of sources. Only a few of the more frequently recurring forms of these attitudes will be mentioned here. Their sources, though implied in some of the descriptions, will be discussed more fully in the next section.

There is, first, a fundamental uncertainty about his actions that seems to plague the teacher at his work. Did the students really understand the explanation he just gave? Are ten problems too many to assign as homework? Should he ignore that slight commotion in the back of the room? Will John's attitude change if his seat is moved, or will that do more harm than good? Questions such as these, ranging from trivial matters to ones of great consequence, crop up many times throughout the day. Moreover, he will never have the answer to most of them, for no matter what effect his actions seem to have, there is always the possibility that things might have turned out the same way despite what he did.

If lack of knowledge concerning the ultimate wisdom of their actions were their only source of discomfort, teachers might consider themselves quite fortunate. For what responsible position in life is free of such risks? Unfortunately, however, the difficulty lies deeper than that. Sometimes the presence of knowledge can lead to as much discomfort as its absence. Often, if the teacher is honest with himself, he must admit that he has made the wrong move, or at least has failed to make the right one. Errors of judgement, in the form of sins of both omission and commission, are all too evident to teachers who take their work conscientiously, and even those who do not cannot be completely oblivious to their own shortcomings.

It could be argued that the situations teachers face, at least insofar as they involve uncertainty and the inevitability of error, are not that much different from those faced by parents as they undertake to raise their children. There are indeed marked similarities between the teacher's role and that of parents, but there are important differences as well.

One of the chief differences, and one profoundly affecting the manner in which the facts of one's own shortcomings are perceived, is that parents occupy the status of amateurs, whereas teachers are defined as professionals. When parents make mistakes, as they inevitably must, they may feel pangs of remorse and guilt, but at least they do not have a certificate hanging on their wall at home or a contract from the Board of Education in their desk to remind them of their professed expertise. Teachers, in other words, must confront the limits of their ability with the additional burden of being publicly perceived as experts who, though not expected to be flawless, are commonly thought to have fewer defects than they truly do.

The teacher's wish for greater certainty, and his natural desire to avoid the discomfort of difficult decisions, are of a piece with two other characteristics that have been noted in several studies of the teacher's personality: deference toward authority figures and feelings of intellectual inferiority (e.g., Getzels and Jackson, 1963; Jackson and Guba, 1957). The apologetic posture of teachers is, in part, a function of their low social status among professional groups, but there is more to it than that. Though society at large does not seem to place a high value on their services, their response to that fact is certainly not one of indignation. Instead, they seem to accept their lot rather meekly (despite signs of growing militancy in some quarters), almost as if they inwardly agreed with the perception others have of them. In the public view teachers are more respected than admired. Like faithful servants, their absence is unthinkable, but their presence is ignored. Strangely enough, teachers do not seem to be terribly unhappy about this state of affairs.

Professional evaluation is a particularly sensitive topic among teachers, and their touchiness about it is yet another aspect of the attitude of defensiveness being discussed here. Many teachers have ambivalent feelings about having their work evaluated. On the one hand, they would like to be told that they are doing a good job; many would also like to know how they might improve in their work. Desires such as these encourage them to welcome outside visitors. On the other hand, they are aware that the criteria of evaluation are notoriously ambiguous; they also know that even the best teacher has his bad days and his awkward moments. This knowledge creates a certain reluctance over the prospect of being evaluated. It accounts for the feelings of nervousness, sometimes bordering on stage fright, that many teachers experience when the principal or a supervisor from the central office enters the classroom. Although things will probably turn out all right, there is always a chance that they will not.

The teacher's vulnerability to criticism, and his misgivings about the quality of his own performance, though they may be thought of as psychological soft spots, are not to be interpreted as signs of pathology. Furthermore, teachers are by no means lone victims of these afflictions. Feelings of doubt and defensiveness are as widespread in our society as the common cold. Yet there is something special about the form and extent of these complaints within the teaching population. It is the way in which they fit the circumstances of the teacher's work that imbues them with special significance to students of education.

Summary

This description of what we have chosen to call *the pedagogical perspective* can be most quickly summarized by briefly restating the central ideas contained in each of the four subdivisions of the section.

First, it was argued that educational thought can be roughly divided into two large families of ideology: one containing variants of the child-centered and progressive approach to schooling, the other comprising teacher-centered and traditional points of view. To the extent that they can be described as holding to any particular ideological position, teachers of young children seem to exhibit a strong leaning toward the child-centered half of this dichotomy.

Second, despite his preference for a child-centered approach, the average teacher does not seem to have worked out an elaborate and complex set of ideas consistent with these doctrines. Instead, what he calls his philosophy of education typically consists of a mixture of teaching lore, aphorisms, and catch phrases useful in summarizing his overall orientation to his task. The gap between what teachers say and what they do, a subspecies of the age-old separation between theory and practice, creates an important source of dissonance in the teacher's work.

Third, the thinking of teachers seems to rest upon a romantic view of the world. This view embraces a focus on individuals, a respect for intuitive modes of thought, a spirit of faith and optimism, and a strong tendency toward sentimentality. It also includes a resistance to generalizations, abstractions, and analytic thought in general, especially when efforts in these directions contradict or transcend the phenomenological base of the teacher's experience.

Finally, the pedagogical perspective was described as containing a noticeable amount of doubt and defensiveness. These qualities affect the teacher's relationship with authority and his attitudes toward efforts aimed at evaluating his performance.

Philip W. Jackson

SOURCES OF THE TEACHER'S OUTLOOK

Having drawn a very tentative sketch of teachers who work with young children, we are now in a position to consider the conditions that might give rise to these characteristics in the first place, or at least help sustain them once they have appeared. There are many ways of setting about this task, all of them involving a lot of guesswork and each emphasizing a particular aspect of the teacher's personal experience. We might, for example, take a purely ontogenetic approach to the problem, tracing the life histories of individual teachers in an effort to discern the formative influences that have made them what they are. Such an approach might help us better understand why certain types of people choose to enter the teaching profession. It might also show us that the teacher's view of his work derives, in part, from his own childhood contacts with teachers.

Alternatively, we could approach the task more globally by focusing, for example, on the social-class origins of today's teachers. This perspective might lead us to a deeper appreciation of the prominence of middle-class values in the teacher's way of thinking. We might also learn, as an example, that some of the teacher's insecurity of which we have spoken is connected with the modesty of his social background.

Though these two lines of approach hold considerable promise and, hence, have been adopted by many investigators, neither takes us close to the forces in operation after the decision to become a teacher has been made. In particular, they overlook the contribution of the teacher's training and the unique quality of the demands and constraints he encounters in the classroom. Because these two sets of influence seem especially relevant in understanding the psychological qualities that have been described, they are the ones on which we shall concentrate our attention.

The Contribution of Professional Training

Most American teachers, and those in many other countries as well, begin their careers as students in colleges of education. In these institutions, over a period of several years, they are slowly inducted into the roles they will perform in their many classrooms. There they hear and read a lot about what the job of teaching entails. Even more important, they are exposed in countless ways to an image of what teachers and teaching ought to be like.

The "oughtness" component of teacher training is both pervasive and subtle. It is not confined to the contents of a few lectures or the italicized passages in an armful of textbooks. Rather, it is reflected in the very *raison d'etre* of the training program, which, presumably, is not simply to supply warm bodies to man the nation's teaching posts but, instead, to send out good and well-qualified teachers to fill those positions. No one, it is hoped, will leave these institutions without having at least a vague idea (though often not much more than that) of what such a good teacher says and does.

The vagueness of these prescriptions and the subtlety with which they are communicated are not without functional significance. If teaching is to be understood as consisting of more than a bag of tricks, its nature and purpose must be transmitted in diffuse and grandiose terms. One way of doing this is by promoting allegiance to an ideology that transcends the mundane and workaday aspects of the teacher's job. Professor William Taylor (1969), an English educator, has the following to say about this tactic:

> One of the major concerns of the colleges is to secure the student's commitment to the task of teacher, to get him to see his future role as not just a job but as a vocation, demanding more of him than mere compliance with instructions and a willingness to work from nine to four. By these means the teacher can be made to assume responsibility for the socialization of the child rather than simply his instruction. A diffuse commitment of this kind is best secured if the teacher's task is not defined in a functionally specific manner, as the communication of a certain amount of knowledge and skill, but in terms of relationships between teachers and pupils; in the jargon of the trade, as a child-centered rather than as a subject-centered activity. (p. 275)*

Whether the dominant ideology *has* to be child-centered rather than subject-centered is a moot point, for the latter view is also capable of being expressed in vague and idealistic terms. A teacher who claims to be engaged in passing on the heritage of man's collective wisdom is no less fuzzy in his view than one who insists that his job is to arrange meaningful learning experiences for his students. Nonetheless, the development of some kind of "diffuse commitment," as Taylor puts it, does seem to be an important goal of the training process.

*This and the next two quotes are from *Society and the Education of Teachers*, by W. Taylor, 1969. Reprinted by permission of Faber and Faber, Ltd., London, England.

Even though a traditional or teacher-centered ideology might well serve as the unifying core of the teacher's preparatory experience, it is certainly true, as Taylor's remarks suggest and as our own description implies, that the child-centered view, in one or another of its many guises, seems to dominate the intellectual climate of most colleges of education. The exact contents of this ideology are, as we have seen, hard to pin down. Taylor, for one, sees them as containing far more than pedagogical doctrines *per se*. Speaking of English teacher-training colleges, he states,

> In these institutions the romantic infrastructure has shown itself as a partial rejection of the pluralism of values associated with the conditions of advanced industrialization; a suspicion of the intellect and the intellectual; a lack of interest in political and structural change; a stress upon the intuitive and the intangible, upon spontaneity and creativity; an attempt to find personal autonomy through the arts; a hunger for the satisfactions of interpersonal life within the community and small group, and a flight from rationality. (p. 12)

If the contents of these beliefs are vague and amorphous, so too are their origins. In Taylor's (1969) view,

> The romantic infrastructure of teacher education is multidetermined. Contributions have been made by the ambiguous position of the teacher in society, as guardians of elite membership without the right of personal entry to the elite; the problem of giving meaning and significance to the education of that majority of individuals who are unlikely to "succeed" in the terms dictated by a competitive, status-conscious society; the uncertain position of the educator of teachers, poised between the world of the school and that of the university, belonging to neither, vulnerable to criticism from both; the history of social and intellectual inferiority that has dogged the colleges of education; the impact of the progressive movement in education, with its stress upon the individual child rather than the curriculum, its liberation of mind and spirit from the shackles of academic formalism; all these have played some part in shaping the system of values that characterizes the way in which teachers are prepared for their task. (pp. 12-13)

The validity of such assertions is open to question, though it will not be challenged here. (One of the most interesting historical treatments of this topic an be found in Cremin, 1961.) Within the present context it is sufficient to note that the vagueness of the teacher training ideology, which includes its uncertain origin, is reflected in the thinking of those who are exposed to it. Upon graduation the newly certified teacher is not only fuzzy about his beliefs, he is also not too sure of where they came from.

The idealistic tone of the teacher's training experience provides an almost inevitable source of friction when he leaves college and enters the reality of the school situation. He may have been partially prepared for this friction by student teaching and planned observation, but none of these experiences is quite like the real thing. Investigators who have been particularly interested in this phenomenon have documented the "reality shock" of the young teacher who begins his work in a slum school (e.g., Becker, 1952). Such encounters are doubtlessly traumatic, but they are only extreme forms of the reality shock to which all teachers are exposed, beginning on that first morning when they realize that the students before whom they are standing comprise the members of *their* class. Preparation surely helps, but it never fully prepares.

Thus, from a setting in which the "oughts" of education are paramount, the teacher is thrust into a world in which the "is-es" of schooling clamor for his attention. Abstract talk about meeting the needs of children begins to look very distant from his new vantage point. Yet, if he is lucky, those vague images of the ideal do not fade away completely. They remain to puzzle, plague, and perhaps even inspire him during those odd moments when he turns his thoughts away from the antics of the boy in the back of the room and the stack of papers waiting to be marked. They also provide him with a way of talking about what he does in purposive terms.

The Press of Educational Reality

The complexity of the classroom environment is impossible to portray in words. In a very real sense a person must be there in order to appreciate it. But even being there is not enough, for the number of things to which one might attend always exceeds the perceptual limits of a single observer. As a result, even the most alert inhabitants of a classroom are only partially aware of what is going on around them. One investigator, J. S. Kounin, has devoted considerable attention to the teacher's awareness of what is going on in the classroom. Kounin has applied the term *withitness* to this quality and has found it to be related to the *work involvement* of the students and the number of *desist orders* the teachers give. Teachers who are "with it" seem to have an easier time in the classroom (as do their students) than those who are not (Kounin, Friesen, & Norton, 1966).

Not only is there a great number of events on which the observer might fix his attention, but many of these are of exceedingly brief duration. Hands go up and down, questions are raised and answered, and interruptions come and go—with a speed that is invariably surprising to those who have not recently witnessed it. Studies of the number of individual interchanges between a teacher and his students, for example, reveal that teachers in the middle grades typically engage in about 200 such interchanges each hour (Jackson, 1968).

To the person responsible for giving shape and direction to the activities within this environment—the teacher, that is—the number and pace of events is something to be reckoned with. These aspects of reality set real limits on the adaptive value of certain forms of problem solving. When the occasions for action come and go in a twinkling, there is little opportunity for careful reasoning and debate. While the teacher is thinking about how to answer one student's question, three others raise their hands. Just as he bends over to examine a student's workbook, a commotion breaks out at the side of the room. In the midst of reading a story to the class, he suddenly remembers that the student he sent on an errand 15 minutes ago has not yet returned. And so it goes. The pressure for quick and decisive action is constantly upon the teacher. He who hesitates may not be lost, but he is bound to experience difficulty in keeping his class running smoothly.

And it is not just the *pace* that keeps the teachers on their toes. In addition to rapidly occurring events, there is an uncertain character about what goes on in a classroom, making it virtually impossible to predict with any accuracy what will happen next. Teachers learn to live with this uncertainty and may even come to relish it, but it militates against a cool and circumspect approach to their surroundings. In the hands of its ablest practitioners teaching is often an unpremeditated art, depending for its success upon what William James (1899) once described as "a happy tact and ingenuity to tell what definite things to say and do when the pupil is before us" (p. 9).

The swiftness and unpredictability of classroom phenomena help justify the teacher's dependence on intuition in guiding him over pedagogical rough spots. These same qualities also partially explain why many teachers are impatient with supervisors and others who would have them draw up detailed plans of exactly what they intend to do. It is not laziness that leads to this resistance (though that may be present as well in individual cases), but the knowledge that such plans are almost bound to go awry ten minutes after the lesson begins. This is not to imply that teachers have no idea of where they are going and what they want to do. It is merely a question of how specific this planning can be. Inevitably, it seems, they are carried along by the drift of events into directions they had not anticipated. When this happens, it is the teacher's native wit, not his planbook, on which he relies most heavily.

The concreteness of classroom events—their physical and social reality—is yet another quality that requires attention in any study of what teaching does to teachers. Many observers have commented, often with a hint of sarcasm, about the teacher's inability or unwillingness to talk abstractly about what he does. When the conversation turns to theoretical matters teachers seem to beat a hasty retreat to the level of their own experience. This transition from the abstract to the concrete is usually achieved by inserting anecdotes that begin, "I once had a student who . . ." or "Yesterday one of my girls said to me . . ." Such a maneuver, which is often frustrating to college instructors, is consonant with the existential vividness of the teacher's world and his personal involvement in it.

Classrooms are not places where teachers can muse peacefully and abstractly about the theoretical underpinnings of their work, even if they had the inclination to do so. Indeed, there is something about the insistence of educational reality that does much to squelch such an inclination should it arise. Dewey (1904) understood this fact when he advocated that the theoretical portion of a teacher's training should precede his practical experience. Once teachers become immersed in the classroom, Dewey noted, it is difficult to lure them back to theoretical studies.

It is not just the instantaneous quality of the classroom environment, its here-and-now-ness, that accounts for its vividness in the teacher's mind, but also the fact that he spends so much time there—approximately one thousand hours each year. To the casual observer in the classroom individual students may be perceived as little more than living embodiments of a formal role. A few of them may stand out as more colorful or unusual than the others but even these are likely to remain anonymous, and the observer would be hard put to recognize them if they should pass him on the street the following day. The teacher's perception of the same class, however, is quite different. He not only knows his students by name, a fact that in itself implies a degree of intimacy, but also can go on to talk about each in a fairly detailed manner. More than this, though he may not wish to admit it, he can also be shown to have developed a genuine sense of attachment or aversion toward particular students in his class (Jackson, Silberman & Wolfson, 1969). It is this familiarity with individuals that gives credibility to the old aphorism about teaching children, not subjects. As much as we may wince at the banality of such a saying, it does express something important about the quality of the teacher's experience. For most, the students who inhabit their world do emerge as sharply differentiated individuals whose lives, for a time, become entangled with the teacher's own. Like parents, teachers develop possessive feelings about their students, who become a source of worry, annoyance, and pride.

Evaluation is fundamental to teaching. Teachers are constantly making judgements about the performance of their students, not just formally, as when they give out test scores and report-card marks, but informally as well. Smiles of encouragement and frowns of disapproval are as much a part of the teacher's stock-in-trade as are pieces of chalk and red pencils. It is not just the students' academic efforts that serve as the objects of these evaluative efforts. They extend to matters of classroom discipline, social courtesies, and general deportment. Nor are they always made public. Even when he does not bother to communicate his judgement, the teacher is often viewing the behavior of his students with a critical eye, noting that now Fred seems to be working well, though Sarah looks as if she were wasting time, and so on.

The evaluative character of the teacher's work exposes him, reciprocally, to the judgement of others. Praise and approval elicit similarly toned reactions from their recipients, as do blame and disapproval. Just as the students' performance is looked upon favorably or unfavorably by the teacher, so is his performance as a teacher graded in turn. As he judges, so is he judged.

The judgments to which the teacher is exposed arise from sources beyond the boundaries of the classroom; they include the views of his colleagues, his administrative superiors, and groups of parents. These separate *subpublics,* as sociologists term them, differ not only in the degrees of their familiarity with the teacher's work but also in the evaluative criteria they apply to it. Students might be chiefly concerned with the teacher's fairness or his sense of humor, whereas administrators might place greater emphasis on his techniques of classroom management and control. Parents, in turn, might care very little about such general attributes, being much more interested in how the teacher gets along with their child. As every teacher knows, it is often difficult to do one's job conscientiously while trying to remain everyone's favorite.

The pervasiveness of the evaluative spirit in education is reflected in the extent to which educational research, almost from its inception, has concentrated on identifying the characteristics of good and poor teachers. The absence of empirically established criteria of effectiveness is often pointed to as one of the chief obstacles to the growth of teaching as a profession. When such a charge is made, it is frequently implied that other professions do not suffer from the same difficulty. The criteria of effectiveness in other fields are not nearly so fuzzy as are those used in education, or so the argument goes. But is this really so? Do doctors and lawyers and engineers and clergymen truly have a clearer image than do teachers of the qualities that contribute to success in their areas of endeavor? Or could it be simply that they are less obsessed with the problem? One can certainly understand why some educational researchers might be interested in questions of teacher evaluation, but the historical prominence of this topic is difficult to understand without keeping in mind all those smiles and frowns in the classroom and the gradebook tucked away in the teacher's desk.

The aspects of the teachers' task on which we have focused thus far—the complexity and uncertainty that attend their efforts, the sharp existential boundaries of their world, and the evaluative context of their work—help to explain the adaptive significance of several of the qualities described in the first section of this chapter. Given these conditions, it is possible to see why they might place a high value on their own powers of intuition, while at the same time be somewhat distrustful of those who would urge them to adopt a more theoretical and systematic approach to their work. These same conditions help us understand why individual students seem to stand out so sharply in their perception and why they might be more inclined to worry about students in a vague sort of way than to hold them up for a close and clinical inspection. Finally, an appreciation of these features of teachers' work helps enlarge our view of the possible sources of some of those unpleasant feelings that belie the calm and confidence of the pedagogical poise.

If each teacher had only one student and if that student had willingly chosen to be instructed, the teacher's task would obviously differ dramatically from what we now know it to be like. Although it might continue to retain many of the features we have already described—complexity, a high degree of uncertainty, an evaluative orientation, and an emphasis on the individuality of the student—it would clearly lack two features that contribute greatly to its unique character: The teacher works with a collectivity of students, all of whom are compelled by law to attend school. The fact that the teacher is faced with thirty students instead of one, none of whom has volunteered for the role although many might accept it without complaint, introduces two very radical conditions that place a particular strain on the idealism with which he might approach his task.

With a classroom full of students most teachers find it impossible at times to give to each the amount of attention he seeks and requires. Though they may desire to treat children individually (the goal of individualized instruction has a long tradition in elementary-school work) this desire is often frustrated by the demands of the total group. At such moments the pronouncements of educational theorists must seem especially remote and divorced from reality, for in their view the unit of concern is the teacher and *a* student. They talk about the *child*-centered (not *children*-centered) approach and the teacher-*pupil* (not teacher-*pupils*) relationship. Though most acknowledge that the teacher has to deal with a class of students, the way in which this might be accomplished without the sacrifice of ideals is left to the teacher's personal ingenuity.

Paradoxically, however, many teachers seem to enjoy this state of affairs. Most do not seem to mind the press of numbers (within reasonable limits) and might even complain if their class size became too small (Jackson & Belford, 1965), apparently because certain activities, such as group discussions and projects, become difficult if the number in the class drops below some optimal limit. Some teachers also speak of the advantages, in terms of heightened interest and variety, of having a mixture of different types of children in their room. But even though they might not want to do away with the crowd of pupils, they are often frustrated by it.

The number of students with which he has to deal might be less of a burden to the teacher and might put less of a strain on his idealistic leanings if the students were all there because they wanted to be and were brimming over with the desire for knowledge. Unfortunately, this is not the usual state of affairs. Students, particularly younger ones, are in school whether they want to be or not. As a result, the teacher must spend a certain amount of time curbing disorder, calling for attention, settling disputes, meting out punishment, and performing many other disciplinary duties that are only remotely related, if at all, to the main business of instruction. Again, this may not be an onerous task for many teachers, and some may even derive a perverse sense of enjoyment from wielding their power in this way. But contradictions seem inevitable between this aspect of classroom reality and grandiose descriptions of what education should be all about. The fact that children are compelled to come to school gives to all the talk about freedom and democracy in the classroom a slightly phony ring.

One of the advantages of working in a classroom without other adults present and with the door usually closed is that many of teachers' weaknesses remain undetected by all except the students with whom they work. Except for the tales these students might tell out of school, the world at large need never know how many mistakes teachers make, how often they lose their tempers, and how far they come from realizing their own ideals.

Yet teachers' isolation is not without its drawbacks. Though they are protected from too many inquisitive eyes, they are also prevented from seeing what others do. Though the world may remain ignorant of their imperfections, they, in turn, must remain largely ignorant of the imperfections of others. Such a situation is ideal for the development of an unrealistic self-image, the belief that one is either much better or much worse than is actually the case. Most important, it adds to the uncertainty that characterizes a teacher's work.

The features of classroom life mentioned in this analysis provide only a partial picture, and a distorted one at that, of the conditions under which teachers labor. The emphasis throughout has been on some of the more demanding aspects of that life rather than on its pleasanter side. Quite a different picture might have emerged if we had focused, for example, on the sources of teacher satisfaction, on the events that buoy their sagging spirits and keep them coming back for more.

But the hustle and bustle of classrooms, their crowded quality, the evaluative climate that pervades them, the compulsory character of their membership, their insular topography, and the length of time people spend in them are features about which relatively little is said in educational discussions. Yet it is only within the context of these demands that many of the characteristic qualities that have come to be associated with the psychological orientation of teachers—their pedagogical perspective—begin to make sense.

CONCLUSION

Those readers who seek simply to confirm their high or low opinion of what teachers are like should be frustrated by the account given here, for it is intended to discourage such simple-minded views. Teachers are neither saints nor sinners but, like most other people, possess strengths and weaknesses in unanalyzable proportions.

Instead of trying to place them on some kind of a good-bad continuum of psychological worth, the approach adopted in this chapter has been to try to understand how teachers of young children view their world and why they might see it as they do. To the extent that this effort has been successful, critics should be left with an increased sympathy for certain pedagogical foibles, whereas champions of a completely uncritical view should find their ardor a bit dampened. We hope that both will have experienced an increased desire to learn more about the psychology of teachers than is contained in these speculative comments.

The limited role accorded rational thought in the image of teaching described here may be particularly disturbing to those outsiders who would like to give teachers a helping hand. If, as has been suggested, teachers are not avid readers of research journals and theoretical treatises, and if they tend to resist the blandishments of all who would have them become more exact in their work, what hope is there for those researchers, theoreticians, and planners who have little to offer but complex ideas and schemes by which a heightened rationality might be achieved? This may not be the best point in the discussion to introduce such a complex question, but having done so requires at least a tentative indication of the direction in which an answer might lie.

First, it must be acknowledged that the situation is not as discouraging as our description, even if accurate, might seem to imply. One source of hope lies in numbers. Remembering what was said in the beginning about the size and diversity of the teaching population, we might take heart in the fact that even if only one teacher in a hundred contradicted the generalization by exhibiting a passion for intellectual analysis, the total number of such atypical cases would run into the thousands. Just as there will always be an audience for serious music and literature, so, it seems, will there always be a sizable group of teachers whose tastes are more cerebral than most. Moreover, there are signs that the number of such teachers is on the increase. Even so, it will probably be a long time before the works of Dewey and Piaget or their intellectual heirs replace the light reading on the average teacher's night table.

A second source of optimism lies in the increasing number of outsiders who, in recent years, seem to have developed a genuine interest in educational affairs. Psychologists, sociologists, economists, philosophers, and many others who heretofore have looked with some disdain on the field of education are beginning to see it as containing problems worthy of serious and concentrated study. Hopefully, as more of the ablest people within these disciplines turn their attention to the phenomena of schooling, the quality of their contributions will be of such a high order that teachers, even those whose interest in theory is weak, will be unable to brush them aside.

All too often, unfortunately, the teacher's disinterest in serious educational literature is not without justification. Much of it is poorly written, intellectually pretentious, and, worst of all, divorced from educational reality. If these features were to change, there is no telling how large an audience might be on hand to welcome the new look.

For even though teachers may be surrounded by a blooming, buzzing confusion much of the day, they also have their moments of reflection and intellectual wonder. Not all of their problems are as ephemeral as whom to call on next in the class discussion or what to write on the bottom of an essay paper. They are also puzzled by how best to group their students, what materials to use, how much emphasis to give to particular subjects, and so on. Over and above these practical concerns, many teachers hunger for a clearer understanding of their work than can be wrested from the complexity of their daily experience. For this they turn to those who are not as caught up as they in the demands of school life.

But a rapprochement between the practitioners and their friends on the outside calls for a push on both sides of the classroom door. If teachers are to overcome their natural suspicion of theoreticians and researchers, they must be given cause to do so. One such cause might be the discovery that the distrusted group now contains many who are aware of the teachers' plight, have a respect for the problems they face, and are trying to speak to them in a language they can understand.

References

Becker, H. S., The career of the Chicago public school teacher. *American Journal of Sociology,* 1952, *57,* 470–477.

Bowra, C. M. *The romantic imagination.* New York: Oxford University Press, 1961.

Cremin, L. *The transformation of the school.* New York: Knopf, 1961.

Dewey, J. The relation of theory to practice in education. *Third Yearbook of the National Society for the Study of Education, Part One.* Bloomington, Illinois: Public School Publishing, 1904, 9–30.

Getzels, J. W. & Jackson, P. W. The teacher's personality and characteristics. In N. L. Gage (Ed.), *Handbook of research in teaching.* Chicago: Rand McNally, 1963, Chapter 11.

Jackson, P. W. *Life in classrooms.* New York: Holt Rinehart & Winston, 1968.

Jackson, P. W. & Belford, E. Educational objectives and the joys of teaching. *School Review,* 1965, *73,* 267–291.

Jackson, P. W. & Guba, E. The need structure of in-service teachers: An occupational analysis. *School Review,* 1957, *65,* 176–192.

Jackson, P. W: & Silberman, M., & Wolfson, B. Signs of personal involvement in teachers' descriptions of their students. *Journal of Educational Psychology.* 1967, *60,* 22–27.

James, W. *Talks to Teachers.* New York: Dover, 1899. (republished: New York: Norton, 1958.)

Kerlinger, F. N. The first- and second-order factor structures of attitudes toward education. *American Journal of Educational Research,* 1967, *4,* 181–205.

Kounin, J. S., Friesen, W. V., & Norton, E. A. Managing emotionally disturbed children in regular classrooms. *Journal of Educational Psychology,* 1966, *57,* 1–13.

O'Connor, D. J., *An introduction to the philosophy of education.* London: Routledge & Keegan Paul, 1957.

CHAPTER FOUR

A Psychoanalytic Approach to Early Education

Jacquelyn Sanders

Often when I have made known my intention of making use of psychoanalytic notions in any educational enterprise, I have been confronted either with suspicion or with an interest discomfitting in its intensity. Which of these reactions people have seems to depend on whether they are worried that I will read their minds or are hopeful that they will acquire the ability to read mine. Fortunately, even intensive psychoanalytic training does not teach mind reading. Seventeen years of work in psychoanalytically oriented institutions for children have taught me, however, the great value of knowing my own mind when attempting to influence the minds of others, and of considering the impact of all aspects of children's environment when planning their education. A major finding of psychoanalytic investigation has, after all, been that forces we do not usually attend to have as strong an effect on our minds and on the minds we are trying to influence as forces to which we normally attend.

In considering the application of psychoanalytic principles to early education, then, these two aspects of the psychoanalytic approach—knowledge of one's own mind and attention to often unnoticed detail—appear to me to be most significant. A third area of the theory's value is the insight it provides into what can best be taught at this particular age. Of course, this insight, is of no use without the first two considerations. Otherwise we are like the mother who knows that it is appropriate for her child to start nursery school, but who, on the child's first days of school, encourages him verbally to go to the teacher while holding him securely on her lap. The child does not leave the mother, and the mother is greatly distressed because she "wants" the child to leave her. Thus, although she knows the right learning experience, she does not know all of her mind—namely, the unacknowledged desire to keep the child with her—nor does she attend to the detail of her holding on to him.

The first part of this chapter presents some observations I made in a preschool when I was a graduate student and my reactions to them at the time. I made these observations with a clinical psychoanalytic eye developed in 13 years of working at the Sonia Shankman Orthogenic School. I attended to detail that quite likely had gone unnoticed but that had important effects on the children. The observations raised questions about preschool education, what its goals might be and the difficulty teachers might have in achieving their goals. The second part of this chapter describes some of my work with teachers at the Center for Early Education in Los Angeles and what we learned from it. We were able there to use some psychoanalytic tools to help teachers and student teachers know their own minds and thereby become able to achieve their goals. The third part of the chapter discusses some implications for curriculum of psychoanalytic theory.

When I had just begun my work in early childhood education, I had the privilege of observing the prekindergarten class of an outstanding private school. At first I was fascinated simply with watching the children, astonished by how much they could do, how quiet they were, and what social creatures they had already become. But then, since I'd become so attuned to the importance of that which is unnoticed, and aware of the profound effect that this first contact with the institution of school has on children, I began to look around more carefully and for a few days watched and took notes. As I subsequently thought about my observations, my thoughts revolved around three features in the classroom and their influence—an influence that I am certain was not consciously intended by the teacher or school. The three features were some pictures on the wall, a white skirt, and a bunny.

The classroom was beautifully equipped. There was space and equipment for both imaginative play and more structured play: blocks, a kitchen, drawing materials, puzzles, a piano, and so forth. All were easily accessible and invitingly arranged. It was altogether bright and cheery. However, there seemed something discordant about several pictures of children on the bulletin boards. I counted and found that of seven pictures five were of one child alone; one showed two children uninvolved with each other; only one was of children playing together. I wondered why, in a place of socialization, there was such a predominance of pictures showing children in isolation. After a time of watching, however, I began to wonder if these pictures were not perhaps appropriate because, to some degree, socialization in our schools began to seem like a socialization by isolation.

For example, the first thing I had observed the children doing was something they did fairly often. Nineteen children, four and five years old, lined up single file—boys in one line, girls in the other—to go from one room to another; to go from classroom to washroom; to go from washroom to classroom; to go inside; to go outside; to go upstairs; to go downstairs. Before these children came to school they walked, ran, or skipped to wherever they were going. They moved as it suited themselves or to suit Mommy, other children, the baby-sitter, or whomever—but certainly not to suit 18 other children and 3 adults. It was obvious, of course, that 19 four- and five-year-olds cannot walk, run, or skip to suit themselves and one another and still arrive at their destination without an overdose of collisions and falls. But was the *single*-file line the beginning of the message: in an institution you are by yourself?

Every day the children rested on the rug. They would come in from play and lie down while the teacher played a record for them. During this time there was a gently but well enforced rule: keep a space between each child. The teacher or one of the teaching asistants would quietly tell them this; more than that was seldom necessary because the watchful presence of three adults silently stated the firmness behind the rule. The reason for this restriction was again apparent: close physical contact would most likely be very stimulating, and how could the children rest if they were stimulated? On the other hand, isn't it possible that by doing this we are telling them: the only way to get along with people who are close to you is to keep your distance?

The same injunction, though less boldly stated, was voiced when the children went for juice. The teaching assistants had carefully arranged glasses for juice on two separate tables. When rest period was over, the teacher called the children up one at a time for their juice. On some days several children would collect around the table at one time as the teacher began to call the children more rapidly. Some children, I observed, would sit down at the table while they drank. But many times, for many children, juice time meant a walk to the table, drinking the juice, and coming back to sit down on the rug. As any parent knows, meal times with even as few as three children can be difficult to manage. Food can be very stimulating, and children with a variety of eating habits can be quite disruptive at times. But is it necessary or desirable to solve the difficulties of this social feeding experience by having them "feed" in isolation?

I could see, of course, that the experiences I mention were not the only socializing ones the children had. But since one of our thorniest problems today is the isolation of the individual in our vast institutions, do we want the picture of the child alone to be at all appropriate in a classroom? In the institution that is most powerful of all in our formative years, do we want, even in a small degree, to convey the message that in order to manage walking with many you have to walk alone? That to manage resting with many you have to rest alone? And that to manage eating with many you have to eat alone? Couldn't there be merit in our concentrating on finding ways for children to walk, rest, and eat together without chaos but without isolation?

The white skirt was an attractive one worn by one of the assistant teachers. My first thought, when I saw it, was that this was rather inappropriate attire for kindergarten. I wondered how she could possibly manage to keep it clean, particularly when I discovered that she was in charge of painting. But I then saw that this teacher managed to stay clean without the need to say anything about it. She never had to protect the skirt, and the skirt never appeared to come first, before the child. So I began to wonder if this were not appropriate attire for this class after all. But as I wondered this, I also wondered if this is the attire that we want to be appropriate in our classes.

When I discussed this issue with a friend, he remarked on another appropriate-inappropriate whiteness—that of hospitals and hospital uniforms. Again I do not speak from immediate knowledge. But if I were in a hospital, knowing I was sick and quite likely to be messy, I think I would find the whiteness a rather unsympathetic color that made so glaring a thing of my sickly mess. I think I would be happier with a color that accepted my state rather than a white that spoke of antiseptic purity to a sick and sullied me.

Certainly one function of our schools is to teach children how to manage to live with others. Another function is to teach them how to manage their own impulses. The natural impulses have to be curbed and channeled before children can become social creatures. The question is, is it necessary or desirable for these impulses to be strongly curbed, and how much do we want to label these impulses alien to the mores of society? In the setting I observed the adults were very effective in curbing the impulses they wished to affect, in a way that was gentle and apparently inoffensive. Perhaps for that very reason, namely, the effectiveness of their teaching, we are made very thoughtful by the issue. Can there be too great a distance between the natural impulse of the child and what is institutionally acceptable behavior? More important, can this distance lead to another kind of isolation—"alienating" the child from his natural impulses?

The painting room was set up so that six children could work there at a time. There was an easel-like arrangement with large sheets of paper for each child. Each easel had before it a place on which to keep cups of paint so that each child could use his own cups. There were enough brushes for each child to have a separate brush for each paint cup. And there was a washroom adjacent to the painting room where brushes were easily washed. With such an arrangement all painting activities could proceed without a single injunction against messing but without a single child becoming at all messy. The trouble is that my understanding of the value of painting over media like crayons or pencil is just this closeness to messing and to the natural inclination of children to mess. Thus, the value of painting is that his natural inclinations, at least towards messing, can be satisfied even while they are being directed into socially acceptable channels. If this is so, then the value of painting lies in the message from society that it can accept, put to use and applaud the child's natural inclinations. However, if no messing is possible, haven't we given up this value, perhaps even reversed it by saying (as the white uniform of the hospital tells the patient): there is no place for messing in this world.

At other times the children were put in positions where the natural impulses were stimulated actively. For instance, the teacher asked who would like to listen to a story; who would like to give a birthday boy a wish; who would like to point something out on the blackboard. Each time several hands went up, and each time most hands that went up had to be lowered in disappointment.

Again, during "free time" the children could play with whatever they chose out of an array of inviting toys. Their day, as an entity, was planned in such a way that there was rhythm and balance to the kinds of activities, and in most structured activities the children were carefully given all the necessary time and help they needed for finishing up. Only in "free play" were things handled differently. This was essentially a children-without-adults activity. Only once did I see a teacher join their play as opposed to giving some restrictive injunctions. And this joining occurred only when a little boy began to beat up a little girl. Since the adults were not part of their activities, none of it was ever terminated by the children's own play timeclock, that is, when their own game ended. Instead, all play followed the institutional timeclock; it ceased at the end of playtime. In other words, the teachers devoted their educative efforts either to the teaching of skills—arts, games or reading—or to preventing chaos. Hardly ever did it go into molding the expression of impulse, the spontaneous interactions of the children in imaginative play. And while to concentrate on skills is our traditional view of the educator's function, like it or not, the school exerts a far greater educative influence. Do we want the content of that influence to carry the message: children's nature is not the concern of adult society; as you grow up it will either be tolerated, controlled, or ignored, but never integrated or accepted as important?

Certainly we want our children to learn how to keep reasonable control of their impulses and how to channel them in constructive ways. But do we want to tell them that while their nature is to be interested in messing, institutions have no place for mess; that their nature is to want whatever is offered, but in institutions this wish can be gratified only by chance; that their nature is to express themselves in fantasy and play, but in institutions no adult is interested in what they express? In short, do we want to tell our children that the appropriate dress for their teacher is a white skirt?

The bunny sat directly in front of me during most of my visiting time. I wondered idly, at first, why I was not taken with this traditional class pet and why I was not taken by the name "Miss Pinky." I also began to wonder why the children did not seem to be too taken by her either. One little boy was making a book about the rabbit. It was not overly rabbitish, but rather a story about his own family. Only after my days of visiting were over did I realize what had troubled me.

I have suggested that two functions of the school are teaching children how to manage with many others and teaching them how to manage their impulses. Certainly a third function is the transmission of the culture, a process dependent largely on symbols. In my own culture the rabbit is a familiar enough symbol. But the very fact that this rabbit sat in a classroom made it impossible for it to exercise its important function—namely, to multiply. In this sense the name was aptly chosen because in the language of symbols there can be no "Miss" rabbit. As soon as she is old enough to have a title at all, she is "Mrs." Thus the name states that this rabbit is a denial of the cultural symbol, just as its presence in the classroom is a denial of its cultural function. Is any animal, in a cage against its will, like the child in the classroom against its will? Is this the real cultural symbol being transmitted?

A parallel issue came to my attention through an activity the children wholeheartedly enjoyed. In their music class they heard a record about Noah and his sons building an ark and about the animals coming in two by two. Afterward they had a delightful time acting out the building of the ark and playing that they were the animals. A day or so later their teacher read a story poem to them about Noah's Ark and suggested that they build an ark in front of which they could do their dances. This all was very charming. What set me to wondering was the last line of the poem. It told of how, when the waters receded, all the animals went back home. My own associations to the Bible and to the moral of the tale were so strong that I did not realize till then that these children might not have known that the story of Noah's Ark is from the Bible. It was only from my own inner response—"But they couldn't go home! Their homes were all washed away!"—that I began to realize this was not being presented as a morality tale at all. Remembering my own efforts to water down the severity of the Bible for some very young Sunday School children, I can well understand the wish to take the sting out of these stories. On the other hand, I wonder what it does if we present a story that is so definitely part of the culture and then comletely dissociate it from its purposes and place in that culture. If this is not the culture the school would like to transmit, if we do not want to scare our children with such tales or to bring religion into the schools, why use the religious symbols of the culture only to negate their cultural meaning?

Teaching children how to manage with a slew of other children, teaching them to channel and control their impulses, and teaching them a culture are all tasks the school, like it or not, does. Early educators are more likely to attend to these tasks than others. What pictures we put on the wall, what skirt we choose to wear, and which animal we keep in the room are important questions not so easily answered.

A while after I had made these observations and had those thoughts I began to work with teachers of very young children. This was an opportunity to discover why teachers with positive intentions give messages that appear so at odds with their conscious intentions. At the same time I was able to see whether some of the methods that had proved so effective with those who worked in a residential setting with disturbed children could also be helpful in a much less intense setting with teachers of "normal children."

A Psychoanalytic Approach

The Center for Early Education in Los Angeles is comprised of a small college for the training of teachers of early childhood, a nursery school, a day-care facility, and a primary unit. Part of the college curriculum consists of student teaching in one of the children's programs. As a member of the college faculty, my first responsibility was, of course, the education of the student teachers, but I also served as consultant to the children's programs in matters of curriculum and management. Since the Center was committed to a psychoanalytic approach, an important part of the curriculum were weekly seminars where the students could bring up problems that troubled them. The topics discussed were left strictly to the students, the only limitation being that they should have something to do with student teaching. There was a clearly designated leader—a member of the college faculty. Because of administrative difficulties one year these seminars were discontinued, which proved to be an impromptu test of their value. That year there was marked student unrest, formation of student protest committees, and general dissatisfaction that had not occurred before that year. The seminars were evidently, of crucial importance. So we resumed the meetings and attended to their content. The three seminar leaders met weekly for discussion, and discovered that even with different leaders and different groupings, there were recurrent themes in these seminars. The kinds of problems discussed are of significance since they are likely to shed some light on problems of beginning teachers, particularly beginning nursery school teachers. The first experiences of beginning teachers are often overwhelming, and any clues as to the cause of problems should be useful.

A problem that arose frequently among the student teachers was related to the issue of being in a position where one is supposed to be an authority, yet is actually a novice. This is common to all beginning teachers. This did not, of course, come up directly, but was reflected, for example, in the following way—some students complained that they were told too much exactly what to do, while others said that they were not told enough; they did not know what was expected of them. These opposite complaints would come from exactly the same kind of situation. Discussion revealed that the students felt they did not know at all what to do, yet would usually feel that they *should* know exactly what to do, and were certain that perfection was expected of them. Through those meetings student teachers came to realize that the high expectations were in their own minds, that no one expected them to know anything. When they recognized this, they could then concentrate on learning what to do rather than worrying about what they could not yet do.

Another set of problems were those created by the impact on the beginner of the primitive behavior of preschool children. In this regard the education of workers with severely disturbed children bears strong similarity to the education of early childhood teachers. For both, the impact of such behavior is very strong; for both, how it is dealt with can largely determine the success or failure of the worker.

One of the most common initial problems for student teachers was the shock of the aggressive behavior of the preschoolers. Many had been motivated to be nursery school teachers because of their enchantment with the idea of the sweet innocence of early childhood. The intellectual understanding that came from course work on normal emotional development helped combat the misconceptions and lessen this shock. However, a much stronger shock for the teachers was their own aggressive feelings. The student teachers frequently were astonished at their own anger at the children, and would find it quite shattering to their image of themselves as loving, giving teachers. The seminars were valuable on the level that the student teachers could recognize their anger, see that others had similar reactions, and realize that to have such reactions was not the end of their teaching careers.

The sucking and messing of the children also typically aroused in the new teachers reactions that they had trouble coping with. Since preschool children have strong sucking needs, it is important that those who work with children of this age be able to deal with such needs comfortably. That there was a great deal of *discomfort* around this issue was evidenced by the fact that, in the developmental course that I taught, there was always a great deal of giggling when it was discussed. Among a wide range of reactions the most predominant was that there somehow was something wrong with it. Discussions were often helpful to those who out of their "enlightenment" thought that they should "permit" the sucking, but actually had a very negative reaction to it. The child would, of course, always sense the negative reaction. Of tremendous value in these discussions was the exchange among students of anecdotes of their own experiences and those of friends. For example, when an obviously well-adjusted young Mexican-American recalled fixing herself a bottle at the age of five, it did much to convince some students that the "normal" age of bottle weaning (according to many physicians—one year) is not necessarily based on "natural" growth.

It was interesting that the students often had a much more accepting attitude to messing. Frequently they would encourage it whether or not it was actually good for the child. When the student became aware in the discussions of her own desire to mess, she was better able to understand the child's needs and decide whether or not to encourage children on the basis of their needs rather than hers.

These seminars repeatedly demonstrated that the primitive behavior of preschoolers aroused feelings in the beginning teacher that were unmanageable until they were recognized. The purpose of the seminars was not to delve deeply into the unconscious of the beginning teacher, but simply to help the teacher recognize what was happening to her emotionally and, thereby, help her to better cope with it.

In addition to being responsible for some aspects of the education of student teachers at the Center, I was also consultant to the regular teachers in problems of management and curriculum planning. It was striking that in both these areas the teachers' lack of clarity in their own minds prevented them from achieving what they thought they wanted. For example, there was an epidemic of swearing among the children that distressed many staff members. This was not the usual giggly anal talk, but more typically adult obscenity. A good number of the staff complained that they objected to it but that other staff permitted it. The director wanted the swearing stopped. It was quite clear that since more than one staff member was involved with the children (particularly the children in day care, since it took two shifts of teachers to cover the day), there had to be some kind of consensus. I called a meeting when all the staff could be present. To everyone's surprise it quickly became apparent that consensus, in fact, did already exist. There was not a single member of the staff who did not want the swearing stopped. So I asked the staff why they thought it should be stopped and what their feelings were about it. It then became clear that the conflict about the issue was not between staff members but within the minds of the individual staff members. Some of the staff, for example, while believing that the language was inappropriate for these children, down deep enjoyed the freedom these children had to swear, as they themselves had never been permitted to do. Other members of the staff thought that there was nothing wrong with the swearing, but that it should be stopped because parents or passersby might be offended. After we discussed such ambivalences, the staff realized how much these feelings were influencing them. We then spent a little time discussing what it might mean to the children, why they might be doing it, and if it was desirable for them. The meeting ended with no vote and no course of action decided upon. Immediately after this meeting, however, the swearing of the children stopped. Once the staff members had clarified their own minds, it was no problem for each in her own way to convey this to the children.

A similar issue pervaded discussions of curriculum planning. That is, factors that the teachers were unaware of were preventing them from achieving what they thought they wanted to achieve. A first step in curriculum planning is, of course, the statement of objectives. Therefore, I would often start our series of curriculum seminars by asking the teacher to state her objective. Many times an objective would actually contain underlying ambivalence—or even an opposite meaning. For example, one teacher stated an objective that the children be able to participate in a group activity. The teacher implied that the value in this was interchange with peers. However, as an example of participation in a "group" activity, she used listening to a story. Anyone who has tried to read a story to a group of preschoolers knows that the problem is to get the children *not* to respond to the other members of the group. Thus, to listen to a story in a group requires the ability to avoid participation in group activity while in the presence of a group. While this teacher's stated goal was participation, underlying this was the goal of nonparticipation. Another teacher had the objective that the children acquire the ability to verbalize their wishes. After saying this, however, she immediately asked what was the use when it does no good—when one child hits another, it simply is ineffective for the second child to tell the first that he doesn't like it. Her objective, thus, was one that she herself thought of little value. This teacher, in fact, was often more concerned with helping children be able to respond to attack physically rather than verbally. With such ambivalences in the mind of the teacher it is no wonder that an objective does not get accomplished.

Our experience at the Center indicated quite clearly that when the teacher is unaware of her own reactions to emotionally difficult situations or of what she really wants to achieve, she is unable to be effective. A solution for both these problems that has been tried and proved effective in two institutions is a meeting of peers for the purpose of discussing such issues. The meeting in all cases was led by an outside-insider—that is, someone very familiar with the situation and its problems but in a position some distance from them. Such meetings have proved helpful to teachers in mastering some of these problems. In meetings with beginning teachers the greatest difficulty was their own reactions to the primitive needs aroused by preschoolers. It is in this area that they need most help.

One might wonder that in discussing a psychoanalytic approach to early childhood education I have not yet referred to the understanding of children. This is not without design—I am convinced that it is impossible to understand others without first understanding oneself. Furthermore, this final aspect of application of a psychoanalytic approach will be a consideration of some implications of its findings in determining the kind of environment we should strive to create for the child.

In *Normality and Pathology in Childhood* Anna Freud systematically shows how the use of psychoanalytic views of development can be applied to the decision about the best time for a child to start nursery school. This decision is usually based on age, but she suggests that other considerations are more important. For example, nursery school teachers frequently discuss the problem of separation from the mother. Anna Freud suggests that children are not ready for this separation that is a necessary part of nursery school attendance until they can hold the image of the mother inside. When a child is very distressed at leaving the mother, it may well be that this stage has not yet been reached and the child is not yet ready for this experience. If one teacher tried to support such children consistently, they would have a figure in the school environment to which they could become attached.

Anna Freud's work also sheds light on another issue frequently raised at nursery schools—"sharing." She notes that a child typically goes through four stages in regard to peers: a completely narcissistic view, wherein other children are seen mainly as interference; the view of other children as objects; the view of other children as helpmates in carrying out a particular task; and finally a view of other children as partners in their own rights. Teachers of young children are frequently frustrated because they believe sharing to be a virtue and find themselves with no virtuous children. Children cannot possibly see sharing as desirable until they have reached the fourth stage of development. While it might be necessary to impose sharing on children before this stage is reached, it will only lead to frustration if it is done with the expectation that the child should *want* to share.

Erik Erikson in *Childhood and Society* has proposed stages of development based on psychoanalytic concepts that can prove useful in determining the kinds of experiences that should be available to children of nursery school age. The preschool child typically is likely to have just mastered the stage called by Erikson "autonomy versus shame and doubt" and to be in the stage of "initiative versus guilt." Each stage represents a focal conflict faced by the child. The issue in the stage of "autonomy versus shame and doubt" is that of control, specifically "who is in control of my body." The healthy resolution of each stage is always a balance—in this case a balance between the child's control of his life and his conformity to external demands. If children do not have a dominant feeling of security in their own ability to control, then they are likely to suffer from very strong feelings of shame and doubt. It is therefore important that children live in an environment where they can feel they have mastery, where they can feel able to make successful choices, where, in effect, they can feel, within reasonable limits, that they are in charge.

At the stage of "initiative versus guilt" the crucial issue is the use of energy—for example, the force that sends four-year-olds charging around a playground. If this force is too critically inhibited, or if its consequences are too destructive, children are likely to suffer from overwhelming guilt. They need opportunities to express their initiative in ways that will not produce destructive consequences.

In my own research I have been concerned with beginning first graders and the application of psychoanalytic concepts to their education. It has become quite clear from this investigation that around the age of six part of the value of school derives from the fact that for psychological reasons the child typically turns away from the family and needs the haven of work. This is a very different attitude from that of the preschooler, and has implications for the recent efforts to build early childhood continuums from ages 3 to 8, for instance. Such curriculum units imply a continuity in development, when actually there is psychologically a very definite discontinuity. That is, children from 3 to 5 still turn toward the family for their main psychological sustenance, while children from 6 to 8 typically turn away from the family. For this reason there is sound logic for the traditional age of starting school.

A psychoanalytic approach to education, of course, means that educators must consider the needs and development of children in planning for them. Before we can do this, we must be certain to know our own minds and to be aware of the implications of the things with which we surround the child. It is then that we can seriously and effectively go about our task of creating environments where children can learn and grow well.

CHAPTER FIVE

Organizational Behavior: A Basis for Relevant Interchange between Psychologists and Educators in Schools

Fredrick F. Lighthall and Joan Zientek

Many advances in psychology imply new curricular content and instructional methods in public elementary and secondary education. McClelland's work (McClelland & Winter, 1969) on achievement motivation suggests that contributions to a strengthened economy might be made through the instructional process. The work of Asch (1953), Crutchfield (1955), and Janis (1971) suggests important curricular contents for social studies courses attempting to deal with problems of participating in a democracy. The studies of Piaget (1951, 1954) and Bruner (Bruner, Olver, and Greenfield, 1966) imply much regarding the sequencing of different kinds of curricular contents for children of different ages in schools. Wertheimer's classic, *Productive Thinking* (1959), has direct implications for instruction in mathematics *and* in social studies. A convergence of recent work by Clarke-Stewart (1973), Kaye and Wood (1974), and Lewis and Rosenblum (1974), suggesting ways in which young learners influence the behavior of

Much of the field work associated with this report was carried out as a part of a training grant from NIMH–(USPHS-5T21 MH 11217) Department of Education, University of Chicago. We gratefully acknowledge helpful criticisms by John C. Glidewell and Benjamin D. Wright of an earlier draft of this chapter. The name of the school and of other persons and groups associated with the school are fictitious. Requests for reprints should be sent to the senior author, Department of Education, 5835 South Kimbark Avenue, Chicago, 60637.

adults who are teaching or socializing them, may have important implications for the sequencing of instructional moves among teachers and learners in school. These advances in psychology—to name only a few—vary in the date of their initial appearance in the literature, but they are all similar in one respect: they have yet to influence educational practice or curricular contents of public schooling significantly.

We seem to have two worlds of activity that have difficulty reaching one another. The world of psychology tends to be at universities; the world of children's classroom learning is in the schools. Each has something to contribute to the other but seems without voice to do so. The "voice," of course, is metaphor for medium of influence. What stands in the way of psychology's influential impact on classroom events? One factor is that psychologists are simply not organized to have influence on educational practices or, for that matter, much else. Another factor is that curricular content is determined by the publishers, and writers for publishers of curricular content are not, for the most part, the scientists who produce the advances in knowledge. A third factor, to which this paper is addressed, is the organizational process through which a decision to change curriculum or instruction must pass if an innovation is to be introduced in a school system.

The separateness of psychologists from engagement in schooling or even in effective educational theorizing seems to be attributable in part to a naive assumption about the organizational processes by which advances in one field migrate to another. If it is possible to assume that psychologists have conceived of their activities as making any contribution to schooling at all, the means of making contributions was apparently that of publishing studies in psychological journals or publishing books intended primarily for other psychologists. It appears that psychology intends to influence education by allowing educators to overhear, if they listen intently, a private conversation among psychologists. Even if psychologists occasionally talk *about* education—as Wertheimer, Piaget, Bruner, Bloom, and relatively few others have done—they talk, with rare exceptions, *to* psychologists. What psychologists were talking (publishing) about was to be picked up by educators from the sidelines and somehow worked into schooling.

Psychology has had a somewhat more direct impact on schooling, we may assume, through participation in the preservice (and sometimes in-service) education of teachers and administrators. The mass media, having derivatives from psychological studies embedded in them, have also contributed something to schooling as well as to everyday behavior of the population at large. But these influences have been indirect, muted.

There has been a single exception to this pattern of relatively weak and for the most part indirect contributions of psychology to schooling. Since the twenties, and in large numbers since the Second World War, the science and profession of psychology has had a direct influence on classroom processes in thousands of school systems through school psychologists. These practitioners, trained for the most part in one- or two-year master's degree programs, have held full-time positions in school systems of towns, cities, counties, and states all over the country.

School psychologists, from their own perspective, have faced a wide variety of psychological problems in the course of their normal work. From the perspective of the entire science and profession of psychology, however, the work of the school psychologist has drawn upon a highly restricted portion of the spectrum of psychological concepts, theories, findings, and methods. Only recently is there evidence that the legitimized activities of school psychologists might go beyond the concepts and methods rooted in the psychology of individual differences and in clinical psychology. The work of B. F. Skinner is unique as a challenge to the typical activities of school psychologists. The spate of published reports by school psychologists conducting "behavior modification" programs in schools attests to the welcome reception given to Skinner's approach (often in a modified form).

But the dominant influence on school psychologists is not that of B. F. Skinner or of the learning theorists Skinner finds so unnecessary—Tolman, Guthrie, Hull, or Lewin. Neither Freud nor Piaget, neither Pavlov nor Vygotsky, has exercised the dominant influence—or *any* appreciable influence—on the activities of school psychologists. The dominant influence is, as it was in 1920, the work of Alfred Binet. To be sure, the actual intelligence test given nowadays may be the more differentiated Wechsler tests, and assessment batteries frequently include some tests claimed to assess children's emotional functioning. Nevertheless, the aims remain the same as Binet's—to quantify individual differences relevant to educability among children. The dominant concept in school psychology remains, as it was in the twenties, intellectual ability. The dominant method remains the same, a method of assessment designed to determine students' positions along a continuum of ability to learn. The dominant question remains the same: "Can the child benefit from regular classroom instruction or should he be separated for special instruction with other children who are also 'handicapped'?"[1]

But even if Skinner, Piaget, Freud, Pavlov, Vygotsky, and all the learning theorists exerted the full influence due them through the roles of school psychologists, the processes through which curricular and instructional changes suggested by these scholars' work would have to pass in order to move from idea to practice would probably remain uninfluenced by psychology. If Skinner himself were to take a position as a psychologist in a school system, he would still have to shepherd his proposals through the organization and would probably attempt to do so *without addressing himself to the organization's change processes themselves.* Certainly school psychologists have not addressed themselves to organizational processes, confining their work, rather, to individual children and to individual child-teacher relations and interactions.

Psychologists who have concerned themselves with educationally relevant phenomena such as learning, or the shaping of behavior, and learning disorders, have concentrated on the learner and to some extent on the behavior of the teacher. That the variables determining the child's learning might operate not in the learner or even in the classroom at all, but in the patterns of organizational behavior among educators outside the classroom, seems virtually to have escaped the attention of educational and school psychologists. Organizational processes like communication, influence, problem solving, and the management of conflict are more difficult to investigate than learning processes. But are these social psychological processes not crucial phenomena with which psychologists and educators must come to grips together if psychology is to contribute to educational change? These are the processes, after all, through which substantive proposals for new curricula and new approaches to instruction must pass before they exert an ameliorative influence on any child's learning.

One important potential resource in any effort to institutionalize a mutual exchange between educators and psychologists that would focus on organizational processes might seem to be the already existing roles of school psychologists. To change those roles so that their activities focus less on individual children and more on adult

[1]The major and minor themes in the activities of practicing school psychologists in the United States are made evident by Barclay (1971), Bennett (1970), Boehm & Weinberg (1970), Magary (1967), and Phillips (1973). Exceptions to major themes in school psychology which emphasize work with adults and with the dynamics of interpersonal and intergroup relationships, rather than with individual children's learning problems, are described by Bergan (1970), Braun (1973), Gallessich (1973), Johnson (1971), Lighthall (1969, 1973), Medway (1975), Meyers (1973), and Singer, Whiton & Fried (1970).

organizational processes, however, represents a formidable program of organizational change itself. If such changes are to occur more than sporadically, the fiscal dependence of the programs of school psychologists on state departments of special education would have to be removed.[2] Departments of special education have no interest in supporting activities related to basic organizational processes; they are charged only with attending to the immediate interests of handicapped children. In some wealthy suburban school districts, however, support of school psychologists is not dependent on reimbursement from state departments of special education. There, possibilities for changing the medium of exchange between psychologists and educators—from insights about individual children to insights into how adults communicate and miscommunicate, alleviate and escalate conflict, and exert and fail to exert influence on one another—would seem to be encouraging. At any rate there would seem to be no substitute for the position of potential influence that school psychologists have gained through the achievement of a position of employment within the school system itself. That closeness of contact with a school system, to be sure, is enjoyed by relatively few school psychologists, most of whom are assigned to a number of schools.

What would actually happen if the role of a psychologist in a single school were developed around the methods and concepts, not of clinical psychology or the psychology of individual differences, but of that part of the spectrum of psychology most relevant to the study of organizational processes—social and organizational psychology? What would happen if a psychologist's role were developed that did not center on the learning problems of individual children or even on classroom processes at all, but on the organizational processes of those administrators and teachers who were most influential in running and improving the school?

Some years ago Lighthall and Glidewell started a graduate training program to prepare what they called "social psychological specialists" for schools (Lighthall & Glidewell, 1967). Earlier, Glidewell had described the functions of a "mental health counselor" from his experience with the school mental health program of the St. Louis County Public Health Department in terms that were relevant to the social psychological specialist's role in schools. The St. Louis specialist provided "consultation on cases . . ., in-service training of teachers, and some informal, *mutual clarification and orientation* interchanges with teachers, parents, and administrators [emphasis added]"

[2]In some cases this requires a change in law by the state legislature.

(Glidewell, 1968, p. 264; see also Glidewell & Stringer, 1967). Diedrich and Lighthall had imagined, in their early conceptions of how a school psychologist might take on a role of "socio-psychological clinician," that:

> implicit in the school psychologist's undertaking of socio-psychological research in his school or system is an additional extension of that school psychologist's role, namely, that of feeding back into the organization the knowledge he has gained about its nature and operation (Lighthall & Diedrich, 1965, p. 109).

Later, after concluding that school psychologists would be constrained by training, predilection, and budgetary dependence on programs of special education from taking on such a role, Lighthall proposed that a social psychologist ought to be trained specifically for school systems and predicted that:

> social psychological help . . . will be rendered only in two ways: (a) by facilitating the group process of setting and reviewing priorities among problems to be worked on and (b) by assisting groups in working on high-priority problems (1969, p. 7).

The graduate training program to prepare the new organizational specialists began in 1968, funded by the National Institute of Mental Health. Both master's and doctoral students worked as interns (half time) in schools in the second year of their program. The internships provided students with valuable experience and provided the program staff with a number of dry runs of the role. The internships produced weak, moderate, and strong enactments of what would now be generally referred to as internal organizational development roles. (See Braun, 1973, for a systematic evaluation of role introductions into five schools.) We now have had experience in one school with such a role enacted intensively over a two-year period.

The two authors developed the role together, but Zientek, a full-time staff member in the school, has been the actual role incumbent. It is impossible in this paper to describe the two years of activities.[3] Our purpose in the remainder of the paper is to provide a glimpse of one kind of problem on which an internal organizational psychologist works and the kind of data that become the "currency of exchange"

[3]See Lighthall (1973) for brief descriptions of the activities of several of our interns and Braun (1973) for extended descriptions and evaluations of the activities of other interns.

between an organizational psychologist and the educators with whom he or (in this case) she works.

The role of the "organizational consultant," as she is called at Trinity High School, grew out of a year-long consultation by the senior author and an associate, Susan Allan, with Trinity High School's administrative council and with the student-faculty advisory council. Trinity is a Roman Catholic high school for girls run by the Blessed Sisters of Trinity. It is located in a predominantly Irish Catholic suburb of a large city, has 2,000 students, and is primarily college preparatory.

During the year's consultation by Lighthall and Allan a new governing structure for the school was developed that called for wider and more intense participation of students, faculty, and parents in the identification and solution of school problems, both curricular and noncurricular. Trinity's administrators recognized a number of problems that were organizational rather than merely personal in their causes, constituent parts, and effects. For instance, students and faculty were dissatisfied with their own and each other's roles and participation in the student-faculty council. Personnel in the business office were not functioning together effectively. A rift had developed between an important segment of the parents and the religion department. Lighthall and Allan worked with the student-faculty council and with the executive group during the previous year to help define and solve a number of such problems. A variety of new procedures and structures emerged as solutions to problems of communication, cooperation, and conflict management among roles and groups at Trinity. One innovation arising from the previous year was a comprehensive set of governing structures for the school. These represented an extension of the movement from a student council to a student-faculty council the year before.

Parallel with the development of the new structure of governance, primarily through the creation of a number of new councils with "problem-sensing" functions, it became clear to the school's administrators that intergroup communication and other organizational problems required a level of continuous attention that the adminstrators rarely had time for. For example, the administrators had a sense that their work on a given problem would be interrupted by another problem, and that the first problem would be dropped. Before the process from an awareness of a problem to implementation of a solution could be completed, it would be preempted by the beginning of a second process and that one by a third, and so on. Each problem-solving process would be abandoned in favor of another, rather than worked to conclusion. The course of given problems through the problem-solving process was unclear to the administrators. Nor was there a way, other than through their own overtaxed and often conflicting memories, for the administrators to keep track of where each problem was in its course from identification to implemented solution. The problem of losing track of problems was one that could be specifically documented by the administrators but required a kind of systematic attention and observation of organizational processes that was outside the limits of their time.

The realization gradually dawned that there was a set of second-order problems, or metaproblems—problems of keeping track of problems or problems of managing communication processes—that operated more regularly and pervasively than the everyday or first-order problems of scheduling, student discipline, curricular innovation, and the like. It was decided, therefore, to release part of the time of a social studies teacher (J. Z.) during the following year to receive training in the University of Chicago's program for social psychological specialists for schools, and to develop methods of addressing these metaproblems.

One of the organizational consultant's first tasks as a first-year intern was to develop a method of keeping track of the course of problems as they moved through the problem-solving process. Just as a manufacturing company has an internal auditor and accounting procedures for keeping track of the movement of products through the manufacturing process, so the organizational consultant would audit the progress of problems through the problem-solving process. What was needed was a problem accounting system. Accordingly, problem-accounting sheets were developed and a member of the newly expanded administrative group was designated and trained as a problem accountant to record the progress of problems. The accounting sheets called for the recording of the date on which the problem was first considered by the three-person administrative team, the form in which it was presented in the meeting (as a proposal, a question, a decision, or a difficulty), the way in which it was (or was not) resolved, the date on which the solution was reached and to whom the solution was sent (or to whom the problem was referred or delegated).

As a part of the development of the new governing structure, during the year before the introduction of the role of organizational consultant, the administrative team was expanded from three members to six members. Four of the new members, furthermore, were to assume and develop a role of "administrator-counselor." In addition to sitting as members of a collaborative executive council (as the team was officially called), they were each to be associated with the girls of one of the four classes in this four-year high school. They were to be responsible for attending to any patterns of disruptive or deviant behavior of girls in their class, taking a "counseling approach" rather than a "punishment approach" to such patterns of behavior. The requirements of the new administrator-counselor role were unknown. In addition, the executive council was twice as large as it had been, though still relatively small.

By the beginning of the second semester (January) of the year in which the new governing structure and the new internal consultant role were being tried for the first time, the executive council decided that its own functioning as well as the functioning of the new administrator-counselor roles should be evaluated. This was not a decision borne of crisis or desperation, but rather in anticipation of modifications that should inevitably be made for the following year.

Our orientation to the motivation of school staff members for working toward changes was that they would be willing to invest energy in organizational problems they themselves experienced. Suggestions for changes in organizational functioning would be most likely to be implemented if the suggestions come from those who would have to carry them out. Therefore, for the most part, we refrained from suggesting changes. Rather, data about the functioning of the four administrator-counselors and about the executive council as a group were gathered and presented, with relatively little interpretation, to members of the executive council. In what follows we will focus on the executive council members' interests in the data regarding their own functioning as a group.

A significant part of the data about the functioning of the executive council came, naturally enough, from the data that had been gathered systematically as a part of the problem-accounting procedure developed by the consultant. In addition to those data, data were gathered from each of the meetings of the executive council from the beginning of the year from tape recordings (openly obtained). Interviews with the executives and ratings by them of a number of items that were, or might have been, discussed in executive meetings provided the rest of the data used in the evaluation session with the executives.

The consultant prepared a number of sheets of data, including quoted comments from interviews that summarized themes in the data. The consultant also prepared tables of frequencies, sums, and ratings in a form easily understood by anyone without the slightest sophistication in statistics. These data sheets became the focus of discussion by the executives as they considered indices of their own behavior or quotes from teachers or students that revealed how they were perceived by an anonymous sample of respondents.

While preparing the data sheets, the consultant noted that amounts of time devoted to discussions of agenda items by the executives varied greatly from item to item, and recalled informal comments by some executives that too much time had been spent in an executive meeting discussing student behavior in the cafeteria. Enough dissatisfaction had been expressed about time taken with trivia in executive meetings to make the consultant wonder about the forces that led mature and able people to spend time on issues that apparently none of them regarded as useful when complaints about the scarcity of time were commonplace. Other things being equal (especially the degree of conflict over the importance of an item), a rational use of such a scarce resource as executive discussion time would seem to vary directly with the degree of importance executives attributed to the items discussed. If an item is important, it ought to receive an important share of the executives' time. Conversely, if an item receives an important share of scarce or premium time, the item ought to be important, that is, ought to be high in the executives' priorities for organizational problems.

This line of thought led the consultant to examine the amount of time executives had spent on each of 11 items taken up in executive meetings during the months of September through December (first-semester items) and each of ten items considered from January through April (second-semester items). Each of the six executives was asked in late January to rate each of the first-semester items on a scale of importance from 0 (little or no importance) to 4 (great importance). Ratings of second-semester items were gathered in July.

The evaluation meeting between the consultant and the executives took place in March. Some of the data we will present later were therefore not a part of their evaluation of their own functioning. One purpose of this paper is to illustrate the kind of data that decision-making educators and participating psychologists can meaningfully confront together, and thus illustrate the basis for a new role of psychologists in schools. This purpose is more meaningfully served if we present data relevant to a single theme of organizational behavior rather than all of the data that were in fact presented at the first evaluation meeting of the executives in March.

Results of an analysis of time spent on 11 first-semester items, together with sums and ranges of the ratings of importance attributed to them, were presented to the executives in the March evaluation meeting. Table 1 is a reproduction of the sheet presented to the ex-

Table 1
Agenda Item Content, Discussion Time, and Rated Importance of Each of 11 Actual Items and 5 Hypothetical Items

Content	*Time Spent*	*Sum of Ratings* [a]	*Range* [b]
1. Intraschool communication: establishing a daily bulletin to read during homeroom.	90 min.	21	2
2. Cafeteria student behavior needs to be regulated—crowd behavior . . . how to control?	65 min.	18	2
3. How well the executive council is performing its functions.	* [c]	18	4
4. Cafeteria: lack of sufficient seating to accommodate students.	60 min.	4	2
5. School policies and procedures for school activities and trips.	43 min.	13	4
6. Determining the admission policy for accepting incoming freshman.	40 min.	19	2
7. How effectively are the school councils functioning?	*	19	3
8. Functioning of homeroom advisors—some are not performing all their duties . . . difficulties of getting cooperation.	40 min.	14	3
9. Stealing—among students, from library, homeroom decorations, etc.	*	17	4
10. Student uniform policy: should the policy be relaxed?	32 min.	8	1
11. Room allocations: what group should be given the use of a room that is no longer in use—as a meeting room, office, etc.?	20 min.	4	2
12. Conflicts between faculty subgroups relative to school policies, departments . . .	*	13	4
13. Evaluation of policies made by the executive council—what procedures, if any, should be used?	18 min.	18	4
14. School parking policies parking lot—which and how much space is given to students? to teachers?	*	2	2
15. Role definitions of executive council positions.	15 min.	21	1
16. School security—police in attendance at school dances, activities, etc.	16 min.	10	2

[a] A high rating (4 on a 0–4 scale) indicated that the item was considered important enough to be discussed at an executive council meeting. The highest possible sum of ratings was 24 for the six executives.

[b] The difference between the lowest and highest rating on a scale 0–4.

[c] Hypothetical items were rated along with other items but never came up for discussion; these were introduced as one test of the extent to which time allocations to items were made on the basis of executives' estimates of importance. These items were omitted from analyses that compared discussion duration to rated importance.

ecutives, except for minor clarifications in the labeling. Five entries in Table 1 were reported without entries in the time-spent column. These items were identified by the consultant as difficulties that were known to members of the faculty and administration but had not been dealt with in executive meetings. We wanted to see whether such items, considered important on the basis of informal comments by faculty and administration, would be rated as important by the executives, and if so, to present data relating the importance of these items to their absence from agenda considered in the executive meetings.

Upon viewing the data in Table 1, the executives voiced concern about how they had been spending their meeting time. They noted an incongruity between the importance they attributed to item 4, student seating in the cafeteria (with a total importance rating of 4 out of a possible 24), on the one hand, and the expenditure of a full hour (one-third of the weekly meeting time) to the item, on the other hand. Item 15 was specifically cited as a contrast, in which only 15 minutes were devoted to an item of great concern to them (with a sum of 21 of a possible 24 in importance), namely, their own various roles as executives.

It became apparent to both the interning consultant and the executives that something other than priorities was controlling their expenditure of time in meetings. The executives wanted to see more data. Similar data were then gathered on second-semester agenda items, as time required by other projects the consultant was involved with allowed. These data were delayed in their preparation beyond a time when they would be relevantly presented to the executives, since the director of the school, Sr. Claudia, who figures prominently in the data, was promoted to another position and a new director was appointed. Discussions of time allocations continued in the group, however, and had other internship projects not delayed Zientek's preparation of these data, they, too, would have been the subject of an executive evaluation meeting. As illustrations of a basis for productive dialogue between educators and psychologists, however, they serve our purpose well. They capture aspects of the behavior of educators who (a) identified aspects of behavior important *to them* and (b) were ready to examine their own organizational behavior as it was captured in data collected by a colleague whose role was to do so. The following analyses, then, extend the self-examination data even if they did not in fact extend that particular self-examination process.

Adding the second-semsester items to the first-semester items increased the amount of data. We also introduced small modifications in the kinds of data analysis presented and the kind of data considered. We summarized the relationship between the time taken in discussing an agenda item and the executives' rating of the importance of that item by computing rank-order correlation coefficients. We also included a different dimension of data. From the studies of Cohen (1958), Kelley (1951), and Read (1962) we knew the truncating effects of power on upward communication. And from the studies of Strodtbeck (1954) and Strodbeck, James, & Hawkins (1957) we knew that differences among group members in their speaking time in discussions is associated with different degrees of influence and status among them. There was a clear difference between the positional power of the director and that of other members of the executive group. But in addition to that difference in position there were other differences in expressiveness or communicative thrust among the members. Those with more power and participative influence, we reasoned, would be more likely to influence the duration of meeting time on any given item than the less powerful or less expressive members. It would be wise then, to differentiate the data with respect to positional power (director versus others) and to degree of participating in the use of the council's time.

To obtain data for differentiating the executives with respect to expressive thrust, we sampled four two-minute segments from each of three executive meetings during the school year (September 22, December 7, and April 2), using the tape recordings routinely made of these meetings.[4] Table 2 reports the number of comments made and the amount of time in commenting by each of the executives and of two staff members who occasionally met with the executives ("others" in Table 2). Using number of comments as a rough index of expressive thrust or ability to influence, a chi-square analysis on the totals across the three meetings shows the different frequencies among the seven categories to be significantly different from chance ($X^2 = 44.5$, df = 6; $p<.001$).

Table 2
Summed Participation over Samples from Three Executive Council Meetings

Executive (staff members)	*Number of Comments*	*Percent*	*Number of Seconds*	*Percent*
Sr. Claudia	30	34%	692	47%
Sr. Patricia	18	21	265	18
Sr. Catherine	16	18	123	8
Sr. Katherine	8	9	173	12
Sr. Mary Ann	6	7	61	4
Ms. Carey	4	5	37	3
(Others)	5	6	89	6

[4]These tape recordings were being provided as a part of a broader study of organizational processes by the Lighthall & Allan.

The frequency data in Table 2 suggested that we should assess the effects of Sr. Claudia's, Sr. Patricia's and Sr. Catherine's ratings of importance of agenda items separately from the ratings of the other executives. Accordingly, we summarized the relations between discussion time on an agenda item and the importance attributed to that item for the three executives who participated most actively in the meetings separately from the ratings of the other executives. The coefficients of rank-order correlation between discussion time and rated importance on the eleven first-semester items was $-.068$ for the three most frequent participants and $+.158$ for the three less frequently participating executives. On the ten second-semester items, the coefficients of correlation between discussion time and attributed importance were .411 for the more frequently contributing executives and .534 for the less frequently contributing executives.

The different frequencies of participation in discussions, taken to reflect a dimension of influence, did not seem to differentiate the magnitude of the correlation coefficients. There did, however, seem to be some degree of differentiation in the coefficients of correlation according to the semester in which agenda items were considered. Our attention shifted, therefore, to time of year as a factor somehow controlling the extent to which the amount of time that executives spent on an item was related to the item's importance to them.

What event or set of circumstances might have led to the apparent increase from the first to the second semester in the positive relationship between time spent on an item and its attributed importance? One factor, which we felt offered only a weak explanation, might have been the March evaluation meeting with the executives, introducing them to the data of Table 1. We were skeptical that a single meeting, even with such relevant data, could bring about a change in executives' behavior, either with respect to their ratings of importance or the extent to which their meeting time was allocated in accordance with their priorities. No changes in procedures or norms had been instituted by the executives that might constrain them to behave differently than they had previously. Furthermore, a number of the second-semester agenda items had been discussed in an executive meeting before the March evaluation meeting in which the data of Table 1 were discussed. Finally, in light of the executives' own desire to improve their performance and the fact that the data were being gathered under their own direction and for their immediate use, it seemed to us incongruous that they would change their ratings of importance, for example, to reduce the apparent dissonance between their rated importance and their behaviors. To the contrary, some members of the group who wanted to underscore what they regarded as a problem to be dealt with might have used the July ratings as an opportunity to magnify the discrepancy.

Another possible explanation emerged from an examination of the substantive contents of, and the persons who had introduced, the items of the first- and of the second-semester meetings. While no pattern of agenda *content* seemed related to time of year, there did seem to be a relationship between time of year and persons who had introduced items. Of the 11 items introduced during the sampled meetings of the first semester, seven were introduced by the director, while the next nearest number introduced by anyone was two. In contrast, during the second semester the director introduced only three of the ten items, while Sr. Patricia, the next most actively participating executive in these meetings, introduced five items.

It was plausible that an item introduced by Sr. Claudia, the director, might consistently receive more attention irrespective of its importance because of deference paid to whatever chief executives say, even if the content of their words may at times be trivial. Such deference might operate only with the person in the most powerful position in a group or organization. And so once again our attention was turned to power as a factor that might be related to the difference between first- and second-semester items and to the apparent change in the time-importance relation.

To pursue positional deference as a source of the weaker relationship earlier than later in the year between meeting time spent on an item and the item's importance, we further differentiated our analysis with respect to the power and participation of the person who had *introduced* an item. We also differentiated our analysis with respect to power and participation of persons *rating* an item. Items had been introduced by Sr. Claudia (ten items for both semesters), by Sr. Patricia, the second most actively participating member (seven items for both semesters), and by Mr. Sullivan (a staff member), and Sr. Mary Ann (who, together, introduced four items). It was possible, then, to have three groupings of items whose rated importance could be ranked and compared with time taken in discussing them: (a) ten items introduced by the most powerful and most actively participating person; (b) seven items introduced by the second most active participant; and (c) 11 items introduced by the second most active participant and two markedly less active participants. Items introduced by the markedly less active participants, the staff member and Sr. Mary Ann, were too few (four) to provide a stable ranking, so these were combined with the items introduced by Sr. Patricia to "water down" the power associated with her items alone.

Data from these three groups of items could be further differentiated according to the level of participation of the person whose ratings of importance were being considered. For example, we considered the importance of the ten items introduced by Sr. Claudia from Sr. Claudia's perspective—that is, using Sr. Claudia's ratings of their importance—from Sr. Patricia's perspective, and so on. We decided to consider Sr. Claudia's ratings of importance separately, to combine the ratings of Sr. Patricia and Sr. Catherine (the next two most frequently participating executives), and to combine the ratings of the other three, less frequently participating executives.

These two classifications of the data, one with respect to the origin (source of initiative) of the item considered and the other with respect to the frequency of use of council time by persons doing the ratings of importance, yielded the data in Table 3. Now, a pattern is clear in these data. When the most powerful and active executive, Sr. Claudia, introduced items for discussion, the longest discussions tended to be associated with the least important items, the shortest discussions with the most important items. Items introduced by the most powerful executive produced a negative relation between the item's rated importance and the length of time the executives discussed it in their meetings. In contrast, when items were introduced by the next most active executive, considered alone or with items introduced by others of still less active participation, the tendency was to spend most time on items of most importance and least time on items of least importance. The pattern is repeated no matter what level of participation

Table 3
Correlations (rho) Between Rated Importance of Items Discussed in Executive Meetings and Time Taken in Discussion, Differentiated According to Frequency of Participation of Persons Introducing and Rating the Items

	ORIGINATOR(S) OF AGENDA ITEMS IN DISCUSSION		
Source of Rating of Importance; by Levels of Power (Frequency of Participation)	*Sr. Claudia: Director*	*Sr. Patricia: 2nd Most Frequent Participant*	*Sr. Patricia, Sr. Mary Ann, and Staff Member: Less Frequent Participants*
Sr. Claudia	−.46	.55	.60
Sr. Patricia and Sr. Catherine	−.41	.56	.62
Three less powerful executives	−.12	.74	.75

characterized the persons whose ratings of importance were considered.[5]

The use of meeting time by these executives tended to be dysfunctional when the attention of the group was directed by the director of the school. It was functional, however, when the group's attention was directed by anyone else in the group or staff. The apparent effect of the director's initiative on the discussion of her own items was antithetical even to her own priorities, as shown by the negative coefficient of correlation (rho) between her own ratings of importance and the time spent by the executives discussing her own agenda items.

Imagine, now, a second evaluation meeting of the executives, in which the data of Table 3 became the subject of discussion, introduced, as before, by the consultant at the request of the executives. Consider, first, the complexity of the data analysis. The only statistical analyses used up to this point have been sums, ranges, a chi-square analysis, and rank-order correlations. All were carried out (and verified) by hand by the interning student-consultant. While no special virtue is to be attributed to the tedium of such handiwork, we have noticed in our experience with the role of organizational specialist that the tendency for intelligent educators to derive personal meanings from data is inversely related to the complexity of statistical manipulations required to carry out the data analysis. The data presented so far are interpretable by the intelligent educator.

The data are not only statistically simple, but also, and we believe far more importantly, capture characteristics of the behavior of the very educators who are to consider them. That is, the data are personally relevant to each educator. The data gathering in this case grew out of previous discussions between the consultant and the executives, and those earlier discussions grew out of the executives' own expressed need for assistance in clarifying their roles and evaluating their first year's functioning as a group.

While the data are simple statistically, they are far from simple in

[5]The foregoing correlational results were obtained when we seperated the importance ratings with respect to *frequency* of participation. If we differentiate the importance ratings according to the *length* of participation, that is, total time taken in participations sampled, then Sr. Katherine, not Sr. Catherine, turns out to be more similar to Sr. Patricia and Sr. Claudia in expressive thrust or participative power. The recomputed rank-order correlation coefficients for the bottom two rows of table 3, with Sr. Katherine's importance ratings being considered with Sr. Patricia's, and Sr. Catherine's grouped with the less active executives, would be (reading from left to right across rows): −.40, .66, and .70 for the two executives and −.16, .76, and .97 for the three less active executives. Ordering the data according to length of participation time rather than frequency of participations, then, strengthens the pattern already found in the data of Table 3.

their social-emotional causes or effects. These data would have been tension-producing for all of the executives, not only for Sr. Claudia. The data bring into focus the effects of positional deference and the extent of participation, two aspects of group functioning not easily confronted by most members of most organizations. Our experience with these Trinity executives over the three years we both have known them, however, suggests that such a confrontation with personally relevant data is well within their individual and at times collective habits of self-examination. Even when data-based feedback is requested by a group, however, and even when individuals in the group have undergone data-based self-examinations before, as both Sr. Claudia and Sr. Catherine had as a part of the consultation with Lighthall and Allan in the year preceding this one, tensions are inevitably generated and persons become vulnerable. A discussion by the executives of the behavior referred to in Tables 2 and 3 would probably change the relationship among them to some degree, perhaps to a marked degree, given that they were the initiators of the concerns behind the data gathering. Such changes are not without energy investment and cost, whatever the benefits turn out to be.

It is in the handling of the readiness for relevant data and of the tensions produced by the data, far more than in statistical data analysis, that sophistication of the consultant is especially required.

We see two major benefits to educators of this new kind and new content of interchange with psychologists in schools. Organizational processes through which the regular programs and indigenous innovations in schools are carried out should become more effective. For example, exploration by Trinity's executives of how they spend their time and why they spend it that way should bring time allocations increasingly under their control, more closely in line with their priorities. Such exploration should also reduce executives' frustration brought about by allocating time in inverse relation to priorities.

Besides benefitting the internal functioning of the school, systematic attention by resident organizational psychologists to communication, influence, planned change, and other organizational processes should also bring benefits from without. To the extent that innovations that reach schools make contact with improved organizational processes in the school, there should be a more effective accommodation of schooling to the most valid of those innovations. Such improved organizational processes may lead to a greater rate of rejection of many of the innovations to which schools now attempt to accommodate themselves—e.g., foreign language classes taught by television and "open" classrooms—and a greater success of those innovations that can stand up to improved examination. Asch, Piaget, and Wertheimer may yet be heard of in the world of schooling.

What benefits might the organizational psychologist in schools bring to the science of psychology? Our view is that theoretically and practically useful constructions of the phenomena of schools as organizations have yet to be formulated, and that experiments in the laboratory or even in the field will be relatively unproductive until they are directed by conceptions derived from close observation of ongoing organizational life in schools. The accumulation of case studies within an organization can build a body of self-correcting data and inferences that can reveal phenomena wholly absent from laboratories. It is true that as one continues the data-based consultations within an organization, the organization itself will change, even at the level of metaproblem. But as data are collected on various groups in the same organization and on comparable groups differing in organizations, we will be able to clarify the uniquenesses and commonalities among settings with respect to their organizational processes. Eventually, like the clinical pathologist in the hospital, we will be in a position to accumulate a file of organizational biopsies, so to speak (dare we call them "slices of life"?). Systematic review of this file should reveal fundamental phenomena and suggest less organic, more variable-centered research of the survey or experimental kind. At present we plan only to continue to build a local science of the processes and the phenomena of Trinity and perhaps one or two other schools. To do so, of course, requires a resident scientist-practitioner who participates as internal consultant in these schools. Without lodging the functions of data collection and analysis in a role within a school, the cumulative benefit of such functions are not felt in the school. Problems of maintaining the integrity of the research function of the role—of preventing cooptation—and of integrating the role within the school organization are very real. The solutions we have developed for these problems constitute another story altogether. The story presented here, in a nutshell, is that psychology can contribute meaningfully and directly to ongoing educational functions by widening its knowledge base beyond the psychology of individual differences to include social and organizational psychology and by extending its attention beyond individual children to include the priorities and process of work groups of the adults in the school building and system.

References

Asch, S. E. Effects of group pressure upon the modification and distortion of judgments. In D. Cartwright & A. Zander (Eds.), *Group Dynamics: Research and Theory.* Evanston, Ill.: Row Peterson, 1953.

Barclay, J. R. Descriptive, theoretical and behavioral characteristics of sub-doctoral school psychologists. *American Psychologist*, 1971, *26*, 257–280.

Bennett, V. D. C. Who is a school psychologist? (And what does he do?). *Journal of School Psychology*, 1970, *8*, 166–171.

Bergan, J. R. A systems approach to psychological services. *Psychology in the Schools*, 1970, *1*, 315–319.

Boehm, A. E. & Weinberg, R. A. (Eds.) *Contributions to the educational enterprise: Innovative psychological services in the schools. Special issue of the Journal of School Psychology.* 1970, *8*.

Braun, J. W. The introduction of a new role into schools. Unpublished doctoral dissertation, University of Chicago, 1973.

Bruner, J. S., Olver, R. R. & Greenfield, P. M. *Studies in Cognitive Growth.* New York: Wiley, 1966.

Clarke-Stewart, K. A. Interactions between mothers and their young children: Characteristics and consequences. *Monographs of the Society for Research in Child Development*, 1973, *38* (No. 153), Nos. 6–7.

Cohen, A. R. Upward communication in experimentally created hierarchies. *Human Relations*, 1958, *11*, 41–53.

Crutchfield, R. S. Conformity and character. *American Psychologist*, 1955, *10*, 191–198.

Gallessich, J. Organizational factors influencing consultation in schools. *Journal of School Psychology*, 1973, *11*, 57–65.

Glidewell, J. C. A design for an experimental program. In R. H. Williams & L. D. Ozarin (Eds.), *Community Mental Health.* San Francisco: Jossey-Bass, 1968.

Glidewell, J. C. & Stringer, L. A. The education institution and the health institution. In E. M. Bower & W. G. Hollister (Eds.), *Behavioral Science Frontiers in Education.* New York: Wiley, 1967.

Janis, I. L. Group think among policy makers. In N. Sanford & C. Comstock (Eds.), *Sanctions for Evil.* San Francisco: Jossey-Bass, 1971.

Johnson, D. W. Students against the school establishment: Crisis intervention in school conflicts and organizational change. *Journal of School Psychology*, 1971, *9*, 84–92.

Kaye, K. & Wood, D. Instructing infants to circumvent a barrier. Unpublished paper, University of Chicago, 1974.

Kelley, H. H. Communication in experimentally created hierarchies. *Human Relations*, 1951, *4*, 39–56.

Lewis, M. & Rosenblum, L. A. (Eds.) *The Effect of the Infant of its Caregiver.* New York: Wiley, 1974.

Lighthall, F. F. A dialogue and three principles. *School Review*, 1970, *78*, 403–413.

Lighthall, F. F. A social psychologist for school systems. *Psychology in the Schools*, 1969, *VI*, 3–12.

Lighthall, F. F. Social psychologists in schools: Some concepts and interventions. *School Psychology Digest*, 1973, *2*, 10–15.

Lighthall, F. F. & Diedrich, R. C. The school psychologist, the teacher, and research: Willing and reluctant cooperation. *Psychology in the Schools*, 1965, *2*, 106–110.

Lighthall, F. F. & Glidewell, J. C. Psychologists for cross-role consultation in schools. Unpublished training proposal to the National Institute of Mental Health. University of Chicago, 1967.

Magary, J. F. (Ed.) *School Psychological Services in Theory and Practice: A Handbook*. Englewood Cliffs, N. J.: Prentice-Hall, 1967.

McClelland, D. C. & Winter, D. G. *Motivating Economic Achievement*. New York: Free Press, 1969.

Medway, F. J. A social psychological approach to internally based change in schools, *Journal of School Psychology*, 1975, *13*, 19–27.

Meyers, J. A. A consultation model for school psychological services. *Journal of School Psychology*, 1973, *11*, 5–15.

Phillips, B. N. Editors note. *Journal of School Psychology*, 1973, *11*, 291–293.

Read, W. H. Upward communication in industrial hierarchies. *Human Relations*, 1962, *15*, 3–16.

Piaget, J. *The Construction of Reality in the Child*. New York: Basic Books, 1954.

Piaget, J. *The Child's Conception of the World*. London: Routledge & Kegan Paul, 1951.

Singer, D. L., Whiton, M. B. & Fried, M. An alternative to traditional mental health services and consultation in schools: A social system and group process approach. *Journal of School Psychology*, 1970, *8*, 172–179.

Strodtbeck, F. L. The family as a three-person group. *American Sociological Review*, 1954, *19*, 23–29.

Strodtbeck, F. L., James, R. M. & Hawkins, C. Social status in jury deliberations. *American Sociological Review*, 1957, *22*, 713–719.

Wertheimer, M. *Productive Thinking*. New York: Harper, 1959.

CHAPTER SIX

Food to Nurture the Mind

Bruno Bettelheim

Wouldn't it be nice if all children could begin their learning in school in the relaxed mood that a good meal, in good company, creates? They would be so much more receptive to what their teachers want them to learn. If, as we are told, an army marches on its stomach, how much more this is true for an army of children, to whom a full stomach alone gives the courage to do battle with and to conquer the challenges of learning. This, the psychological impact of eating, of how we eat, and of how we eat together, as different from what we eat, has received far too little attention.

In my work with severely disturbed children I encountered daily some to whom, theoretically, an abundance of the best food had been offered, but who had been starving themselves because it was offered under conditions that were utterly detrimental to their self-respect. They rejected food that, for psychological reasons, had become unacceptable, had become degrading to them—so much so that even forced feedings could not keep them alive. The only way we could restore them to both physical and psychological health was to create conditions that made eating acceptable and enjoyable to them.

Such publications as *Why Child Nutrition Programs Fail* and *Their Daily Bread* tell the appalling story of how food programs fail. From my experience I am convinced that everything these booklets report is true, but they tell only part of the story. They fail to take account of

Reprinted with permission from the *School Review*, 1975, *83*, 433-448. This chapter was originally delivered to the Children's Foundation in December, 1969.

some of the psychological factors that explain why food programs meet with resistance and why they are so inadequately administered by the school system.

The answer is, I believe, that those who institute and administer the programs, well motivated as they are, do not create the emotional climate that would assure their success. Because somebody is hired as a cook and accepts the job because he or she needs the money does not mean that this person likes to prepare and serve meals to others, least of all to rambunctious children.

Let me illustrate by a situation that exists in a school with which I am familiar. The school is only about a decade old, quite new as school buildings go. But its kitchen is not much larger than the rather spacious one in my home. In this kitchen, where meals are prepared for 400 children, the stove, refrigerators, dishwashing machine—everything—is much larger than in my home, which leaves very little space for the cook and her two helpers to work. As much as she may have been originally motivated to prepare good, attractive, and nutritional meals, the daily struggle with impossible working conditions has aggravated the cook, annoyed her, made her short-tempered. Only rarely do the children get meals they really enjoy; most of the time they are served things like gooey beef, which young children typically do not like though they contain all the desirable nutritional elements. Worse, they are served by a cook who is often so angry that she practically throws the food at the children. She does not talk, but screams at them for the slightest reason. If a child arrives at the pay station without his money because, for example, an older brother or sister has it, she bawls him out: "Why isn't he here? Why don't you stay in line with him?" And she sends him back. For everything the children do or don't do they are angrily scolded. To even a reasonable question the cook screams: "Don't ask me any questions!" Her behavior is the consequence of the hours of aggravation that she and her helpers have to live through in impossible working conditions.

Though this is a new school building, it has no lunchroom. The place where the children eat has to serve triple duty as lunchroom, gymnasium, and assemby hall. Thus the time for eating is very short. Tables and chairs have to be set up and removed in a hurry, a hurry that characterizes and defeats the entire lunch program. When the 12 o'clock bell rings, 400 children who want lunch have to wait in one long line along the walls of this room. It means that those who are last have to wait a half-hour or more until they can squeeze through the all too narrow space in front of the counter to get their meal. The result is that they jostle each other for a place in the line; the longer they have to wait, the more unruly they become. They push and fight to get ahead of each other, the natural consequence when children are frustrated by being kept in line for far too long.

Not that things are more pleasant once they've gotten their food. As the children eat, there is an awful noise: older children are pushing big, noisy, metal containers into which they drop the vast amounts of uneaten food. Their job, to scrape other people's plates, is not pleasant, and they are careless so the containers immediately become filthy, increasing the generally unpleasant atmosphere. Is it difficult to predict that after such waiting for the meal and after having eaten it under such unpleasant circumstances this nutritionally valuable fare would remain largely uneaten?

In this noisy and disorderly lunchroom, with all the standing in line, fighting for long periods before the meal, and squabbles while eating it, several teachers are forced to police the area. Because of the lunch program they have had to give up their own free lunch period. Now it is one thing to be convinced of the importance of good nutrition and it's another to have to give up, day after day, the lunch hour in which you can rest and eat relaxedly, while socializing with your colleagues. Teaching in general, and in particular in low-income schools, is not such a simple or pleasant task that, come 12 o'clock, the teachers do not feel they are entitled to that hour's rest and peace.

TEACHERS NEED PREPARATION

School food programs like this one, as desirable as they may seem, were imposed on schools that were both physically and psychologically ill-prepared to take on this additional task. All too many new tasks have been assigned to the schools by law, or by community expectations, with scant concern for the fact that to put more and more burdens on the teacher is to make it harder and harder for her to function adequately. It is one thing to realize that something is socially desirable or necessary, such as good nutrition, but it is another to expect people to do more and more, especially when they have been given no larger understanding of the meaning of these programs than that the children need to be fed. To my knowledge, nowhere has it been explained to teachers why and how the food program could help them in their teaching, how it is not good nutrition per se, but being fed pleasantly in class by the teacher—as opposed to food being thrown at him in the lunchroom—that helps a child to learn in class, particularly from the teacher who feeds him. If we had made concentrated efforts to explain all this and much more to teachers, maybe they would be more cooperative, more willing to spend their own free time on feeding the children, even willing to make feeding a central point in their relation to the children, rather than viewing it as another unfortunately necessary but onerous task.

Let me give an example of how such preparation can be effective. During the war years when the Kaiser Company was building the liberty ships, they employed large numbers of poor whites who had migrated to the shipyards near Seattle. An entire city of trailers fed its many children into a special school system where school failures and truancy were the rule until a new superintendent decided that the children's main problem was that they did not get enough sleep in the crowded trailers, where at all times of the day and night some adult was coming back from one shift and another getting ready for the next. He arranged for some large tables to be set up in the rear of each classroom and some blankets to be provided. He then encouraged the children to lie down for naps whenever they felt like it. A fine idea, but the teachers resisted, fearing that the example of the sleeping child would demoralize those who still paid attention, would interfere with the learning of those who lost out on listening to the teacher by sleeping. It took the superintendent many weeks of hard work to persuade the teachers. After that, throughout the school day several children slept in each class. Others who had never attended began to come to school because they found there more restful sleep than in their trailer homes. After he had won the positive cooperation of the teachers, absenteeism dropped from the old rate of nearly 50 percent to less than 10 percent. More important, the morale among the children and among the teachers improved greatly. And while the children were, on the average, academically two to three years behind their chronological age, after a year of this new arrangement there was no longer more academic retardation to be found in this group of deprived children than in the well-established middle-class neighboring Seattle school system. Thus, letting children sleep in class was not only good for their physical health but was an outstanding academic success. Severly deprived children performed, because of this program, as well an nondeprived children. But it worked so well not because the opportunity to sleep had been added to the class routine. It worked because the teachers had become convinced that the new system could help them to teach and maintain discipline. They had become convinced because special efforts had been made to win them over—necessary efforts, though the teachers had been convinced that children need sleep, as our present teachers are convinced that children need good nutrition.

Another example will help to point out how, while teachers accept the importance of a new function added to their load, their efforts will fail without the proper psychological preparation. When sex education was added to the program of many schools, there was little question that it was desirable for the children. But, while teaching materials and courses of study were made available, no efforts were made to prepare teachers for this extremely difficult task. Nothing was done to remove their anxieties or prejudices about sex or to correct outright misinformation they believed to be gospel truth; nothing was done to help them understand that sex means something entirely different to the child than to the adult and that it will not do to approach them with the adult attitudes toward sex. This, incidentally, is also what is wrong with the food programs: nutritional problems are seen from an adult point of view, without recognition of the psychological meaning of food to the child, particularly to the deprived one.

The result of sex education is that many children now receive information that is not only short on enlightenment but is utterly confusing, and outright damaging to some. Simply to feed into the child's vast distortions and anxieties what seems to the adult correct sex information doesn't clear the air of the confusion but only adds to it. One of the oldest agencies concerned with sex education recently asked my advice because they were unable to find anyone who could properly prepare teachers to give sex information. All the material on it that is available, correct as it is, neither helps teachers with their own difficulties with the subject nor helps them to understand how vastly different is the child's view of sex. You might dismiss this example by saying that sex is, after all, a touchy subject for most people, while nutrition is not.

So let me use another example from my experience. In a fairly good course of study on nutrition that was made compulsory in all Chicago public schools, teachers were given no help in understanding what is emotionally involved in such a course because it was assumed that they all knew how important good nutrition is, as indeed they did. I happened to work at that time with a group whose assignment included teaching this course. A teacher, fully convinced of the importance of good nutritional habits, reported how she had taught the children what a well-balanced breakfast should consist of, and why, and that all her children had understood it. She had stressed, among other things, the importance of drinking some juice, such as orange juice, in the morning. She then asked the class who had orange juice for breakfast, and, to her surprise, in this underprivileged group nearly all children raised their hands. She did not question them any further because she did not want to make them self-conscious about it, which speaks well of her sensitivity to her children's feelings. I encouraged her to go back to her class and, instead of just stressing the desirability of having orange juice for breakfast, discuss with the children the economic difficulties that make it very hard for many parents to provide the kind of nutrition that they would like to offer. Thus to what she had been teaching originally, good nutrition, she now added discussions of the difficulties parents encounter in providing it for their children. I further suggested that after adding this elaboration of the economic and psychological issues to those already in the curriculum on nutrition, she might then ask children, individually and privately, when they had last had a glass of orange juice for breakfast. The problem approached in this way revealed that, while most of them had at one time had a glass of orange juice, none of them in the class had it regularly for breakfast. One youngster, for example, explained that he had raised his hand because indeed, last Easter, he had—once—had orange juice for breakfast.

EATING HELPS LEARNING

A few years ago I spoke to a group of school administrators about how eating while learning helps to reduce children's anxieties about it and often permits even nonlearners of long standing to overcome their fears so that they suddenly become able to achieve. How intimately connected to food learning to read is! We are feeding knowledge to the child while feeding him food. I illustrated this connection with a story of a nonreader who finally learned to read when, after he had been hand fed by his teacher for weeks, he said, "Feed me," when he meant, "Read to me." Without recognizing it, he was saying that we have not only to teach but to feed the whole child, feed food to his body as we feed knowledge to his mind.

An elderly gentleman told me excitedly that I had helped him to finally understand an experience he had had as a very young man. While teaching in a little red schoolhouse in his native Montana, a blizzard had isolated him and the children for two days. In class he had a 10-year-old boy totally unable to read despite his best efforts to teach him. But this time he not only tried to teach him to read; he also had to feed him for two days. While he was feeding the boy some sandwiches he had prepared for him, the boy who was looking at the pictures in a book suddenly began also to read it. The educator told me how all his life had been baffled by this experience, which now finally made good sense.

This man now has become an outstanding educator. If it took this long lecture, coming at the end of his rich educational experience, to understand the connection between a teacher feeding her children and their learning from her, how can we expect average teachers to understand all this without instruction? But this is what we do when we simply add food programs without regard for their feelings about the added burden, not to speak of other unconscious feelings they may harbor about the children which may stand in the way of their administering the food program properly.

Children have unconsciously a deep understanding of what food means to them, a better understanding than some of their teachers, though they cannot put it into words, and maybe even a better understanding than the well-meaning legislators who pass the empowering legislation. They feel, though they cannot or will not tell, that food given unwillingly, without love, is not good nutrition but an insult. Forced by hunger under psychologically unacceptable conditions, and hating the school that tempts them to do something that runs counter to their self-respect, they may eat a little, but they will not be well nourished.

Eating and being fed are intimately connected with our deepest feelings. They are the basic interactions between human beings on which rest all later evaluations of ourself, of the world, and of our relationship to it. Therefore, when we are not given food in the right way, with the right emotions, questions arise on the deepest level about ourselves and about those who give it to us. That is why food given by the school without regard for the child's self-respect poisons his relation to school and learning.

Let me explain the psychological reasons for this. Breast feeding remains the best paradigm of how only the interactions of the two partners around food can lead the infant to develop a sense of trust in our persons and the world. For it is neither mother love, nor food itself, nor the skin contact between mother and child that accounts for the essence of the nursing experience. Certainly this essence does not lie in its being an "oral" experience related to a particular part of the body, the mouth. While mother love is very important, it becomes significant as it conditions what goes on around feeding and being fed. What conditions the later ability to relate—which, after all, comes from within us—is our inner experience during these eating interactions with the world.

When the infant is nursed by an unwilling mother, when he is fed without positive feelings, he becomes flooded with impotent rage, a helpless victim of inner tensions. According to Erikson this experience is "the ontogenetic source of the sense of being bad, of a 'basic mistrust' which combines a sense of mistrustfulness, and of untrustworthiness." He reminds us that the psychiatric literature is full of references to the "oral character," which is a characterological deviation based on unsolved conflicts around eating. Whenever oral pessimism becomes dominant, infantile fears, such as that of "being left empty" or simply of "being left" and also of being "starved," can be discerned in the depressive forms of "being empty" and of "being no good." Such fears, in turn, can give behavior that particular avaricious quality which in psychoanalysis is called "oral sadism," that is, a cruel need to get and to take in ways harmful to others. But there is an optimistic oral character, too, one from which the child, from the way he has been given and he has received food, has learned to make giving and receiving the most important thing in life.

How one has been fed as an infant and the circumstances that surround eating in infancy have a larger impact on the personality than any other human experience. To convey this message to teachers and the others concerned with school food programs should not be too difficult. But to my knowledge it is neglected in favor of stressing physical hunger, as if our greatest hunger were not for being accepted, for feeling important and worthwhile. If teachers would understand the psychological meaning that feeding children has, we would not encounter situations where teachers threaten little children not to give them their meal ticket if they do not behave or do not finish assigned work on time. In defense of teachers, I must say that I did not once witness such a threat actually carried out. In the end, all were given their meal tickets. But the teachers were not aware of the terrifying psychological threat that was implied in their remarks. If they had, they could never have made them.

Let me repeat: eating experiences condition our entire attitude to the world, not so much because of how nutritious is the food we are given, but because of the feelings and attitudes with which it is given. Around eating, attitudes are learned, or not learned, that are the preconditions for all academic achievement—the ability to control oneself, to wait, to work now for future rewards. Only after many experiences in which he is pleasantly and well fed does the infant stop screaming for his next feeding because he has learned to wait patiently for it, certain that it will come in good time. With that he has begun to acquire those inner controls required for all later learning.

For example, the injunction not to grab and eat a cookie right away is a typical experience around which inner controls are further developed and made secure. But such learning will be effective only if the child gets praise and affection for the postponement, if his hunger has been pleasantly and fully sated in the past, and because he fears that uncontrolled grabbing will lose him the source of all this reliable satisfaction. No praise will work if the hunger is unstilled, no demand will be effective without the child's conviction that to postpone is the way to greater gains (satisfaction and praises) and certainly not to any loss. Therefore no postponement is possible if my whole experience tells me that "what I don't grab now I'll never get."

That is why the underpriviledged child needs to grab, cannot wait for food, and should not be expected to wait in long lines for it. Too much of his life he has found that if he doesn't grab it now, he won't get it later on. One reason that an education that takes so many years from which to achieve results (jobs, money) does not reach children who do not believe that future rewards can result from energy spent now is because they have not learned that food will always be there for them, and hence they don't need to grab it now.

WASTE MAY BE NECESSARY

In my efforts to teach teachers this seemingly simple principle I have nearly always been up against their puritanical ethic, according to which waste is sinful and will be punished by scarcity in the future. This belief has served them well, has enabled them too make it through college and become teachers. Their own past experience makes them believe in it strongly. What they have long ago forgotten is that their present ways are the consequence of their having been fed early and consistentle in their life, and on time. That is why they now can wait in line, need not grab, and need not waste.

But most underprivileged young children are uncontrolled. They grab (and may one day graduate to looting) when the teacher distributes food (or paper, or pencils), though they then often don't use it—even throw it away. In the teacher's eyes they waste supplies, which she feels is wrong. All the good food going to waste upsets the cooks, the more so since they may not have enough to feed their own families, another source of resentment which they may be discharging in their screaming at the children.

The teachers' and the cooks' morality requires an economical use of food, but this clashes head-on with the children's own experience that delay may mean no satisfaction at all, to the point where they cannot help but waste. What the teachers and cooks fail to realize is that these children, by wasting food and asking for more all the time, are trying to find out what is of vital importance to them, to their view of life, and the world: Are the food supplies adequate, will there be more, even if they don't grab it now?

Only on the basis of such pleasurable satiety, with repetitions of the experience that, despite waste, enough is left so that we can feel that this is a good world, will we feel that it is worthwhile to come to terms with its demands. But the teacher expects the children to have such convictions long before they have learned to make them their own. She is critical of their wastefulness, which only reinforces their conviction that "there isn't enough, and we'd better grab it now."

At the Orthogenic School of the University of Chicago there is a tremendous waste of food. It took many months of patient teaching to convince the cooks and helpers that it is so important for emotionally, and often also physically, deprived children to be able to waste and to have their wastefulness positively accepted, because it is for them such an important testing of whether this is a friendly or an unfriendly world. After they understood, they no longer minded the children's wasting large amounts of food, though they had to economize in their own families. We all can accept such behavior in others only after we have really understood its causes and its consequences, but we cannot accept it just because we are told to do so.

FEEDING SHOULD BE PRIMARY CONCERN OF SCHOOLS

Sufficient satiation is a prerequisite for all learning because, if the deprivation is too great, learning becomes too difficult a task. What then is needed is not so much a head start in academic learning, not even a cultural enrichment program (though all this certainly is desirable and helpful), because culture cannot be appreciated on an empty stomach. Instead the application of a few old saws is required, such as the one I mentioned initially of an army marching on its stomach or that "it is easier to fill the stomach than the eye." and finally that "the way to a man's heart (and much more so to that of a child's) is through his stomach."

Therefore in order to make school attractive and learning feasible, we should first concentrate on feeding the children. And by this I do not mean the food programs that exist and provide food as food, nor do I mean to add feeding as just one more part of the educational enterprise. Instead I suggest centering the school experience around satiation of the children's needs, building the school day around meals, with breakfast in the morning, a snack at midmorning, lunch at noon, and another snack at the end of the day. Money spent on such a program would pay off much better than that spent on practically any other expense, be it textbooks or teaching machines. I would give it priority even over school buildings. But this program would have to be entirely different from the mass feedings that are characteristic of most of our food programs. The meals I have in mind are not just a filling of the stomach but an enrichment of the total personality around a common meal, which requires that only a small group should eat together and eat with those who are supposed not only to educate their minds but to nurture their total personalities.

If, for example, teachers eat a different fare and in a separate room, then from the beginning of the educational enterprise a class system is created, and all children, not only the deprived ones, are made to feel a group apart from the established order, as represented by the teacher. Food is the greatest socializer—that is why all great social events require a shared meal which is often made the central feature of the occasion. If we would do that in our classes, they would attain a very different meaning, particularly for the child whose deprivation is a social one, of feeling excluded from the great and meaningful social occasions.

School is the first great encounter of the child with society. It represents to him society and what it stands for. While the middle-class child can accept to some degree that the teacher's teaching is a giving of knowledge to him, for the deprived child what the teacher does seems only to be making demands on him. Thus it is even more important that we convince such children from the moment they come into contact with society that it both gives and demands, and gives first before it demands. And there is no more obvious giving to the child than the giving of food. But a giving from which one excludes oneself, a meal that is given but not shared, is in many ways a condescending giving and hence degrading.

Here an experience might be mentioned that I have had repeatedly:

The social climate of a mental institution changes immediately if the entire staff, up to the top of the hierarchy, takes its meals with the patients. While such practice obviously presupposes a change in attitude of the staff, which should not be overlooked in the effectiveness of such eating together, the fact that patients, staff, and doctors eat together, and eat the same fare, immediately reduced the levels of tension, the potentiality of violent outbreaks. And this not just at mealtime but all during the day and throughout the institution. Now, the teacher's taking her meals with the children also presupposes a change in her inner attitude; but this change, I believe, is the precondition for helping children learn to feel satiated, and with it to learn in general.

Of course, for some time they will waste food, and some may gorge themselves so that they throw up. But when handled correctly, this will be a most important lesson in how beneficial it is to learn controls, and not only for the rare child who stuffed himself so fast and furiously that his stomach revolted, but even more for the other children who watch it and whose natural disgust will teach them control more than any verbal teaching could. But for them to learn this lesson the teacher must not be disgusted; she must use the event to help the sick to feel better and to point out that, while gorging oneself is understandable when one is deprived, controlling one's desires is to one's advantage.

I think the school day in our inner-city schools should begin not with the Pledge of Allegiance, but with a hearty breakfast, eaten in class, with the teacher. Eating together is what makes for allegiance between people, and eventually to one's country. Nothing is more divisive than when people eat a different fare, in different rooms, the one of inferior, the other of superior, quality. But this is exactly what is typical in our schools at lunch, and it is the school cafeteria where most discipline problems are born.

I could cite innumerable examples of children who for years were unable to learn anything in school but who began to learn while they were hand fed by their teacher. The person who feeds us is simply the first teacher in our life and remains our best teacher later on. But a few will have to do as one nonreader did. He had to hold food in one hand while holding the flash card in the other before he could begin learning to read because, as he said, "Food is the only good thing in life and only if I get more in one hand can I learn more [meaning reading] with the other."

The degree to which very deprived children will experience food as a symbol of all pleasure, instead of just nourishment, is typified by the statements a perennial truant made during our early efforts to keep him in school. "You know," he said, "I'm one of those people who has to eat. Sometimes when I've just eaten a lot, I run out of the room and I get hungry again and I want some more food. And then, a little later, I'll need more, even before it's time to eat again. I just like to eat; I just have to have food around."

Food is thus what first attaches many truants to the school; the security of a regular food supply is the great domesticator. Some children who became runaways as soon as they outgrew their infancy were first able to accept school on such a basis.

So closely and intricately interwoven into a single strand within the individual are both our physical nature, which requires food, and the nurture which we call intellectual development, that it will not do to keep them separate. The distinction between physical and emotional need, between body and intellect, is, in reality, a false one. Although schools are concerned with the children's intellectual development, the two are not separable, certainly not in the actual life of the individual. Piaget, the foremost student of the child's intellectual development, makes this point as explicitly as Freud, the foremost student of emotional development would have made it: "There is never a purely intellectual action; numerous emotions, interests, values intervene—for example, in solving a mathematical problem. Likewise, there is never a purely affective act, even love presupposes comprehension." Thus, Piaget is convinced that "there is a close parallel between the development of affectivity, and the intellectual functions." So we can understand why many a child who cannot count just by looking at how many cookies are on the table will know whether there are enough to go around. And I have taught more children to count by counting pieces of candy than in any other way. It is the oldest mathematics, and still the most effective.

Food, for children, is the main source of security. If we want them to engage in what are scary experiences for them, such as learning to read, we have to supply them well with gum, candy, cookies. We have to do that for them when we want them to begin the dangerous exploration of letters and words, as we would have to fill their knapsacks full of good food if they were going to explore the wilderness. Spending as much money on food as on all other teaching material would be a reasonable distribution of expenditures if we want to make learning easy and acceptable.

Once we feed our children as we teach them to read, the two activities will become identified and the children will recognize that just as real food nourishes the body, the intellectual food feeds the mind. If we could realize this and with it what is required to have children learn in school, then the school food programs would become truly successful in feeding body and mind at the same time, and the children so fed will grow intellectually and emotionally into the succesful citizens our society needs.

CHAPTER SEVEN

Relation of Early Parent-Teacher Socialization Influences to Achievement Orientation and Self-Esteem in Middle Childhood Among Low-Income Black Children

Diana T. Slaughter,

In an article published in *Socialization and Society* in 1968, Clausen suggested that childhood socialization is a cumulative process. In his view too few child development researchers have studied the *interactive* effects of diverse socialization agents on the child's development in nondeviant populations. For those of us interested in childhood socialization, particularly the interface between child development and early education, Clausen's comments have particular significance. We need to know how to design studies so that they yield maximal information about the relationships between family, schooling, and childhood outcomes. We also need data that will permit development of realistic expectations and goals, relative to program planning, for educational intervention into the lives of minority youth and their families. This paper may provide some insights into both of the above issues.

In 1967 Coopersmith defined self-esteem as the attribution of positive or negative attitudes toward oneself. Among the social experiences antecedent to the development of positive self-esteem, he included the individual's history of successes, relative to his own values and aspirations, and the amount of respectful, accepting, concerned treatment he receives from significant others. However, he concluded from his research with middle-class white preadolescent males that parental factors almost singularly contributed to this development of self-esteem. Although his book is entitled *The Antecedents of Self-Esteem,* it is devoted to the *parental* antecedents or correlates of this aspect of childhood personality.

Katz (1967), reviewing his experimental studies of black youth in fifth and sixth grades, noted that academically unsuccessful boys engaged in significantly more self-criticism than successful boys, even when the experiment was designed so that both groups would succeed. He concluded that such self-criticism could be an effort to reduce anticipatory anxiety in achieving situations, due to a prior history of negative reinforcements from parents. This interpretation was quite consistent with the existing literature, which has emphasized the adversive influences of low-income black parents' child-rearing practices upon the socialization of achievement motivation and cognitive processes in their young children. (See reviews by Freeberg and Payne, 1967; Hess, 1970; and Deutsch, 1973.) For example, Roberts (1971), in another longitudinal study of black American children in Nashville, Tennessee, attributes the mean decline in these children's Binet I.Q. over a five-year period to familial patterns of socialization of achievement motivation, particularly academic achievement motivation.

In an unpublished review of 13 studies of black high and low school achievers of ages four to 16, Lang (1969) concludes that higher achievers differ from their lower-achieving peers primarily in the areas of self-esteem, positive responsivity to adult authority figures, and verbal fluency, rather than in familial background variables, including attitudes and values. Coleman (1966) and others have reported similar findings, suggesting that a sense of personal control or personal efficacy regarding the ability to influence others and confidence in one's own ability are the most important correlates of minority students' school achievements. Lane (1973) reports that retrospective examination of the childhood records of 22 black college graduates from poverty backgrounds revealed that, by comparison to siblings, these students showed a marked increase in average I.Q. scores around the eighth grade. Lane believes this suggests early outside influences that extend beyond the immediate family.

Klaus (1973), however, in a recent longitudinal study of black and white New York school children, concludes that emphases in the educational area as to the importance of teacher expectancies and behaviors to the development of academic competencies in low-income black youth may be exaggerated (see, for example, Clark,

1965; Rosenthal and Jacobson, 1968; Rist, 1973). He notes that in his study teacher knowledge of I.Q. neither affected teacher expectancy nor pupil test performance. Race of teacher was also not a factor in pupil test performance. He implies that the parents of lower-achieving children lack the mechanisms for appropriate socialization of achievement behaviors in that, while they aspire to college attendance for their children, they also believe that their children should pursue "anything which would make them happy" (page 149). Similar data are introduced by Rosen (1959) in his comparative study of parental achievement values among diverse ethnic groups. He concludes that while black American mothers had high aspirations for their children, they were more likely, by comparison to mothers from other ethnic groups, to accept lower-status positions for their children in the broader society.

Despite efforts by Minuchin et al. (1969) in this area, studies of white middle-class students do not reveal an impact of the school experience upon these children and their families (Wallach, 1971). In fact, Jencks (1972) has concluded that for American pupils there are *no* long-term effects of schools upon pupils. Perhaps only in England have Himmelweit and Swift (1969) been able to document the relationship between type of school attended (roughly equivalent to high school) and long-term occupational outcomes independent of familial social class background.

This longitudinal study attempts to explore some of the assumptions in the preceding studies, specifically (1) the power of the parent, in this instance the mother, relative to achievement behaviors and achievement test outcomes in a sample of low-income black youth; (2) the potential role of teacher evaluations in these outcomes; and (3) the relationship between self-esteem and achievement orientation to the children's academic performance. A longitudinal design is employed because we are especially interested in an examination of the hypothesis of *discontinuity* between the home and school contexts as experienced by low-income blacks, but perhaps not middle-income whites, upon formal school entry.[1]

We envision at least six areas in which the school experience could affect family life through the mother as related to her child. In each area the themes of perceived self-esteem, potency, and resources are salient, as these are the psychological counterparts of the sociological issues of prestige, power, and privilege raised by the social status of these families in relation to the schools many of their children attend. These areas, to be explored in the present study, include: (1) the maternal expectations or aspirations held for the child; (2) the expressed educational philosophy of the mother; (3) the perceived sense of maternal potency relative to the school social system; (4) the quality of personal-social communication between mother and child relative to educational processes; (5) the participation of the family in the broader community; and (6) the stability of the child's family life.

We envision at least three dimensions of child behavior that are related to positive, adaptive, coping behavior in the school environment: the capacity (1) to relate constructively to peers and teachers; (2) to be independent and self-reliant relative to schoolwork; and (3) to be interested in competing and doing well against standards of excellence in an academic context. We believe that the child's history of successes or failures in these areas, as perceived by significant others, may have an influence on his own sense of self-worth. We assume that, at least in the early years of schooling, parents and teachers constitute the child's most significant others.

METHOD AND PROCEDURES OF THE STUDY

Sampling Procedures and Sample Characteristics

The sample for this research consists of 56 middle school children and 40 of their mothers. Thirty children are males and 26 are females. In 1965 90 mother-child dyads (45 males, 45 females) were studied by this researcher when the children entered an eight-week summer Head Start program in Evanston, Illinois. At that time all of the families met the poverty guidelines for urban areas of the Office of Economic Opportunity. In 1965 48.2 percent of the 56 families relocated in 1971 were composed of father-present/mother-working parents; in 1973 this percentage had dropped to 43.6. In 1965 8.5 percent of the 56 relocated families received welfare payments; in 1973 16.4 percent received such payments. No child was included in the 1965 study who had been identified by teachers or school social workers as having severe learning or emotional problems.

In 1971 64 of the 90 dyads were relocated, and 56 agreed to participate in the present study. Relocation was facilitated through examination of school records. Four parents refused to permit their children to be part of the 1971 study, and two children refused when contacted after parental permission had been given. Two children apparently left the school system during the intervening period between relocation in the summer of 1971 and the initiation of child interviews in the summer of 1972. (The delay was unavoidable because of the funding status of this research, which did not permit simultaneous hiring of large numbers of staff.)

Of the relocated and participating families sixteen mothers were not interviewed. Seven could not be contacted by two part-time interviewers before the end of the data collection period. Two families moved. Four families granted permission for their children but not for themselves. Our interviews with the children of these families have given us no reason to believe that these mothers are dramatically different from the other 40 who were interviewed.

The 56 present and 34 attrited samples were contrasted on all possible early variables given in the present report. There were no significant differences in mean scores on maternal attitude measures between the two groups. Mothers of children in the present sample were significantly older in 1965 (31-35 years) than mothers of children in the attrited sample (26-30 years). They were significantly less well educated, but had the same average number of children in the household.

There was a tendency for the 56 study children to have been judged as more intellectually competent, by standardized test data ($p \leq .05$), and more motivated for school achievement, by Head Start preschool teachers ($p \leq .05$), than the 34 attrited children.

In addition to examining mean differences between present and attrited samples on maternal and child variables from 1965, we also examined intercorrelation matrices. We found the correlates of maternal and child variables to be similar for both samples except that there was a significant positive correlation between maternal age and maternal control style and between maternal education and value for school achievement in the present, but not attrited, sample. Number of children in the 1965 household was positively correlated with Binet Mental Age in the attrited, but not present, sample. In the present sample, but not the attrited group, number of children in the 1965 household was positively correlated with Head Start teacher ratings of higher levels of verbal-social participation in the classrooms.

We found no preschool classroom effects on any maternal or child variables, and we also found that attrition, by elementary school attended, was random. The 56 remaining children attended 14 of 16 possible elementary schools, with a maximum of nine children and a minimum of one at any one school.

In general, comparisons of the present and the attrited samples suggest that the latter sample of children was composed of children less psychologically mature than our current group upon school entry. Their mothers tended to be younger ($p \leq .05$), to have more formal education ($p \leq .05$), but not necessarily better parenting strategies, than mothers in the present sample. Klaus (1973), reporting similar findings for his New York children, had additional evidence that his attrited group was, in fact, *downwardly mobile.* We believe we have a similar situation for at least two reasons: first, in 1965 the present sample constituted the somewhat better organized children; second, the school system they currently attend has an excellent academic reputation.

The subsequent academic achievements of the 56 study children, as measured by standardized tests administered in grades kindergarten through 4, were not impressive. With each year an increasing percentage of children achieved below national norms on the tests used. This percentage increased from 68.9 at the end of kindergarten to approximately 93.5 by grade 4. In the summer of 1965 the Binet I.Q.'s of these children ranged from 58-129, with a mean of 92.7 (s.d. = 14.9). Data on these students in 1969 (grade 4) must be considered in historical school context.

When these students entered grade 2 in 1967, the Evanston school system began a systematic program of school transfers toward the goal of integration of the 16 elementary schools servicing grades K-5. The four middle schools (grades 6-8) had been desegregated for some time. In August, 1971, just prior to the initiation of this study, the Evanston Educational Testing Service (ETS Mid-western branch) published a longitudinal report, *Integration in Evanston: 1967-71.* This report indicates that grade 4 reading scores on the Sequential Tests of Educational Progress (STEP) in 1969 for the student population were as follows: (1) mean score for 848 white pupils = 251.0 (s.d. = 16.5); (2) mean score for 243 black pupils = 235.4 (s.d. = 9.2); (3) the range of scores for the 1,091 students sampled was 303-226. The mean score on STEP at grade 4 for our own students, all black, was consistent with these findings: 234.9.* The Evanston Testing Service reported that Evanston norms for black students were lower than for whites but similar to those of the black pupils of the ETS Growth Study of 35,000 pupils. However, Evanston white students were consistently performing above the ETS Growth Study norms.

Our student population had, by grade 4, experienced an eight-week Head Start program and desegregation for two years, by comparison to earlier cohorts (i.e., 1967 and 1968), but their academic perfor-

*Some children did not reach grade 4 until 1970. These data are treated as grade 4 data, although it was year 5 for the child. No child was advanced beyond his original grade placement.

mance had been only slightly affected. There were no significant differences between the academic test performances of children in the present sample and a matched non-Head Start control group in grades K-4. The Evanston Integration Study reported that this cohort performed slightly better than the cohorts of the preceding years, before the elementary schools were desegregated.

We believe it important to indicate, since this particular study included no direct classroom observations or study of teacher attitudes, the conclusions of the Evanston Integration Study. Classroom observations in 1968-1969 of first and second graders (our children were in the third and fourth grades at the time) revealed that white children were physically active in the classroom relative to schoolwork activities such as moving from their seats to the teacher's desk or to reference shelves. Black students gave more attention to persons other than the teacher; black boys, in particular, were least likely to interact with anyone of the same race or sex as themselves. Both groups of students seemed to share in participation of planning of classroom group projects. Teacher perceptions of positive student traits were almost uniformly attributed to white, rather than black students.

At the time of maternal and child interviews in 1972-1973, the children were concentrated in one of four possible middle schools, the one traditionally servicing the poorer classes of families in this affluent community. Twenty-seven of 56, or 48.2 percent, of the children attended this one school, while 12, 7, and 10 children attended one of the other three schools. The two-and-one-half-hour interview with each child during the third time period of this study was administered at each child's school. Maternal interviews in both instances were at the home.

In the present sample there was a dramatic increase in the number of children in the household from 1965-1972 in only two instances among the 40 mothers reinterviewed. One mother had five more children; a grandmother who was, in 1965, rearing all five of one daughter's children was joined by another daughter who had five children of her own. Five other families reported an increase of one child. Twelve reported one to three fewer children in the household. Since the "mother" of the child was identified for purposes of the 1965 study as that female who had primary responsibility for the daily care and welfare of the child, current households with fewer children reflect the discrepant ages of the mothers interviewed as well as, perhaps, altered living arrangements in some instances so that fewer relatives shared the same household.

A record of each child's birth order relative to living children was not obtained in 1965; however, the 40 reinterviewed mothers were queried about the target child's birth order in 1973. Nine children were only or first-born; nine were second-born, nine third-born, 13 fourth- or later-born.

To summarize: in 1973 the mothers in the present sample averaged 40 years of age (range 28-58 years), and had 10.7 years of formal education (as of 1965), with six mothers reporting school attendance since 1965, though no additional degrees were awarded. They reported an average of 3.9 children in their households (range = 1-10). Birth orders of their children averaged 2.9 (range = 1-6). There was a net loss of two fathers in the 56 households, and relatively few instances of economic or educational gains made by parents. Twenty-eight of 40 mothers (70 percent) reinterviewed reported major changes in their family over the intervening years, 1965-1973. Families either survived at their original level of economic and psychosocial balance or had been challenged by new crises that were not always favorably resolved. The families lived in a striving and economically prosperous white middle- to upper-middle-class community of 80,000 and had, according to our parent interviews, assimilated many of the values of that community. Blacks constituted approximately 16 percent of the population. Many of the families in our study, if not most, did not have the resources to implement these valued life styles. The findings are probably generalizable to all such comparable black American populations. They are probably not generalizable to either severly deprived low-income urban or rural communities or to comparatively affluent black middle-class communities.

Maternal Variables and Measures

Chart I presents the list of maternal variables assessed from interview data in 1965 and 1973. In a principal component analysis of the 1965 data variables 5, 3, and 2 loaded on Factor I in that order of priority; variables 4, 6, and 1 loaded on Factor II.[2 3]

Variables 5, 3, and 2—Warmth expressed toward the child; Cognitive controls used with child; Individuation of the child's personality—emphasize the quality of personal communication between mother and child. Variable 2 focuses on maternal awareness of the child's age-related personal and social needs; 3 on the style of monitoring of the child's experiences; and 5 on the amount of encouraged sharing of these experiences. Factor I refers to dimension (4), personal-social communication, as outlined on page 104 of this chapter.

Variables 4, 6, and 1—Value for school achievement; Social contacts of the mother; and Concepts used in family problem-solving—emphasize the quality of the family's relationship with the broader community as perceived by the mother. Variable 4 focuses upon the expectations or aspirations the mother might have for her child as well as on her apparent investment in their realization; 6 on the degree of differentiation of the mother's current life space, relative to the broader community; and 1 on the mother's tendency to use part and present experiences to form guidelines for decision making. Factor II refers to dimensions (1), aspiration, and (5) community ties, as outlined on pages 103-104 of this chapter.

Variables 9, 10, 11 emphasize maternal attitudes toward the school. Variable 9 assesses the mother's perceived influence on the school; 10 an aspect of her educational philosophy, the degree of emphasis on learning the "3 R's"; and variable 11 her regard for teachers and school curricula. Variable 9 refers to dimension (3), potency; Variables 10, 11 to dimension (2), educational philosophy.

Variable 12, assessed only in 1973, attempts to indicate the amount of perceived discontinuities in family life during the child's early school years. This variable refers to dimension (6).

Specific definitions of the first eight variables, listed in Chart I, are presented in two coding manuals that can be obtained from this researcher, one for 1965 and one for 1973. The manuals present definition, measures, and coding criteria.

The most important aspect of the procedures of the study, relative to assessment of maternal variables, was the attempt to establish comparability between identical psychosocial processes assessed at two different periods in the parent and child's development. Initial measure-

Chart I
Maternal Variables Assessed

	Time I (July, 1965)	*Time III (January, 1973)*
1. Concepts used by mother	X	X
2. Individuation of the child's personality	X	X
3. Cognitive controls used by the mother	X	X
4. Value for school achievement	X	X
5. Warmth toward the child	X	X
6. Social contacts of the mother	X	X
7. Cooperation with the interviewer	X	X
8. Maternal Individuation*	X	X
9. Potency with schools	X	X
10. Traditionalism in educational orientation	X	X
11. Esteem for teachers and curriculum	X	X
12. Changes in family life over the years 1965-1973		X

*Measurement of this variable is the average sum score of variables 1-3.

ment in 1965 of the maternal variables, the first eight presented in Chart I, employed a technique used by Dyk and Witkin (1965) to evaluate maternal interview material. The presence of specific *indicators* was used to determine whether or not a mother could be viewed as "high" or "low" on a particular variable. These indicators were chosen as age-appropriate indices of a particular kind of maternal-child interaction and were theoretically determined by this researcher. They assessed specific attributes of mother-child interaction that were thought to be important "signs" of the presence of certain psychosocial processes in the child's home. These indicators could never be more than probability statements of what might actually occur.

In both the 1965 and 1973 manuals the indicators presumed to be associated with each of the first six variables are delineated, and the presence (+) or absence (−) of each of these is tested. The final rating is the sum of the "plus" indicators, with a score of 1 indicating that no indicators are present and a score of 7 indicating that all indicators are present.

Comparability in 1972-1973 was defined in primarily two ways: (1) identical interview item and (2) revision of the item(s) for age-status and school experience. For example, a mother was not asked in 1973 what she would do if her child refused to go to bed, but what she would do if he refused to do his homework. During all coding each variable was rated on all cases before proceeding to the next variable. At no time were the coders aware of the children's scores on the diverse measures.

The median percent agreement per indicator scale on 18 percent of the cases at Time I and 30 percent of the cases at Time III was .810 in 1965 (range = .762 - .929) and .842 in 1973 (range = .703 - .904). Rank-order correlations of actual scale scores were, of course, much higher.

Variables 9-11 were assessed with items derived from principal component analysis of a 26-item Educational Attitude Survey developed by Hess and Shipman (1969) and cross-validated by Slaughter in 1970. Mothers are to indicate agreement or disagreement on a 5-point scale relative to four short items per variable. The maximum factor score, the positive end, is 5.0. This score is obtained by dividing the respondent's factor sum score by the four items in each factor.

Variable 12 was assessed through questions of the mother as to major changes in life, such as moving to different housing, illness of a family member, financial problems, and so on. A high score of 7 indicates that the mother reported changes in all six areas of inquiry, while a low score of 1 indicates no reported changes.

Child Variables and Measures

In addition to child achievement performance measures used here, including the Binet in preschool, the Metropolitan Reading Readiness Test at the end of kindergarten, and the Sequential Tests of Educational Progress at the beginning of grade 4, Chart II presents the list of child personality variables assessed. Three were assessed from teacher and observer ratings of classroom behavior in 1965 and observer ratings of interview data in 1973. In 1973 three direct measures of the child's attitudes toward self, school, and life were taken: (1) the Coopersmith Self-Esteem Inventory, (2) the Meadors-Slaughter Satisfaction with School Inventory, and (3) the three Coleman report (1966) personal-control items. These variables emphasize the child's personality characteristics, as judged from self or other's perceptions. The Kuder-Richardson 20 reliability for the Coopersmith Self-Esteem Inventory with this population is .98; test-retest reliability is .68. The Spearman-Brown internal consistency coefficient for the Satisfaction with School Inventory is .55.

At Time I teacher and observer ratings on Verbal-Social Participa-

Chart II
Child Variables Assessed

	Time I (July, 1965)	*Time II (Sept. 1965-June 1971)*	*Time III (July, 1972)*
CHILD PERSONALITY VARIABLES			
Verbal social participation*	X		X
Independence*	X		X
Achievement motivation*	X		X
Self-esteem			X
Satisfaction with school			X
Sense of potency			X
CHILD ACHIEVEMENT VARIABLES			
Teacher evaluation—reading		X	
Teacher evaluation—language		X	
Teacher evaluation—mathematics		X	
Teacher evaluation—conduct		X	
Test evaluation—reading skills		X	
Test evaluation—mathematic skills		X	
Test Evaluation—verbal aptitude		X	
Test evaluation—quantitative aptitude		X	
Test evaluation—intelligence quotient	X		

*These ratings were made by both teachers and observers trained in child development in preschool; however, in 1972 resources were available only for repeat of the child development observers' evaluations. Dates are reported as of initiation of data collection period.

tion, Independence, and Achievement Motivation correlate .68 (Pearson r), .30, and .26, respectively. For this reason they are treated separately in data analyses; apparently the child development observers and the preschool teachers entered different criteria into their judgments of the personality characteristics of each of the children. In 1973 agreements between two observers on 20 cases were .81, .65, and .76, respectively, for the Verbal-Social, Independence, and Achievement Motivation scales.

At Time I each of these three variables was assessed on a seven-point rating scale adapted from the Zigler Behavior Inventory. This adapted 23-item instrument had been used to rate 177 black preschool children in three different preschool settings. Observer and teacher ratings were factored by principal component analysis (Hess, Kramer, Slaughter, et al., 1966). Three of the five factors, those identified above, were used in the 1965 study, where the primary focus was on the cognitive performance outcomes of the children rather than on their personal-social development. Each factor contained four items, to be rated on a seven-point scale. The Verbal-Social Participation and Independence scales range from 1 (high) to 7 (low), while the Achievement Motivation scale ranges from 7 (high) to 1 (low).

The four rated dimensions of Verbal-Social Participation include: (1) talks eagerly to adults about his own experiences and what he thinks; (2) likes to talk or socialize with the teacher; (3) is eager to inform other children of the experiences he has had; and (4) asks many questions for information about things, persons, etc. The rated dimensions of Independence include: (1) tries to figure out things for himself before asking adults or children for help; (2) does not need attention or approval from adults to sustain him in his work; (3) appears to trust in his own abilities; and (4) goes about his activities with a minimum of assistance from others. The rated dimensions of Achievement Motivation, expressed in the Zigler Inventory from the perspective of low Achievement Motivation, include: (1) discontinues activity after exerting a minimum of effort; (2) when faced with a difficult task, either does not attempt it or gives up quickly; (3) seems disinterested in the general quality of his performance; and (4) is lethargic or apathetic, has little energy or drive.

Because observational data were not available at Time III, an extensive effort was undertaken to establish comparability of observer perceptions.[4] This involved simultaneous selection by this researcher and two observers of potential interview questions that could elicit information related to each factor item, a series of meetings to reach consensus on these questions and the respective coding criteria, as well as the final rating of 20 cases of Evanston children not in this longitudinal study, but matched with this sample for race, socioeconomic status, year of birth, and length of time in the Evanston school system. These 20 cases were randomly selected from an additional pool of 31 interviews available.

Charts II and III also describe our use of teacher grades in this study to index the history of the child's successes and failures relative to teacher-student interaction.

At the end of each academic year each child's teacher evaluated the progress in three academic areas: reading (reading readiness in kindergarten), language, and mathematics (number readiness in kindergarten). This information was recorded on the cumulative record cards as Doing Well, Making Acceptable Progress, or Needs

Chart III
Categories by Grade of Judgments of Pupil Progress

	Reading	*Language*	*Mathematics*
Kindergarten	Interested in stories, poems, and books; recognizes likenesses and differences; interprets the meaning of pictures	Listens to learn; follows directions; contributes to discussion and planning; learns and uses new words	Recognizes numerals 1-10; is learning the meaning of numbers
	4*	4	2
Grade 1	Shows desire to read; is acquiring a slight vocabulary; comprehension; word attack skills	Listens attentively; speaks easily and to the point; forms letters correctly; spaces letters and words; writes stories	Uses numbers with understanding; writes numerals correctly; is learning number combinations
	4	5	3
Grade 2, 3	Shows desire to read; slight vocabulary; comprehension; phonics and word attack skills	Listens attentively; speaks fluently; uses correct English; forms letters correctly; spaces letters and words; organizes written work	Uses numbers with understanding; number combinations; growth in accuracy; understands and solves thought problems
	4	6	4
Grades 4, 5	Comprehension; interpretation; vocabulary; word attack skills	Oral expression; written expression	Number facts; reasoning; computation
	4	2	3

*Number of subcategories (distinguished by each new semicolon)

Improvement. The subcategories, by grade, under which these judgments were made, are listed in Chart III. Doing Well was coded as 3; Making Acceptable Progress as 2; and Needs Improvement as 1. The maximum score in each area, therefore, was three times the number of subcategories. For example, the maximum score for reading readiness in kindergarten = 3 × 4 (number of subcategories) = 12, while the maximum score for mathematics in grade 5 = 3 × 3 = 9. The corresponding minimum scores are 4 and 3. In the few instances where there was no information on a particular subcategory a 2 (the equivalent of Making Acceptable Progress) was recorded.

In the instance of grades 2 and 3 an *average* score was computed, and similarly for grades 4 and 5 for each of the three areas: reading, language, and mathematics. This was possible because the cumulative rating forms for grades 2 and 3, and grades 4 and 5, are identical.

A *profile* of each child's progress was then constructed. Each of the frequency distributions of the 12 variables above were separately inspected and divisions made according to those scores in the following percentiles: (1) 1-20; (2) 21-40; (3) 41-60; (4) 61-80; (5) 81-100. A child whose score placed him in the top 20 percent is therefore a child whom 80 percent of his classmates are behind. It is important to emphasize, however, that percentile comparisons were introduced by the research and *not* in the original teacher evaluations.

In the research each child was given a percentile standing from 1 (high) to 5 (low) in the subject area for each grade (i.e., on the 12 variables listed in Chart III). The median percentile standing for each of the three subject areas was then computed for each child. *Any movement of two or more percentile standings in either a positive or negative direction was defined as a significant change.* Movement from the top 20 to 60 percent, for example, was considered a significant change, while movement from 20 to 40 percent was not. It was hoped thereby to somewhat compensate for error of measurement and regression factors in repeated individual evaluations.

All profiles and other academic information on each child were then examined according to the following criteria: (1) evidence for a significant percentile standing change in teacher evaluations between the kindergarten and fourth and fifth years and at any points in between; (2) evidence of the direction of the change, if any; (3) whether or not the child was retained by the school during the primary grades; and (4) whether the retention seemed to result in improved evaluations (i.e., at or beyond the level of performance prior to the problem year (s) *or* average standing. In one or two instances children were identified during the kindergarten year and performance was judged improved to average standing in later years. Most children were identified after either grades 1 or grade 2 and revealed no significant improvement after retention.

The following *patterns* were identified for the *56 children reinterviewed* in the present study:

Pattern 4 (N. = 24): No change; average or above average in teacher academic evaluations throughout the years kindergarten to grade 5.

Pattern 3 (N = 5): Change from low standing to at least average standing; children typically identified in early years, kindergarten or grade 1, retained, and judged later as improving by teachers.

Pattern 2 (N = 12): No change, below average in academic standing from earliest years; retention did not result in later improvement, according to teacher evaluations.

Pattern 1 (N = 15): Change from average or above standing to a lower standing; typically never identified by school personnel for special services.

Other, theoretically possible patterns did not occur with any observed regularity. These four patterns constitute the *Index of academic consistency relative to teacher-student interaction.* The patterns form a *nominal* scale. Each is viewed as a discrete, separate entity. The distributions by patterns according to children whose *mothers were also reinterviewed* are as follows: pattern 4 (N = 17); pattern 3 (N = 4); pattern 2 (N = 8); pattern 1 (N = 11).

For purposes of this report pattern 4 students will be referred to as *achievers;* pattern 3 students will be identified as *proachievers;* pattern 2 students will be identified as *nonachievers;* and pattern 1 students will be identified as *antiachievers.*

RESULTS

The results of this study are presented in Tables 1-9b. Table 1 presents the correlations between maternal and child variables for the 56 dyads in 1965 at Time I of the study. Maternal variables and child personality variables were assessed within the first four weeks of the 1965 summer Head Start program. The Stanford-Binet was also administered at that time. The Metropolitan Readiness Test was administered at the end of kindergarten in spring, 1966. There is a rather striking relationship between reported maternal behaviors and attitudes and the children's achievements upon school entry. There is

Table 1
Intercorrelations of Maternal and Child Achievement Variables at Time I

Child Variables (Preschool)	*Binet MA (Preschool) (56)*	*Binet IQ (Preschool) (56)*	*Metropolitan Readiness (Kindergarten) (56)*
1. Verbal-social participation (Teacher)	−35**	−25**	−31**
2. Verbal-social participation (Observer)	−34**	23*	−17
3. Independence (Teacher)	−18	−12	−23*
4. Independence (Observer)	−08	04	−09
5. Achievement motivation (Teacher)	46**	40**	57**
6. Achievement motivation (Observer)	25*	17	32**
Maternal Variables (Preschool)			
7. Mo concepts	26*	29*	03
8. Mo individuation of child	25*	28*	13
9. Mo controls with child	42**	39**	37**
10. Mo value for school achievement	25*	34**	19
11. Mo warmth	14	14	14
12. Mo social contacts	21*	22*	11
13. Maternal individuation	40**	41**	22*
14. Mo potency †	43*	34**	45**
15. Mo trad. educ. orientation †	33**	30**	50**
16. Mo esteem for teachers & curriculum †	53**	41**	71**

**p =01
*p =05
† =N's = 53−50

N. B. Child personality: Significance levels of 05 or better occurred only between maternal control style, teacher/observer perceptions of achievement motivation, and teacher perception of the child's verbal-social participation.

also a relationship between observed behavioral attributes of the children, particularly their observed verbal-social participation and persistence on tasks in the classroom, and their own performance outcomes in test situations. Maternal control style (variable 9) and teacher/observer perceptions of achievement motivation were significantly correlated (.39 and .35 respectively, $p \leq .05$). Similarly, maternal control style and teacher's perceptions of the child's verbal-social participation in the classroom were significantly correlated (- .25, $p \leq .05$).

We believe that subtleties in expression of independent behavior at this early age level account for the absence of significant findings relative to this variable. Specifically, our rating does not adequately distinguish children who are emotionally dependent from those who are instrumentally dependent when, presumably, it is the latter that is most important in educational contexts. Some children may have been perceived as emotionally dependent and uncertain when in fact they sought task-related assistance in ways that were quite appropriate to their ages.

Whether or not the mother chooses to monitor her child through personalized forms of control, as contrasted with age or sex normative prescriptions for behavior, seems to be related to both child achievement and personality characteristics in educational contexts in this four- to five-year-old period. Maternal affect per se, or educational aspirations for the child, may be less important. Conversely, maternal attitudes toward the school are also related to child performance outcomes.

Table 2 presents the stability coefficients (Pearson r) in the diagonal of each maternal variable assessed at the two time periods—1965 and 1973.[5] The right side of the table presents the correlations of all Time III maternal variables, while the left side presents the correlations of Time III variables with every other maternal variable except itself (presented in diagonal) at Time I. The four variables for which there is the greatest stability between Time I and Time III in order of magnitude are: Social contacts of the mother, Warmth toward the child, Value for school achievement, and the summary score (variables 1-3) indexing Maternal individuation. Table 3 presents data as to the relationship between children's achievement performance in grades K-4 and maternal and child attributes assessed in 1973 (grade 6).

Data in Tables 2 and 3, jointly considered, suggest a variety of important points. First, insofar as the stability of maternal behaviors has

Table 2
Intercorrelations of Time III Maternal Variables with:
(a) Time I Maternal Variables and (b) Time III Maternal Variables

Time I (N = 40)	*Scale*	*Time III (N = 40)* 1	2	3	4	5	6	7	8	9	10
Mo concepts	1	20	48**	53**	52**	36*	53**	83**	14	04	−15
Mo individ of child	2	14	16	37**	20	26	20	75**	−04	−06	−11
Mo controls with child	3	23	17	15	51**	54**	36*	80**	−10	−05	05
Mo value for schl. ach.	4	22	32*	33*	36*	35*	26	54**	20	−10	32*
Mo warmth	5	29	07	24	27	42**	50**	47**	15	−08	00
Mo social contacts	6	26	01	07	32*	00	43**	44**	11	24	−08
Maternal individuation	7	25	24	27	33*	51**	36*	30*	−00	−04	−03
Potency with schools	8	32*	−04	−06	13	05	02	02	−00	−05	32*
Traditional ed. orient.	9	−04	16	08	19	00	−09	08	−01	−17	04
Esteem for teachers and curriculum	10	−01	−03	−03	15	01	−29	04	−29	09	19

***p = .01*
**p = .05*

Table 3
Relation Between Selected Child Achievement Measures and Child and Maternal Variables at Grade 6

(Correlations)

	CHILD ACHIEVEMENT VARIABLES						
	Binet MA (Preschool) (56)	*Binet IQ (Preschool) (56)*	*Metropolitan Readiness (Kindergarten) (53)*	*STEP Reading (Grade 4) (50)*	*STEP Math (Grade 4) (51)*	*SCAT Verbal (Grade 4) (46)*	*SCAT Quant. (Grade 4) (42)*
Child Variables (Grade 6)							
Verbal-social participation	−10	−01	−25	−24	−07	−30*	−36*
Independence	−38**	−36**	−33**	−46**	−10	−38**	−28
Achievement motivation	31**	27*	24	38**	13	12	18
Self-esteem	44**	39**	47**	34**	17	29*	24
Satisfaction with school	10	14	01	02	−20	−02	−06
Potency	27*	18	16	12	04	32*	−06
Maternal Variables (Grade 6)[1]							
Mo concepts . . .	04	−02	15	−06	07	−01	22
Mo individuation of child	31*	24	34*	13	33*	32	36*
Mo controls with child	22	24	41**	15	16	08	11
Mo value for schl. ach.	46**	43**	40**	23	15	09	27
Mo warmth	30*	37**	23	04	22	14	22
Mo social contacts	10	18	−00	−22	09	−09	00
Maternal individuation	24	19	36*	11	23	16	24
Mo potency	−01	07	−28	08	27	−19	01
Mo trad. educ. orient.	03	C3	04	20	23	−03	06
Mo esteem for teachers & curriculum	17	08	20	38*	06	−08	27
Mo change in family life over eight years, 1965−1973	−38**	−37**	−14	−18	03	−21	−02

**p = 01
*p = 05

[1]N's on maternal variables range from 40-30.

relevance for the achievement performances of their children, expressed maternal affectivity and aspirations are most important, rather than explicit styles of monitoring the child's behavior, the latter perhaps being much more subject to the immediate social and developmental context. Even the relatively high stability over an eight-year period of mothers' levels of participation in the community has little import in relation to the child's early or later school performance.

Second, recency of assessment has little to do with the relationship between child performance and maternal attributes. The attributes that are significantly correlated are related to performance in the earlier years of schooling, not in the later years.

Third, the assessment of similar child attributes at the sixth grade level is related to child achievement in the early and later years of schooling, particularly in the areas of reading and verbal skills. We found no relation between child and maternal attributes assessed at the sixth grade level, except for a correlation of .31 between maternal warmth and child independence in the school context ($p \leq .05$).

Fourth, maternal attitudes toward the school are extremely unstable, by comparison to the other variables. There is essentially no relationship between early and later attitudes toward the school, or between these later attitudes and children's achievements at any grade level. In short, it is not possible to account for the achievement performance, achievement motivation, and self-esteem of these children after school entry by consideration of maternal background factors prior to that entry.

Assuming that our measures of maternal and child variables at both Times I and III are valid, these data suggest some intervening forces have influenced achievement performance outcomes in the children after school entry. We believe these "intervening forces" to be the history of successes and failures the children have experienced in relation to teacher-student interactions.

Data in Table 4 lend some support to this hypothesis, suggesting that the *trend* is for maternal attitudes, as expressed when the child was enrolled in middle school, to be associated with teacher evaluations of that child's performance in the earliest years (grades K-1) of schooling. These descriptive data do not elucidate why this trend exists. It is possible that the mother simply *reacts* to expressed teacher judgments; it is equally possible that teacher judgments are formed around subtle perceptions of family instability at the point of school entry, an instability that mothers themselves report at Time III and that seems to relate to some aspects of the child's early school performances (see Tables 3 and 4). It is also possible that mothers react to perceived

Table 4
Relationship Between Teacher Evaluations in Grades K-5 and Maternal Variables in Preschool (Time I) and Grade Six (Time III) (Correlations)

MATERNAL VARIABLES

Teacher Evaluations	*Value for School Achievement*		*Warmth Towards Child*		*Social Contacts of Mother*		*Maternal Individuation*		*Potency*		*Traditional Educational Orientation*		*Esteem for Teachers and Curriculum*		*Perceived Change in Family Life over eight years*
	T1 (44-48)	T3 (33)	T1 (44-48)	T3 (33)	T1 (44-48)	T3 (33)	T1 (44-48)	T3 (33)	T1 (40-42)	T3 (32-34)	T1 (40-42)	T3 (32-34)	T1 (40-42)	T3 (32-34)	T3 (40-32)
Kindergarten															
Reading	04	43**	04	27	02	15	21	14	−25	18	07	00	15	11	−16
Language	13	48**	14	26	12	08	34*	20	−10	−03	06	−14	14	08	−38*
Mathematics	10	31	−06	16	08	03	15	−05	−06	−17	07	03	−19	16	11
Conduct	20	37*	29*	36*	19	07	50**	16	−19	−05	−05	−16	12	10	−39*
Grade One															
Reading	−08	20	03	20	06	08	20	−08	−00	19	02	−03	−09	20	−27
Language	−11	22	08	20	06	08	20	−08	12	27	02	−17	05	23	−32
Mathematics	03	46**	13	51**	11	12	29*	06	−02	16	10	−29	01	19	−43**
Conduct	−11	22	08	49**	15	18	18	11	−08	06	15	−03	02	06	−26
Grades 2-3															
Reading	−06	−08	−10	02	10	02	01	−14	04	−18	02	−12	−22	27	−14
Language	−04	09	−02	29	19	05	13	−00	12	−04	10	−11	−05	10	−41*
Mathematics	−20	−10	−06	09	−11	−12	02	−12	09	04	15	14	10	21	−18
Conduct	−09	26	16	25	00	−20	22	13	25	05	09	−24	−10	24	−11
Grades 4-5															
Reading	−05	−08	18	33	05	08	−04	10	09	10	−12	08	−06	03	−21
Language	−21	08	02	−09	08	−21	04	03	14	−02	−19	−35*	06	05	−32
Mathematics	00	−01	34*	37*	08	12	17	16	00	19	06	02	11	22	−50**
Conduct	−03	−12	07	02	11	−23	08	07	30*	−08	−20	−17	−30*	−15	−09

**p = 01
*p = 05

Table 5
Relationship Between Teacher Evaluations and Child Personality Variables in Preschool and Grade 6 (Correlations)

	CHILD PERSONALITY VARIABLES											
	Verbal-Social Participation			*Independence*			*Achievement Motivation*					
Teacher Evaluation	*Teacher (Preschool) (48-45)*	*Observer (Preschool) (48-45)*	*Observer (Grade 6) (48-45)*	*Teacher (Preschool) (48-45)*	*Observer (Preschool) (48-45)*	*Observer (Grade 6) (48-45)*	*Teacher (Preschool) (48-45)*	*Observer (Preschool) (48-45)*	*Observer (Grade 6) (48-45)*	*Coopersmith Self-Esteem (Grade 6) (48-45)*	*Meadors-Slaughter Satisfaction with School (Grade 6) (48-45)*	*Coleman-Potency (Grade 6) (48-45)*
Kindergarten												
Reading	−28	−07	−15	04	04	−09	32*	24	03	38**	07	12
Language	−43**	−21	−24	−43**	−21	−30*	47**	31*	10	34**	08	13
Mathematics	−24	−15	−14	−15	−09	−24	13	−06	32*	35**	37**	23
Conduct	−20	−11	−07	−11	−04	−27	36**	31*	09	10	18	02
Grade One												
Reading	−28	−10	−20	−25	−25	−34*	26	15	32*	19	−02	14
Language	−02	06	−21	−02	06	−37**	17	18	28	07	03	01
Mathematics	−13	02	−04	−25	−10	−17	33*	16	21	12	05	04
Conduct	−18	−18	−02	−02	−23	−09	10	17	18	20	06	09
Grades Two - Three												
Reading	−16	−15	−27	−26	−11	−41**	21	05	32*	26	10	16
Language	−22	−24	09	−22	−24	−07	38**	14	27	23	14	11
Mathematics	−27	−06	−25	−14	−07	−32*	38**	12	52**	22	−00	18
Conduct	08	05	−01	−02	−21	−09	20	−07	11	34*	22	13
Grades Four - Five												
Reading	−19	−17	−29*	−18	−22	−44**	18	11	28	21	16	20
Language	−05	02	−16	−05	02	−23	15	01	09	13	−17	08
Mathematics	−32*	−31*	−29*	−17	−05	−57**	42**	13	23	13	−01	12
Conduct	12	18	−14	−17	−27	−38**	20	06	18	18	24	12

**p = 01
*p = 05

changes in the child that have been initiated by the teacher. The important point for us is that there is some *discontinuity* between the influence of the parents of these children before and after school entry.

Data in Table 5 indicate that children's independence in school contexts at grade 6 is associated with teacher evaluations of academic performance. Self-esteem at grade 6 is associated with teacher evaluations in kindergarten. The child's verbal-social participation is not consistently associated with teacher evaluations at any grade level. Conversely, preschool teacher evaluations of achievement motivation tend to be important throughout grades K-3. Observer evaluations of achievement motivation at Time III do not seem to be associated with teacher evaluations of academic performance. In short, positive teacher evaluations do not increase the motivational levels of these children, but they do appear to encourage a greater self-confidence in their own abilities and their capacity to function competently in the school setting.

Data in Table 6 present our attempts to characterize the differences in maternal and child variables by history of teacher-student interaction, as indexed by our index of academic consistency. Recall the distinctions between the four groups presented. *Achievers* (Group IV), according to teachers' judgments, have been consistently average or above average in academic standing relative to other children in this sample from kindergarten through grade 5. *Proachievers* (Group III) have typically been judged by their teachers as improving in their academic performance over the intervening years; typically, they were identified as having academic difficulties in K-1, retained, and then judged as having improved after the retention experience. *Nonachievers* were below average relative to this group as a whole and remained in this standing, whether retained or not, from the earliest years of schooling. *Antiachievers* have consistently changed over the years from average-or-above standing, according to teachers' judgments, to a lower standing. Typically, they have never been identified for any special school services. The question addressed in Table 6 is whether these four groups differed in any way, upon school entry, on either maternal or child personality variables.

Two significant differences are reported in Table 6. Mothers of proachievers typically had a more "traditional" view of schools than other mothers; they preferred that schools spend more time on reading, writing, and arithmetic and reduce time on sports and games; these parents see to it that children work hard in school and do not interfere with teachers' right to teach. The second difference must be interpreted cautiously insofar as we believe it may be associated with a

Table 6
Differences in Time I Maternal and Child Variables by Subsequent Child Achievement Group

		Group I Antiachievers (N = 15)	*Group II Nonachievers (N = 12)*	*Group III Proachievers (N = 5)*	*Group IV Achievers (N = 24)*	*F Ratio*	*Significance*
1. Concepts used in family problem-solving	mean	3.07	2.50	3.40	3.21	0.8635	NS
	s.d.	1.53	1.09	0.89	1.44		
2. Individuation of child personality	mean	4.33	3.67	4.60	4.37	0.6088	NS
	s.d.	2.09	1.67	1.34	1.44		
3. Maternal control style	mean	4.13	3.08	3.60	4.29	2.0188	NS
	s.d.	1.41	1.31	0.55	1.65		
4. Value for school achievement	mean	4.13	3.67	5.00	4.25	1.3272	NS
	s.d.	1.19	1.37	0.70	1.39		
5. Warmth to child	mean	3.73	4.58	4.00	4.91	1.9217	NS
	s.d.	1.67	1.44	1.58	1.56		
6. Diversity of maternal social contacts	mean	3.73	2.83	3.40	3.33	0.9876	NS
	s.d.	1.47	1.58	1.14	1.16		
7. Maternal individuation*	mean	3.82	3.16	3.86	4.09	1.9536	NS
	s.d.	1.37	0.94	0.70	1.02		
8. Maternal potency in schools†	mean	2.84	2.96	2.60	2.77	0.3006	NS
	s.d.	0.77	0.76	0.50	0.64		
9. Maternal traditional view of school†	mean	2.36	2.52	1.42	2.55	3.0344	$p = .05$
	s.d.	0.77	0.76	0.50	0.64		
10. Maternal esteem for school†	mean	1.85	1.98	1.68	1.97	0.7163	NS
	s.d.	0.50	0.37	0.70	0.37		
11. Teacher — verbal-social participation	mean	4.20	5.50	4.20	4.38	1.8427	NS
	s.d.	1.82	1.09	1.64	1.64		
12. Observer — verbal-social participation	mean	4.93	6.00	4.20	4.62	3.1758	$p = .05$
	s.d.	1.38	0.85	2.17	1.44		
13. Teacher — independence	mean	4.13	4.33	4.20	3.42	2.1002	NS
	s.d.	1.50	1.23	1.48	0.88		
14. Observer — independence	mean	4.33	4.17	3.20	3.50	1.9256	NS
	s.d.	0.90	1.19	2.17	1.35		
15. Teacher — achievement motivation	mean	5.53	4.91	5.00	5.67	2.1951	NS
	s.d.	0.64	1.24	1.41	0.76		
16. Observer — achievement motivation	mean	5.40	4.92	4.80	5.42	0.9194	NS
	s.d.	0.91	1.31	0.83	1.14		

*Measured by the average sum score of variables 1-3.
†N's = 14, 12, 4, 21 respectively for Groups I-IV.

lack of homogeneity of variances. The child development observers viewed the subsequently identified nonachievers as being more reticent, relative to other peers and their preschool teacher, than the other children upon school entry. No other differences are observed in these four groups regarding maternal attitudes and reported behaviors or child personality variables upon school entry.

Conversely, data in Table 7 reveal four significant differences between these four groups. There are also consistent trends that seem important. By grade 6 mothers of Achievers report expressing higher

Table 7
Differences in Time III Maternal and Child Variables by Previous Child Achievement Group

		Group I Antiachievers (N = 10)	*Group II Nonachievers (N = 8)*	*Group III Proachievers (N = 4)*	*Group IV Achievers (N = 18)*	*F Ratio*	*Significa*
1. Concepts used in family problem-solving	mean	4.20	3.88	5.50	3.94	1.1032	NS
	s.d.	1.62	2.03	1.29	1.47		
2. Individuation of child personality	mean	5.00	4.38	5.25	5.11	0.4353	NS
	s.d.	1.94	1.68	1.71	1.41		
3. Maternal control style	mean	4.00	3.25	5.00	4.33	1.2181	NS
	s.d.	1.33	2.19	1.82	1.53		
4. Value for school achievement	mean	4.90	3.50	4.75	4.39	1.1576	NS
	s.d.	1.66	2.00	0.50	1.61		
5. Warmth to child	mean	4.80	4.25	3.75	5.72	3.0255	p = .0
	s.d.	1.62	1.62	1.91	1.17		
6. Diversity of maternal social contacts	mean	4.80	3.62	4.50	3.89	1.0799	NS
	s.d.	1.69	1.68	1.91	1.41		
7. Maternal individuation*	mean	4.41	3.80	5.28	4.43	1.1444	NS
	s.d.	1.35	1.70	1.26	1.11		
8. Maternal potency in schools	mean	3.49	3.92	3.82	3.60	0.5328	NS
	s.d.	0.99	0.51	0.24	0.85		
9. Maternal traditional view of school	mean	3.52	3.40	3.40	3.37	0.0738	NS
	s.d.	0.84	0.85	0.91	0.76		
10. Maternal esteem for school	mean	3.01	3.30	3.50	3.37	0.8459	NS
	s.d.	0.69	0.47	0.58	0.71		
11. Observer — verbal-social participation†	mean	3.47	4.42	3.20	3.33	1.8899	NS
	s.d.	1.06	1.31	1.30	1.58		
12. Observer — independence†	mean	3.40	5.00	3.40	2.96	5.9217	p = .
	s.d.	1.24	0.95	1.14	1.65		
13. Observer — Achievement motivation†	mean	3.73	3.08	3.80	4.25	2.4858	p = .0
	s.d.	1.16	1.16	1.30	1.26		
14. Self-esteem†	mean	74.67	60.67	74.40	73.42	2.7151	p = .
	s.d.	13.79	14.70	10.90	15.05		
15. Satisfaction with school†	mean	61.60	58.25	61.00	62.70	1.0384	NS
	s.d.	8.30	5.05	8.12	7.16		
16. Sense of potency†	mean	7.60	6.67	7.60	7.25	0.9936	NS
	s.d.	1.50	1.67	1.67	1.33		

*Measured by the average sum of variables 1-3.
†N's = 15, 12, 5, 24 respectively for Groups I - IV.

levels of affection toward them than mothers of children in the other three groups. Their children have consistently higher levels of independence and achievement motivation. Nonachievers are consistently viewed as having lower levels of independence in the school context, lower levels of self-esteem, and a tendency toward a lower level of achievement motivation. Data in Table 3 suggest that these latter three variables are significantly correlated with reading and verbal skills in grade 4, as measured by achievement performance tests. Nonachievers also express the least amount of satisfaction with school and the least amount of potency relative to personal influence in general life events. It appears that the school experience has maximized differences between the two groups of children in areas of importance to their personal-social development.

However, data in Table 8 reveal that the Achievers and their families may be experiencing only the *illusion* of academic competency. In actual fact the average level of reading performance in grade 4 of all groups *most closely approximates that of the Nonachievers, despite initial differences in presumed intellectual competence.* For example, mean reading achievement scores of Proachievers show a difference of only one point from that of Achievers, despite an initial difference of nearly 10 points in Binet I.Q. Differences between Achievers and Nonachievers, upon school entry, were nearly 20 points in the Binet I.Q.; the difference between these two groups after six years of schooling is only about eight points. The apparent reading achievements of the two groups do not differ, despite initial differences in potential for early reading achievement. The same is true for those identified as Antiachievers by comparison to Nonachievers. Finally, it is important to note that there is a tendency for the Achievers to have experienced more stability in family life, by

Table 8
Differences Between Teacher-Identified Achievement Groups by Achievement Test Performance and Maternal Perceived Stability in the Home

		Stanford Binet IQ (Preschool)	*STEP Reading (Grade 4)*	*MO Perceived Change in Family Life (Grade 6)*
GROUP I (Antiachievers)	mean	97.6	234.6	2.33
	s.d.	12.88	4.24	1.32
	N	15	14	9
GROUP II (Nonachievers)	mean	79.1*	230.4	2.12
	s.d.	10.49	3.22	0.99
	N	12	9	8
GROUP III (Proachievers)	mean	88.8	236.8	3.50
	s.d.	18.33	5.62	1.29
	N	5	4	4
GROUP IV (Achievers)	mean	97.2	237.8	1.82
	s.d.	13.56	8.43	0.88
	N	24	23	17

*p = .05 for differences between Group II and Groups I and IV respectively.

comparison to the other groups. Those whose relationships with teachers improved (the Proachievers) showed the greatest amount of early instability. These data, we believe, support the hypothesis of an *interactive* effect between family, school, and child outcomes, once the child enters the formal school environment.

Data in Tables 9a and 9b lend even greater support to the hypothesis of discontinuity. Table 9a indicates that when mothers with higher and lower levels of individuation are identified from 1965, their children differ by nearly 23 I.Q. points upon school entry.[6] Later, although mothers maintain their relative standing, the children do not differ in average level of reading performance. In fact, these children seem to approximate the level of Nonachievers in actual reading per-

Table 9a
Differences Between Early (1965) High and Low Individuating Mothers by (a) Children's 1965 Stanford-Binet I. Q. Scores; (b) Children's 1969 STEP Reading Scores; and (c) Later (1972–1973) Level of Maternal Individuation (N=40)

	Maternal Individuation (1965)	*Stanford-Binet* I. Q. (1965)*	*STEP Reading (1969)*	*Maternal Individuation (1972-73)*
Group I Mothers				
mean	5.47	103.2	236.2	4.76
s.d.	0.30	9.30	5.09	0.99
N	9	9	9	9
Group II Mothers				
mean	2.18	80.4	233.5	3.76
s.d.	0.50	7.68	4.76	1.30
N	7	7	6	7

Table 9b
Differences Between Later (1972–1973) High and Low Individuating Mothers by (a) Children's 1965 Stanford-Binet I. Q. Scores; (b) Children's 1969 STEP Reading Scores; and (c) Early (1965) Level of Maternal Individuation (N=40)

	Maternal Individuation (1972–73)	*Stanford-Binet* I. Q. (1965)*	*STEP Reading (1969)*	*Maternal Individuation (1965)*
Group I Mothers				
mean	5.92	93.9	237.6	4.38
s.d.	0.11	13.93	8.69	0.92
N	12	12	11	12
Group II Mothers				
mean	2.61	88.7	234.4	3.43
s.d.	0.18	14.29	3.10	1.31
N	10	10	7	10

**p* = .01

formance. This is in striking contrast to the school norm for white pupils on the same test, reported earlier as 251.0. Five of the nine pupils in Group I were identified as Antiachievers, four as Achievers. Two of the seven pupils in Group II were identified as Achievers, three as Antiachievers, and two as Nonachievers. The children in both groups attended six different elementary schools, with a maximum of two students in any one of those schools. In all, nine different schools were attended by the 16 students at the extremes of our distribution relative to Maternal Individuation in 1965. There was an overlap of three schools between the two groups, accounting for five pupils in Group I and three pupils in Group II.

Data in Table 9b enable us to consider the possibility that changes in level of maternal individuation influenced the 1970 performance outcomes presented in Table 9a. It seems, however, that more individuating mothers, as identified in 1972-1973, do not have children who are significantly different in performance outcomes at either Times I or III. These mothers essentially constituted our "average" group in 1965. Their increased participation in their children's intellectual life at this later time essentially is ineffective as regards the children's academic performance. Rather, it seems that at the later time period the earlier individuating mothers are now more facilitative or supportive of their children's academic efforts (see Table 2). We believe that the data suggest the hypothesis of developmental changes in maternal role behavior relative to children's academic efforts, particularly since the trend of both Tables 9a and 9b is toward higher-individuating mothers having higher-achieving children. The obtained significant correlation of .31 between maternal warmth and children's independence at Time III, primarily due to differences between Achievers and the other groups (Table 7), also supports this view.

Children in Group I in Table 9b attended nine different elementary schools, with a maximum of two in three different schools; children in Group II attended six different schools with a maximum of two in four different schools. In all, 12 different schools are represented. There was also an overlap of three schools between these two groups, accounting for six pupils in Group I and five in Group II.

Whereas specific school effects are probably random, it is important to note the sex differences between Groups I and II. In Table 9a only three of the nine children in Group I are male, while five of the seven in Group II, are male. In Table 9b six of the 12 children in Group I are male, while seven in Group II are male. The data in Table 9a suggest that females are the most vulnerable to the impact of the schooling experience. Male children tend to be the poorer achievers in this sample, as in white elementary school populations. Males are more often Antiachievers, or students whose later academic performances do not meet prior standards, regardless to original level. However, it is the subsequent lower levels of performance by females after school entry that seem most dramatic, given initial assessed potential, relative to the total group.

SUMMARY AND CONCLUSIONS

These longitudinal data suggest an early impact of the schooling experience upon these children and possibly their families. This impact is evident despite the status, relative to both maternal and child attributes, prior to kindergarten entry and before the expeience of desegregation per se. This suggests that for this population the schooling experience is discontinuous with early childhood development. The impact has implications for both personal-social and cognitive performance outcomes, insofar as both are school-related. Teacher evaluations and judgments interact with parental influences to produce these outcomes. Parent-to-child or teacher-to-child models are too simplistic for characterization of minority children's achievement behaviors, particularly once they are engaged in formal schooling for an extended period. Furthermore, it is even more imperative than ever that educational psychologists develop reliable and valid procedures for assessing school achievements since the current feedback mechanisms may influence children's personal-social development, and may be spuriously related to actual skill acquisition. Finally, we have assumed our test measures to be valid indicators of the children's potential and actual school achievements. Even if this assumption was useful for purposes of this study, it is apparent that these tests have little diagnostic value.

These findings do not imply that early education is without *intrinsic* value. Clearly, mothers who in 1965 reported behaviors that are cognitively stimulating had children who, upon school entry, were better prepared for a variety of intellectual efforts. But the findings do imply that early education—without direct intervention into, and assessment of, the primary grade classrooms that minority children attend—could have unrealistic programmatic expectations. Sustained intellectual growth and development once the child enters school depends, we believe, upon the quality of the relationship established between parent, teacher, and child. The child's personal history of successes in the context of this triadic relationship will probably determine whether his initial urge to learn will become formalized into a structure of personal educational desires and aspirations. Early educators will wish to design follow-up studies to examine this issue. It would be extremely important to establish in any follow-up studies that receiving schools and teachers are unaware of the children's earlier preschool activities.

In conclusion, we need research designs that *simultaneously* characterize the interpersonal ecology of both home and school environments, if we are to understand children's school achievements. Such studies may have to be longitudinal, but they will be multivariate. We need programs that simultaneously emphasize the ecology of home and school contexts, if they are to influence patterns of achievement socialization. We need to consider the reciprocal interactions between the child and all his significant others, if we are to encourage his personal-social development. Most important, perhaps, we need to reconsider Durkheim's (1911) early proposition that education is but the mirror of society. This would be a reconsideration from the perspective of childhood development and outcomes, rather than societal and school social structures, as originally intended by Durkheim himself.

References

1. Bloom, B. *Stability and Change in Human Characteristics.* New York: Wiley, 1964.

2. Clark, K. *Dark Ghetto.* New York: Harper, 1965.

3. Clausen, J. Perspectives on childhood socialization. In J. Clausen (Ed.), *Socialization and Society.* Boston: Little, Brown, 1968, pp. 130–181.

4. Coleman, J., et al. *Equality of Educational Opportunity.* Washington, D.C.: U.S. Office of Education, 1966.

5. Coopersmith, S. *The Antecedents of Self-esteem.* San Francisco: W. H. Freeman, 1967.

6. Deutsch, C. Social class and child development. In B. Caldwell & H. Ricciuti (Eds.), *Review of Child Development Research.* Chicago: University of Chicago Press, 1973, pp. 233–282.

7. Durkheim, E. *Education and Society.* Glencoe: Free Press, 1956 (first published in 1911).

8. Dyk, R. & Witkin, H. Family experiences that are related to the development of differentiation in children. *Child Development,* 1965, *36,* 21–55.

9. Freeberg, N. & Payne, D. Parental influence on cognitive development in early childhood: A review. *Child Development,* 1967, *38,* 65–89.

10. Hess, R. Social class and ethnic influences on socialization. In P. Mussen (Ed.), *Carmichael's Manual of Child Psychology.* New York: Wiley, 1970. Vol. II, pp. 457–558.

11. Hess, R., Kramer, R., Slaughter, D., et al. Techniques for assessing cognitive and social abilities of children and parents in Project Head Start. Unpublished report of Research Contract OEO-519, July, 1966.

12. Himmelweit, H. & Swift, B. A model for the understanding of the school as a socializing agent. In P. Mussen et al. (Eds.), *Trends and Issues in Developmental Psychology.* New York: Holt, Rinehart and Winston, 1969, pp. 154–181.

13. Hsia, J. *Integration in Evanston, 1967-71: A Longitudinal Evaluation.* Unpublished report of Educational Testing Service (ETS), Midwestern Office, Evanston, Illinois, August, 1971.

14. Jencks, C., et al., *Inequality.* New York: Basic Books, 1972.

15. Katz, I. The socialization of achievement motivation in minority group children. In D. Levine (Ed.), *Nebraska Symposium on Motivation.* Lincoln: University of Nebraska, 1967, pp. 133–191.

16. Klaus, P. *Yesterday's Children.- New York: Wiley, 1973.*

17. Lane, E. Childhood characteristics of black college graduates reared in poverty. Develop. Psychology, 1973, *8,* 42–45.

18. Lang, S. *Research relating to personality differences between high and low achieving black children.* Unpublished report to the Institute for Juvenile Research, 1969.

19. Minuchin, P., et al., *Psychological Impact of the School Experience.* New York: Basic Books, 1969.

20. Rist, R. *The Urban School: A Factory for Failure.* Boston: MIT Press, 1973.

21. Roberts, S.O. Longitudinal performance of Negro American children at five and ten years on the Stanford-Binet. In R. Wilcox (Ed.), *The Psychological Consequences of Being a Black American.* New York: Wiley, 1971, pp. 146–153.

22. Rosen, B. Race, ethnicity, and the achievement syndrome. *American Sociological Review,* 1959, *24,* 47–60.

23. Rosenthal, R. & Jacobson, L. *Pygmalion in the Classroom.* New York: Holt, Rinehart, and Winston, 1968.

24. Slaughter, D. Maternal antecedents of the academic achievement behavior of Afro-American Head Start children. *Educational Horizons,* Fall 1969, 24–28.

25. Slaughter, D. Parental potency and the achievements of inner city black children. *American Journal of Orthopsychiatry,* 1970, *40(3),* 433–440.

26. Wallach, M. Book review: The psychological impact of the school experience. *Harvard Educational Review,* 1971, *41(3),* 360–363.

Notes

A chapter presented at the Biennial Meetings of the Society for Research in Child Development, Denver, Colorado, *April 10-13, 1975.* The work reported in this chapter was partially supported by the Early Education Research Center of the University of Chicago, formerly a Subcontractor under the National Program on Early Childhood

Education of CEMREL, Inc., a private nonprofit corporation supported in part as a regional educational laboratory by funds from the United States Office of Education, Department of Health, Education and Welfare, and a small grant from the Social Science Research Council of New York, New York.

[1]Data to be reported here do not include the results of a detailed analysis of child and maternal perceptions of schooling and the school experience: they will be reported later.

[2]Variable 7, Cooperation with the interviewer, was a control variable and will not be discussed in this paper.

[3]Variable 8 is the average rating of variables 1, 2, and 3. Variable 8 is discussed in a 1969 article by this author, published in *Educational Horizons*. It refers to the mother's report of behaviors thought to be cognitively stimulating to young preschool children. Since factor analyses revealed one of the three variables to be loaded on a separate factor (variable 1), data are presented independantly for each variable 1, 2, and 3.

[4]At time III the three observer scales had a median intercorrelation of .53. The Coopersmith Self-Esteem Inventory correlated .31 (p v .05) with the Meadors-Slaughter Satisfaction with School Inventory and .47 (p v .01) with the Coleman personal control or potency score. Observer ratings and direct measures of self-other perceptions were not significantly correlated.

[5]Of 36 possible correlations between Times I and III on child personality measures, four reached significance at the .05 level. These were (1) teacher and (2) observer ratings of Achievement Motivation at Time I, with observer ratings of Independence at Time III; (3) observer ratings of Verbal-social-participation at Times I and III; and (4) observer ratings of Independence at Time I, and perceived School Satisfaction at Time III.

[6]Groups were identified as one standard deviation above or below the group mean for N = 40.

CHAPTER EIGHT

Attention Dysfunction and Child-Care Attitudes among Mentally Ill and Well Mothers and their Young Children[1]

Bertram J. Cohler, David H. Gallant, Henry U. Grunebaum, Justin L. Weiss, and Enid Gamer

Mental illness has been demonstrated to affect an individual's styles of receiving, regulating, and modifying external and internal stimuli that together comprise that psychological function known as "attention" (Shakow, 1962, 1963; Silverman, 1964; Wachtel, 1967). Socialization research has demonstrated that parental attentional styles are associated with differences in the child's capacity for both selective and sustained attention (Seder, 1957; Witkin et al., 1962; Wynne & Singer, 1963a, 1963b; Singer & Wynne, 1965a, 1965b, 1966; Kagan & Kogan, 1969). Since mothers typically spend a greater amount of time than fathers with their young children, maternal influence on the child's socialization is particularly significant. Partially as a result of inheritance, and particularly as a result of socialization, the children of mentally ill mothers appear at particularly high risk for the development of deficits in the ability to deploy as well as to sustain attention (Marcus, 1972).

In the present report the attentional style of young children of mentally ill mothers is contrasted with that of children whose mothers have never sought psychiatric assistance. Within each of these two groups of mothers and children individual differences in the children's capacity for selective and sustained attention are examined in relation to both maternal attentional styles as well as maternal attitudes toward child-care. Maternal beliefs concerning importance of the child's achievement of greater interpersonal reciprocity, greater competence in transacting with the environment, and increased individuation from the mother are viewed as important dimensions in understanding socialization during the preschool years (Sander, 1962, 1964, 1969; White, 1963; Mahler, 1968).

MATERNAL MENTAL ILLNESS AND ATTENTION DYSFUNCTION

The research to be reported in the present paper derives from an ego-psychological perspective on psychopathology, in which attention dysfunction with regard to either selective or sustained attention is viewed as a major factor in the development of the disturbance of an individual's adaptation to reality (Cohler, 1972a, 1972b; Wachtel, 1972b). This adaptative perspective was first explicated by Freud (1911) who observed that:

> A special function was instituted (in the course of development) which had periodically to search the external world in order that its data might be familiar already if an urgent internal need should arise—the function of attention. (p. 220)

Later theorists (Hartmann, 1955; White, 1963; Schachtel, 1954, 1973) have emphasized the importance of attention in the child's development of a "primary relation to reality" (Buhler, 1954), in which, over time, the young child develops both an increasingly stable concept of objects and an increasingly sophisticated understanding of reality. This theoretical position has been applied by Silverman (1964) in the interpretation of a variety of laboratory studies of impairment of attention among schizophrenics. However, this same theoretical approach may be applied more generally to the understanding of psychopathology, which is viewed as evidence of failure to attend to reality (Gardner, 1962; Witkin, 1965; Wachtel, 1967; Santostefano, 1969).

The concept of attention includes two separate but closely related elements. *Selective attention* refers to an ability that Freud (1912) referred to as "evenly hovering attention," that Schachtel (1954) has termed "focal attention," and that Gardner et al. (1959) have termed "focusing." In order to attend selectively, or to focus, it is necessary to discriminate between the several elements of the stimulus and to develop simultaneous awareness of these several elements (Freud, 1911). As Wachtel (1967) has observed in this regard:

> The study of attention is essentially the study of selectivity in perception and cognition and of variations in the overall responsiveness to stimulation. (p. 417)

While selective attention represents deployment of attention in order to consider disparate aspects of the stimulus, separate and differentiated from each other, *sustained attention*, or concentration, represents the ability to maintain deployment of attention over time, even though there may be distracting thoughts or distracting and competing external stimuli. As Rapaport et al. (1968) observe in discussing this element of attention:

> Concentration may be characterized as an active relationship to outside reality. When one finds himself unable to take in freely what the flow of a book, a lecture, or a conversation brings to him, he may exert a conscious effort to keep out of consciousness all material that is not directly pertinent. (p. 108)

Sustained attention permits maintenance of focal attention by preventing intrusion of distracting stimuli.

Examples of these two related abilities are provided by two of the Wechsler subtests of verbal intelligence. Arithmetic consists of a series of "story problems" of increasing difficulty. Digit-Span requires repetition of strings of numbers that increase in length over successive trials; a second part of this subtest requires backward repetition of the string of numbers. The most appropriate set to maintain in responding to arithmetic items is that of "focal or selective attention," which results in the discovery of the logical steps required in order to solve the problem. While some concentration or sustained attention is required in order to keep a story-problem in mind, the important task is that of providing a solution for the problem. Digit-Span is more directly a test of concentration, for one must be able to exclude all distracting thoughts that might interfere in hearing and repeating the string of numbers.

THE IMPACT OF MATERNAL MENTAL ILLNESS UPON CHILDREN

To the extent that maternal psychopathology influences the child's psychological development, it is likely to have a serious impact on his developing adaptation to reality (Lidz, 1965; Wynne & Singer, 1963a, 1963b; Singer & Wynne, 1965a, 1965b). Most of the empirical work in this area has concerned children of schizophrenic women, for whom the risk of developing schizophrenia is approximately 10–16 percent, as contrasted with the risk in the population as a whole of about 1 percent (Reisby, 1967). Other data suggest that as many as 60 percent of the children of schizophrenic mothers may show some behavioral deviation during later childhood or adulthood (Heston, 1966; Rosenthal, 1966, 1973).

While there is little comparable data regarding children of depressed or psychoneurotic mothers, Beisser et al. (1967) report that the children of nonschizophrenic mentally ill mothers also show behavioral deviation, and that both groups of children whose mothers are mentally ill may be differentiated in elementary school from children in a "normal" control group. This study, which is based on both parental reports of symptoms as well as teacher ratings, shows that daughters of mentally ill women are even more socially maladjusted than sons, a finding that is consistent with theories of the development of identification (Lynn, 1962; White, 1963; Meissner, 1972; Miller with Cohler, 1971).

Results of other studies have also suggested that children of mentally ill mothers show greater social maladjustment during the years between six and 12 than their peers (Higgins, 1966; Rolf, 1973). Rolf's report includes carefully selected groups of children of schizophrenic, depressed, and well mothers, together with two groups of behavior-disordered children. His results show that children of schizophrenic mothers, particularly daughters, are rated by peers as less socially competent than children in any other group, with the exception of antisocial children. Analysis of teacher ratings also shows that daughters of schizophrenic mothers were judged as less socially competent than daughters of well mothers; however, neither sons of schizophrenic mothers nor sons of depressed mothers were rated by teachers as less well adjusted than well sons of well mothers.

Since a deficit in the ability to sustain attention has been reported to differentiate between adult psychiatric patients and nonpsychiatric groups (Shakow, 1962, 1963; Silverman, 1964), several investigators have studied the children of mentally ill mothers in order to determine if this deficit is transmitted either genetically or as a result of deviant patterns of intrafamily communication. Both McClelland and Pugh (1962) and Mednick and Schulsinger (1968) have reported that, compared with children of well mothers, children of schizophrenic mothers manifest greater intellectual impairment, particularly on those measures such as Wechsler subtests that are believed to reflect the ability to sustain attention.

Studies that have examined the impact of age on differences in the ability to sustain attention within children of mentally ill and well mothers have reported contradictory findings. Gale and Lynn (1972) report a linear relation between age and the ability to concentrate among normal children between the ages of seven and 13. Gallant (1972a, 1972b) reports a difference in the ability to sustain attention between the five-year-old children of schizophrenic and well mothers, but notes that this difference was not observed among the six-year-old children of mentally ill and well mothers. Fish (1963) and Fish and Alpert (1962, 1963) both report differences between the children of schizophrenic and well mothers in the ability to sustain attention, and also note that such group differences appear to diminish as the children grow older. Marcus (1973), reporting cognitive data for the same children used in Rolf's study of social competence, finds that within the very limited age range in his sample age was associated with increasing impairment in the ability of children of mentally ill mothers to sustain attention.

Marcus also shows that the children of both schizophrenic and depressed mothers perform less well on these attentional tasks adapted from Shakow's (1962, 1963) segmental set of studies with adults than was true either of children of well mothers or those with behavior disorders. However, even within the two groups of mentally ill mothers, children of depressed women were better able to improve their performance, when provided with an incentive for doing so, than children of schizophrenic mothers, who were unable to improve their ability to sustain attention under any condition in which help was provided.

Overall, these studies of children of mentally ill and well mothers suggest that maternal psychopathology influences children's social adjustment as well as their ability to maintain concentration on a task. In addition, data reported by Anthony (1968) and by Gallant (1972a, 1972b) suggest that the children of schizophrenic mothers also show greater impairment in selective impairment than children of well mothers. The children of these mentally ill mothers show a preference for global rather than differentiated and articulated perception of stimuli in an embedded figures test.

THE SOCIALIZATION OF ATTENTION

Largely because adult schizophrenics have been differentiated from nonschizophrenics on the basis of the ability to sustain attention, research regarding the impact of maternal psychopathology on the child's cognitive development has been concerned primarily with impairment in the child's ability to concentrate. Such impairment is viewed as a possible precursor of subsequent mental illness in the offspring of mentally ill mothers. From the perspective of the present study this concern with the impact of maternal mental illness on the child's ability to sustain attention is only part of a larger interest in the extent to which maternal personality and cognitive style influence the child's cognitive development.

Concern with the role of family characteristics in the socialization of attention has increased because of renewed interest in factors such as family, social class, and ethnicity that appear to affect the child's ability to learn in school. For example, Bee et al. (1969), in a study of lower- and middle-class black and white four-year-olds and their mothers, found that specificity of maternal suggestions, the extent of her praise, nature of her feedback to the child regarding his performance, and the degree of her involvement in the task were all associated with the child's ability to focus upon and complete a task. This finding is consistent with Hess and Shipman's (1965) observation that in specific test situations the mother's capacity for verbal conceptualization is a major influence on the child's ability to sustain attention.

Most research concerning the socialization of attention among well mothers and children has focused on selective rather than sustained attention, where selective attention is viewed as the selective perception of particular segments of a complex stimulus field, requiring simultaneous inhibition of response to other aspects of the field.

Much of the research in this area derives from the work of Witkin and his associates (1962, 1971) on selective attention viewed as field dependence versus independence or global versus differentiated and articulated psychological functioning. This cognitive style is believed to reflect a more pervasive manner of construing experience. In discussing psychological differentiation, Witkin (1967) observes that:

> Perception may be conceived as articulated, in contrast to global, if the person is able to perceive [an] item as discrete from [the] organized ground when the field is structured (analysis), and to impose structure on a field, and so perceive it as organized, when the field has little inherent organization (structuring). . . Articulated experience is a sign of developed differentiation in the cognitive sphere. . . . [It] is a consistent feature of a given individual's manner of dealing with a wide array of perceptual and intellectual tasks. Because it represents the characteristic approach the person brings to situations with him, we consider more global or more articulated functioning to be an individual's cognitive *style*. (pp. 234–245)

In reviewing published and unpublished research on psychological differentiation, Witkin comments that persons who show an articulated cognitive style are also likely to demonstrate an articulated and differentiated body concept, as measured by figure drawings, and a more highly developed sense of separate identity; such persons demonstrate a more differentiated manner of functioning (Witkin et al., 1971). Using a perceptual task in which the person is required to differentiate or disembed a figure from a complex background (Witkin 1950), it is possible to place the person at any point on the continuum between field dependence or global functioning and field independence or differentiated and analytic functioning. Furthermore, Karp (1963) has demonstrated that selective attention, viewed as psychological differentiation, is orthogonal or independent of the ability to concentrate or sustain attention.

In the reports published by Witkin's group (Witkin et al., 1962; Dyk and Witkin, 1965) highly significant relationships were shown between the extent of the child's field independence, or ability to overcome embeddedness, and ratings based on maternal interviews of the extent to which mothers inhibit or foster psychological differentiation. However, in these studies the criteria for classifying a mother as more or less inhibiting in fostering differentiation were not specifically cognitive, and included the following: the degree to which the mother was able to foster the child's individuation or sense of separate identity (a concept closely related to Mahler's (1968) concept of separation-individuation); the extent to which mothers reported that they could care for children without undue self-sacrifice in their own life; and the level of sophistication that mothers showed in human figure drawings.

Seder (1957) analyzed child-rearing questionnaires administered to parents of field-dependent and -independent children and found that boys who were more field dependent had more authoritarian and punitive mothers who were more likely to push their children to perform in accordance with strict standards.

The correlation between parental and child field independence, an indication of the extent to which parental cognitive style is transmitted to the child, has yielded more ambiguous results. In the studies of Witkin and his colleagues (Witkin, 1962; Dyk & Witkin, 1965), there was little correlation between maternal scores on the Embedded Figures Test (EFT) and the scores of their children on the comparable Children's Embedded Figures Test (CEFT). Corah (1965), controlling for age of the child and verbal intelligence, found cross-sex field-independence relationships for fathers and girls and mothers and boys. There was little same sex correlation between mothers and daughters and fathers and sons. Goldstein and Peck (1973), using the Rod-and-Frame test, an experimental measure of field independence, report that maternal selective attention is more strongly related to that of sons than that of daughters. Kagan and Kogan (1970), in discussing the issue of cross-sex correlations for field independence, suggest that such results are consistent with Seder's (1957) observation that the father was more often the primary disciplinarian for field-independent boys and the mother for field-dependent boys. Scallon and Herron (1969) report that enuretic boys attending a psychiatric clinic had Embedded Figures Test scores that more closely approximated those of their mothers than was true for mothers and sons in the control group, suggesting the hypothesis that maternal psychopathology may increase the correlation between selective attention of mothers and children. Finally, it should be noted that both Anthony (1968) and Gallant (1972a, 1972b) report that children of schizophrenic mothers are more field dependent than children of well mothers.

MATERNAL PERSONALITY AND CHILD-CARE ATTITUDES

In the present study attitudes toward child care are viewed as one aspect of maternal personality which, in turn, directly affects the child's socialization. Following McClelland (1955), attitudes are viewed as the component of personality that orders or schematizes the interpersonal world and that serves as a guide to action with regard to specific interpersonal interactions. As Smith, Bruner, and White (1956), Katz and Stotland (1959), and Sarnoff (1960) all show, attitudes represent a set of constructs employed for evaluating events in terms of a person's own needs and concerns, and reflect both present and past life experiences. In the context of her relationship with her child, child care attitudes influence the mother's appraisal of transactions between her child and herself and determine the range of responses that are possible regarding particular actions on the child's part.

One relevant evaluation that a mother makes regarding her child's development is that of his competence in dealing with the environment. Mothers differ in the extent to which they regard infants and young children as competent to maintain interpersonal mutuality and to explore and order the world about them (White, 1963), just as mothers differ in the extent to which they believe that children's needs and intents may be differentiated from their own needs (Levy, 1943; Mahler, 1968). Mothers also differ in the extent to which they can recognize and accept the ambiguities and complexities involved in rearing children in contemporary urban society (Minturn & Lambert, 1964).

Such variations in maternal attitudes are believed to affect children's cognitive and socio-emotional development, including their ability to attend selectively and to sustain this attention. However, there has been little direct study of this problem. Cross-cultural socialization data reported by Witkin (1967), together with earlier studies of the antecedents of field independence in maternal socialization practices (Seder, 1957; Witkin et al., 1962; Dyk & Witkin, 1965) provide some support for this view. In the one published report of the relationship between child care attitudes and maternal and child cognitive style Byrne (1964) reports largely negative results using a group of college students and their mothers and an instrument that emphasizes primarily attitudes regarding the issue of authoritarian control among mothers of young children.

STATEMENT OF HYPOTHESES

Although there has been some study of the relationship between maternal and child-selective attention among well mothers and children, there has been little consideration of this relationship among mentally ill mothers and their children, and very little consideration of the relationship between maternal and child ability to sustain attention among either mentally ill or well mothers and children.

In the present study it is hypothesized that:

1. Mentally ill mothers and their children, as contrasted with well mothers and their children, will show greater impairment both in the ability to selectively attend and to sustain this attention.

2. The relationship between maternal and child attention style will be greater for both selective and sustained attention among mothers and daughters than among mothers and sons, and the magnitude of this relationship will be greater within the group of mentally ill mothers and their children than within the group of well mothers and their children.

3. Maternal attitudes regarding attainment of appropriate closeness with the child and acceptance of ambivalent feelings regarding child care will be related to an increased ability to sustain attention among both children of mentally ill and well mothers; within each of these two groups greater belief in the importance of fostering reciprocity between the child and the environment, and in the attainment of appropriate closeness with the child, will be related to more articulated and differentiated performance by the child on a measure of selective attention.

METHOD

The Samples

The data were taken from a larger study in which intensive nursing aftercare was provided for psychotic mothers with young children, following the mother's discharge from a psychiatric hospital (Grunebaum et al., 1971; Hartman et al., 1973). The goal of the intervention study was to help these mothers to function more effectively in their adult roles and to prevent rehospitalization by providing supportive home treatment.

Women hospitalized for mental illness following childbirth were originally referred to the aftercare project by state or private mental hospitals in the Greater Boston area. Over the course of two years a sample of 47 mothers was recruited for the present study, comprising nearly all those referrals who were married, with intact families, had a diagnosis of psychosis, and had at least one child below age five. These former patients may be described as a group of chronically inadequate women with a poor premorbid history, numerous prior hospitalizations, and extended periods of stay during each hospitalization. According to the formal diagnosis approximately two-thirds of these patients showed schizophrenic or schizoaffective psychoses, with one-third showing manic-depressive or depressive psychoses.

The 48 well women wo had never sought psychiatric assistance were recruited by means of newspaper advertisements. Previous research with this means of obtaining a sample (Cohler et al., 1968) has shown that relatively few differences appear between subjects volunteering in this manner and other samples of young adult women. Hospitalized mothers were matched with nonpsychiatric controls on the basis of the husband's occupation, wife's education, age, parity, religion (Catholic/non-Catholic), and age and sex of the youngest child.

Demographically, these two groups were quite homogeneous. The typical husband in each group had at least some college education and worked either as a clerk or salesman (patients), or as a clerk, small businessman, or lesser professional (controls). On the basis of occupation and education, these men can be described as middle class. The typical wife also had some additional schooling beyond high school.

Most families in each group included at least two other children, and at the time the children were tested their ages ranged between 59 and 78 months (14 children of mentally ill mothers and 15 children of well mothers failed to attain the age of 59 months by the end of the study, and were not tested). These children had originally been identified at the the beginning of the study as the "index" child, as it was their birth that had preceded the mother's most recent hospitalization. The children were tested at specific landmark birthdays (within six months either of their fifth or sixth birthday, depending on the child's age at the mother's entrance in the study). Since the patient and control groups were equated on the age and sex of the index child, the distribution of age and sex of the index child in the two groups is identical.

THE MEASURES

The Maternal Attitude Scale (Child Care Attitudes)

The Maternal Attitude Scale (MAS) is a 233-item Likert-type instrument constructed according to Sander's (1962, 1964, 1969) formulation of the developing mother-child relationship in the first years of life. The construction of the Maternal Attitude Scale is described in greater detail by Cohler et al. (1970) and by Cohler (1974). Developed as a result of extensive pretest studies, the MAS is scored by computer on the basis of norms obtained from a sample of over 200 mothers of young children. As Table 1 shows, this instrument yields five second-order orthogonal or *independent* factors (high scores on a factor are in the direction of the scale title).

Shipley-Institute-of-Living Scale (Maternal Intelligence)

A brief screening measure of the mother's current level of intellectual functioning was obtained with the use of the Shipley scale. This self-administered and objectively scored measure consists of 20-item vocabulary and abstraction scales in which the subject must determine a pattern of responses and complete the pattern. Several investigators have reported correlations between this measure and the full-scale WAIS score in the .80s and .90s (Cohler et al., 1970), making this a suitable measure for estimating verbal intelligence.

Wechsler Preschool and Primary Scale of Intelligence (Childrens' Intelligence)

Children in both groups were individually administered the Wechsler (1963) Preschool and Primary Scale of Intelligence (WPPSI). The subtests were administered in one setting with frequent rest periods, and verbal tests were alternated with performance tests. Particular care was taken on the vocabulary subscale to be sure that children understood the test requirement, and sufficient neutral prompts were used to ensure that the child's optimal performance was being evaluated. The WPPSI was scored for verbal and performance subscale IQ, full-scale IQ, and the mean level of intertest scatter across all subscales.

The Continuous Performance Test (Sustained Attention)

The ability to sustain attention (concentration) was measured by the Continuous Performance Test (CPT), a laboratory procedure in which letters (older children and adults) or colors (younger children) are individually displayed on a revolving drum for a duration of 0.2 seconds before a viewing window at which the subject sits (Rosvold et

Table 1
Schematic Description of Child-Rearing Attitude Factors
Maternal Attitude Scale[a]

Factor	*Adaptive Attitude*	*Maladaptive Attitude*
(I). Appropriate versus inappropriate control of child's aggession[b]	Intent of agressive impulse should be recognized, but it is important to modulate expression of agression by providing alternate channels.	Overly restrictive attitudes or, less commonly, overly permissive.
(II). Encouragement versus discouragement of reciprocity[b]	Babies can communicate with their mothers, and mothers should encourage development of a relationship between mother and child.	Babies cannot communicate with their mothers and are unable to develop a reciprocal social relationship or to respond to appropriate cues from their mothers.
(III). Appropriate versus inappropriate closeness with the child	A mother can enjoy and care for a baby without sacrificing herself, without becoming overly binding or overly protective, and without yielding to the baby's demand for an exclusive relationship (Mahler, 1972)	Pregnancy, delivery, and child care are seen as burdensome, depleting, and destructive of self; vacillation between the wish to be the sole caretaker, perpetuating the mother-infant symbiosis, and the wish to relegate all aspects of child care to others, a pattern similar to that described by Levy (1943) as the "overprotective mother."
(IV). Acceptance versus denial of emotional complexity in child care	Acceptance of ambivalent feelings about child care, of some feeling of inadequacy as a mother, and of uncertainty regarding some aspects of child care, all without loss of self-esteem.	Denial of any concerns regarding child care and of inadequacy in the maternal role, together with highly conventional and stereotyped beliefs and the feeling that mothers require little child care assistance from others.
(V). Feeling of compitence versus lack of competence in perceiving and meeting the baby's needs	Mothers can understand the infant's physical needs and meet them adequately.	Babies are unable to let others know what there physical needs are, and mothers find it very difficult to understand and meet these needs.

[a]Factors scores are expressed in standardized form based on a larger normative sample, with mean = .000 and standard deviation = + 1.000.

[b]Scores on the first *two* factors have been reflected so that a positive score indicates more adaptive attitudes.

al., 1956; Orzack & Kornetsky, 1966, 1971; Gallant, 1972b). The subject is asked to press a button, which rings a bell whenever the critical or criterion color or letter appears at the viewing window. Each mother and child participated in 10 trials (revolution of the drum) and was scored on *total errors of omission* (failure to respond to critical stimulus) and *total errors of commission* (responding to an incorrect stimulus).

The Embedded Figures Test (Selective Attention)

Selective attention (field independence or psychological differentiation) in mothers and children was measured by an embedded figures test (Witkin 1950) that evaluates an individual's ability to respond to particular segments of a complex stimulus field while simultaneously inhibiting response to other aspects of the field. The embedded figures test material consists of a series of complex cards or pictures in each of which a more simple form is embedded. The subject's task is to locate the simple form in the more complex picture. In the original Embedded Figures Test (EFT) (Witkin 1950; Witkin et al., 1962) the individual's score was the length of time required to identify the simple form in the complex stimulus.

Since the EFT proved to be a difficult test for children below age 10, Goodenough and Eagle (1963) developed a modification, for children, with more attractive figures. This test is suitable for use with children age five through nine, but is complex to administer. Karp and Konstadt (Witkin et al., 1971) further modified this children's embedded figures test, creating visually appealing and colorful cards in which the simple form is either a tent or a house and developing a set of demonstration instructions that make the procedure suitable for use with children as young as five (CEFT). According to the manual (Witkin et al., 1971), the EFT and CEFT measure much the same domain. When both tests were administered to children of age 9-12 (Dreyer et al. 1969), the median correlation between measures was .79 ($p<.01$). The CEFT has a median internal consistency coefficient (alpha) of .88.

Since the use of a stopwatch made some children anxious, the authors of the CEFT used a score based on the number of figures correctly identified. However, recent reports (Campbell et al., 1967; Mumbauer & Miller, 1970) have combined the scoring procedures of the EFT and CEFT, so that scores are obtained both for time to correct identification and number of cards on which the simple form is correctly recognized. This modification of the scoring system was used in the present study.

In order to make the parent form of the embedded figures task as comparable as possible to the childrens' series, the CEFT was modified so as to provide an adult form also containing the tent and house figures. Maternal responses to this modified form of the CEFT were also scored on time to correct identification and number of correct cards.

FINDINGS AND DISCUSSION

Maternal and Childrens' Selective and Sustained Attention

Scores of women in the two groups were compared on both the selective and sustained attention measures, as well as on measures of verbal intelligence and attitudes toward child care. The results of this comparison are shown in Table 2. Compared with well mothers, mentally ill mothers show greater impairment regarding both selective and sustained attention. These mentally ill mothers are more likely to fail to respond to the critical stimulus and tend to respond more often to the incorrect stimulus. Consistent with the first hypothesis, formerly hospitalized mothers are both more global and field dependent and less able to sustain attention than well mothers.

In view of these group differences in attention it is particularly important that women in the two groups do not differ with regard to verbal intelligence. Zigler (1963), Wachtel (1968, 1972a), Kagan and Kogan (1970), and Vernon (1972) all have noted that differences in performance on embedded figures tasks may merely reflect differences in verbal intelligence.

Differences in child care attitudes between mothers in these two groups show that patients believe less in the possibility of establishing a reciprocal social relationship with the baby (Factor II) and tend more often to deny ambivalent feelings regarding child care (Factor IV). These mentally ill mothers also believed to a lesser extent than well mothers in the possibility of differentiating between a mother's own needs and those of her children and to a greater extent than well mothers that child care demands extensive self-sacrifice (Factor III). However, these formerly hospitalized mothers did believe to a greater extent than well mothers in their ability to understand and meet a ba-

Table 2
Comparison of Hospitalized and Nonhospitalized Mothers on Selective and Sustained Attention Measures, Verbal Intelligence, and Attitudes Toward Child Care

Mothers Scale	*PATIENTS (N = 47)*		*CONTROLS (N = 48)*		*t-test*	*p*
	Mean	*S.D.*	*Mean*	*S.D.*		
CPT						
Errors of omission	7.26	8.79	3.88	5.51	2.09	.04
Errors of commission	8.26	7.24	5.60	6.53	1.74	.08
EFT						
Time to correct	444.9	167.6	381.8	156.2	1.80	.07
Number of failures	5.00	3.71	3.16	2.81	2.00	.05
Shipley Scale						
Vocabulary scale	29.02	6.7	30.8	5.4	1.30	NS
MAS						
Appropriate control (I)	0.02	0.96	0.15	1.37	0.55	NS
Encouragement of reciprocity (II)	−0.16	1.01	0.46	0.74	3.43	.001
Appropriate closeness (III)	−0.50	1.05	0.12	0.83	3.16	.002
Acceptance of complexity (IV)	−0.83	1.36	−0.16	1.08	2.64	.01
Meeting baby's needs (V)	0.51	0.70	0.19	0.86	2.02	.05

Table 3
Comparison of Children of Recently Hospitalized and Nonhospitalized Mothers on Attention Measures

Attention Measure	GROUP: Patient Boys (N = 18)		Patient Girls (N = 11)		Control Boys (N = 18)		Control Girls (N = 11)		(A) F Ratio Group	(A × B) (B) F Ratio Sex	F Ratio Inter-Action
	Mean	S.D.	Mean	S.D.	Mean	S.D.	Mean	S.D.			
CPT											
Errors omission	25.83	18.67	18.60	11.18	19.83	13.00	14.13	8.19	2.42	3.69[a]	0.05
Errors commission	41.56	37.18	31.87	28.04	31.00	21.28	18.20	14.92	3.28[b]	2.83	0.54
CEFT											
Time to response	618.7	136.6	594.1	137.0	549.1	158.2	559.5	102.7	2.38	0.04	0.27
Number of failures	7.11	3.95	8.67	3.20	6.89	3.48	5.13	2.30	5.20[c]	0.02	4.04[d]
WPPSI											
Verbal scale	106.22	15.25	102.18	13.44	109.83	13.47	104.64	10.23	0.69	1.59	0.03
Performance scale	108.94	15.52	101.52	13.56	108.78	12.53	107.46	8.10	0.66	1.52	0.74
Full scale	108.39	16.43	102.00	13.59	110.17	12.52	106.46	7.85	0.74	1.94	0.14

[a] F-Ratio significant at $p = .06$.
[b] F-Ratio significant at $p = .07$.
[c] F-Ratio significant at $p = .02$.
[d] F-Ratio significant at $p = .04$.

by's physical needs; as long as the baby requires only physical care, these mothers believed they could meet the baby's needs. Problems arise only when the baby makes demands for a more reciprocal relationship.

Compared with mothers in the nonhospitalized group, formerly hospitalized mothers showed greater impairment both in selective and sustained attention. According to the first hypothesis, these differences were also expected for children of mentally ill and well mothers. Data reported in Table 3 provide some support for this first hypothesis. This aspect of the first hypothesis was examined using a two-way analysis of variance since, although Witkin (1962, 1971) reports no sex differences in selective attention for children below age eight, data reviewed by Kagan and Kogan (1970) suggest that such sex differences probably exist.

Considering first results for sustained attention, children of mentally ill mothers responded to a significantly greater number of incorrect stimuli than children of well mothers. However, across diagnostic groups boys of both mentally ill and well mothers were significantly less accurate than girls in these two groups in responding to the critical stimulus. The findings for selective attention were less ambiguous. While the children in the two groups did not differ with regard to the time to response, daughters of former-patient mothers failed a greater number of cards than boys or girls in the three other groups.

This finding suggests that maternal mental illness may affect a daughter's capacity for selective attention in a manner different from that of sons, and that of daughters may be at greater risk than sons for impairment in this area of adaptation.

It should be noted that group membership, sex, and interaction effects are not significant for the verbal scales, performance scales, or the full-scale measures of intelligence among the children in the two groups. A number of previous studies have shown that children's performance on the CEFT is related to verbal intelligence (Crandall & Sinkeldam, 1964; Maccoby et al., 1965; and Mumbauer & Miller, 1970). Since the groups in the present study do not differ in intelligence, however, it may be concluded that the reported attention differences are not merely a result of differences in intellectual functioning among children of mentally ill and well mothers. Finally, it should be noted that, in contrast with the reports of Mednick and Schlusinger (1968) and McClelland and Pugh (1962), there is little indication that maternal mental illness directly affects the child's intellectual functioning.

RELATIONSHIP BETWEEN MATERNAL AND CHILDREN'S SUSTAINED AND SELECTIVE ATTENTION

The second hypothesis predicted that there would be a significant relationship between both selective and sustained attention of mother and child but that, consistent with theories of identification, girls' attention scores would be more highly related than those of boys to the attention scores of their mothers. It was also expected that this relationship would be greater for the children of mentally ill mothers than for those of well mothers.

The data reported in Table 4 are generally consistent with this hypothesis regarding selective and sustained attention of mothers and children.[2] Significant relationships between attention measures for mothers and children are restricted to the same domain of attention: there is no instance in which maternal selective attention is related to child sustained attention. Within the group of mentally ill mothers and their children the highest correlations for the selective attention measures are between mothers and daughters, rather than mothers and sons. Particularly when considering the measure of number of stimuli failed, this relationship is significant for mentally ill mothers and daughters, but not for well mothers and their daughters, confirming at least a part of the second hypothesis. Mentally ill mothers who take a longer time to overcome embeddedness have daughters who fail a greater number of CEFT cards, although there is little relationship with the time measure of field independence for daughters. Once more the data suggest that daughters of mentally ill mothers appear to be at greater risk than sons for impairment in selective attention. These results regarding selective attention are generally consistent with the hypothesis, derived from Scallon and Herron's (1969) study, that psychopathology in either parent or offspring may increase the magnitude of the intergenerational correlation for measures of selective attention.

In contrast to Witkin (1962, 1965), who found little relationship between selective attention of mothers and children, the data from the present study indicate that this relationship does exist and that it is especially salient among mothers and daughters. Only further study will indicate the extent to which explanations based on genetic or socialization (identification) factors are more parsimonious in terms of the

Table 4
Intercorrelation of Mother and Child Attention Measures Among Mother-Child Pairs in Hospitalized and Nonhospitalized Groups

Child Attention Measure		MOTHER ATTENTION MEASURE							
		CPT				*CEFT*			
		Errors of Omission		*Errors of Commission*		*Time to Correct Response*		*Number of Failures*	
		Patient	*Control*	*Patient*	*Control*	*Patient*	*Control*	*Patient*	*Control*
CPT									
Errors of omission	Boys[1]	.61*	.25	.46	−.02	.46	−.13	.21	−.24
	Girls	.17	−.03	.00	.16	.17	.19	.19	.49
Errors of commission	Boys	−.08	.63**	.22	−.35	.22	.07	.26	.26
	Girls	−.03	−.16	−.10	.37	.03	.18	−.05	.19
CEFT									
Time to correct response	Boys	−.32	−.22	−.03	−.13	−.13	.11	−.14	.16
	Girls	.23	.01	.12	.19	.62*	.83**	.62*	.29
Number of failures	Boys	−.24	−.23	−.18	−.26	.21	.04	−.11	.15
	Girls	.33	−.01	.33	−.45	.58**	.11	.59*	.17

[1]Patient-Boys (N = 18), Patient-Girls (N = 15), Control-Boys (N = 18), Control-Girls (N = 15).
*$p < .05$.
**$p < .01$.

data. It should be noted that these results show the importance of possible sex differences in selective attention, even with children as young as five, an age at which Witkin does not believe such sex differences in psychological differentiation should appear.

Findings with regard to sustained attention are somewhat more ambiguous. While the relationship between maternal and child ability to concentrate is significant between mothers and sons but not between mothers and daughters, there are group differences in the measure of sustained attention that shows this relationship. Among mentally ill mothers and sons this relationship between the two generations appears for the measure of failure to respond to the critical stimulus, while among well mothers and sons this relationship appears for the measure of responding to incorrect stimuli.

Differences in the domain of attention for which correlations appear among mothers and sons and mothers and daughters may reflect sex differences in the child's cognitive development. Data reviewed by Maccoby (1966) and by Vernon (1972) suggest that girls and women generally score lower than men and boys on visual-spatial tasks such as the embedded figures test. On the other hand, boys tend to be more impulsive than girls (Maccoby, 1966; Kagan & Kogan, 1970), a trait that would deter them from maintaining concentration to the extent required for tasks such as the CPT. For example, considering the CPT scores of boys and girls of mentally ill and well mothers—data presented in Table 3—it can be seen that boys in both groups failed significantly more often to respond to the correct stimulus. In addition, within the well group boys were more likely than girls to respond to the incorrect stimulus ($t=1.96$, $p=.06$). Among both the children of mentally ill mothers and those of well mothers, boys also show somewhat more variable performance on these measures of concentration.

To summarize these findings regarding attentional styles of mentally ill and well mothers and their children, we have found that, although a relationship exists between maternal and child attention, the extent of the relationship depends both on the nature of the task and the sex of the offspring. For girls it is selective attention that shows the greatest mother-child correlation, and the magnitude of this relationship is in general greater among mentally ill mothers and daughters than among well mothers and daughters. For boys it is sustained rather than selective attention that is most directly related to maternal attention, and this relationship obtains among boys in each group.

MATERNAL ATTITUDES AND MOTHERS' AND CHILDRENS' COGNITIVE STYLES

The third hypothesis concerns the relationship between child care attitudes and the socialization of the child's capacity for selective and sustained attention. Before considering this hypothesis, it is useful to consider the relationship between child care attitudes and the mother's own capacity for selective and sustained attention.

Maternal Attitudes and Mothers' Cognitive Style

Since both maternal cognitive styles and maternal child care attitudes are related to intellectual performance (Cohler et al., 1973; Wachtel, 1968), correlations are presented between child care attitudes and selective attention with and without intelligence controlled.[3] These data are presented in Table 5. Considering sustained attention, the only significant correlation was among the well mothers, and shows that mothers who believe to a greater extent that they can differentiate between their own needs and those of the child make fewer errors either of omission or commission.

The relationship between child care attitudes and maternal selective attention appears to be much more striking, although the partial correlations suggest that this relationship is at least somewhat mediated by maternal intelligence. Within the group of mentally ill mothers greater maternal psychological differentiation (fewer cards failed and shorter time to correct solution) is associated with more adaptive attitudes regarding four of the five MAS factors. These results suggest that, particularly for those attitudes that concern fostering reciprocity (Factor II), achieving greater differentiation between her own needs and those of children (Factor III), recognizing and tolerating ambivalent feelings regarding child care (Factor IV) and, to a lesser extent, regarding modulated control of the child's aggression (Factor I), mothers who are more field independent, or who demonstrate greater psychological differentiation, are more able to differentiate between self and child and to foster the child's feelings of effectiveness in dealing with the environment.

Among well mothers the major correlate of greater selective attention or field independence is that of acceptance of ambivalent attitudes regarding child care (Factor IV) and, to a lesser extent, belief in the im-

Table 5
Correlation Between Child Care Attitudes and Maternal and Child Measures of Sustained and Selected Attention

	MATERNAL ATTITUDE SCALE FACTOR									
	Appropriate Control (Factor I)		*Encouragement of Reciprocity (Factor II)*		*Appropriate Closeness (Factor III)*		*Acceptance of Complexity (Factor IV)*		*Meeting the Baby's Needs (Factor V)*	
Mother Measures	*Patient*	*Control*	*Patient*	*Control*	*Patient*	*Control*	*Patient*	*Control*	*Patient*	*Control*
CPT										
Errors of omission	−.03	−.07	−.12	−.16	−.15	−.39**	−.18	−.13	−.14	−.04
Errors of commission	−.02	−.02	−.13	−.18	−.18	−.38**	−.05	−.03	−.17	−.05
EFT										
Time to correct	−.24	−.25	−.29*	−.16	−.36	−.17	−.35**	−.47**	−.05	−.11
Correct-partial IQ	−.14	−.06	−.27	−.08	−.35*	−.09	−.31*	−.35*	−.06	−.10
Number of failures	−.31*	−.38**	−.36*	−.18	−.31*	−.27	−.31*	−.45*	−.03	−.01
Failures-partial IQ	−.22	−.21	−.35*	−.09	−.29	−.21	−.26	−.32*	−.03	−.01
Child Measures										
CPT										
Errors of omission	.07	−.24	−.29	−.56*	−.06	−.11	−.37*	−.50*	−.43*	.26
Errors of commission	−.20	−.21	−.34	−.35	−.30	−.12	−.28	−.11	−.14	.12
CEFT										
Time to correct	−.22	.15	−.32	−.25	−.49**	−.12	−.45*	−.02	−.29	−.36
Number of failures	−.09	−.42*	−.38*	−.14	−.34	.02	−.53**	−.20	.05	−.09

Note: For mother measures, patients (N = 43), controls (N = 45); for child measures, patients (N = 28), controls (N = 17).
*p < .05.
**p < .01.

portance of modulating the child's aggressive impulses (Factor I). The relationship between psychological differentiation and the capacity to admit to complex and ambivalent feelings regarding child care supports the view of Witkin et al. (1962) that field independence represents a factor of psychological differentiation in which there is decreased reliance upon more primitive and global defenses such as denial in dealing with inner conflicts.

Maternal Attitudes and Children's Selective and Sustained Attention

The small size of the group receiving both the attention measures and the MAS makes it difficult to examine this relationship separately within boys and girls. However, previous work with the MAS (Cohler et al., 1970) has not shown that the attitudes of mothers of girls differ in any notable respect from those of mothers of boys.

It had been expected that the MAS factors of Appropriate Closeness (Factor III) and Acceptance of Complexity (Factor IV) would be related to the child's ability to sustain attention, among both the children of mentally ill and well mothers, while within each of these two groups Encouragement of Reciprocity (Factor II) and Appropriate Closeness (Factor III) would be related to the increased ability to attend selectively.

This hypothesis was largely supported within the group of children of mentally ill mothers. Those who more often failed to respond to the critical stimulus had mothers who were less willing to admit to complex and ambivalent feelings regarding child care and who believed to a lesser degree that they could understand and meet the baby's needs (Factor V). Within the group of children of well mothers maternal attitudes were also associated with errors of omission, and while maternal ability to admit to ambivalent feelings regarding child care was associated with fewer errors, the extent to which the mother believed in fostering reciprocity was also associated with fewer errors of omission.

The third hypothesis was largely supported considering the relationship between maternal attitudes and the development of psychological differentiation among the children. Among the children of mentally ill mothers, greater psychological differentiation (shorter time to correct identification or fewer card failures) was associated with maternal attitudes supporting greater competence (Factor II), greater differentiation between her own needs and those of the child (Factor III), and greater willingness to admit to ambivalent feelings regarding child care (Factor IV). As with the mothers themselves, greater maternal psychological differentiation in the domain of child care attitudes is related to greater psychological differentiation or more field-independent performance among the children.

Within the group of well mothers the third hypothesis was less clearly supported. The only significant correlation was between the MAS factor of Appropriate Control (Factor I) and fewer card failures on the CEFT. This finding is, however, consistent with Seder's (1957) data, which suggest that mothers of field-independent children were more consistent in their child-rearing techniques and that they engaged in less harsh and authoritarian discipline than mothers of more field-dependent children.

CONCLUSION

Consistent with the findings of other research, the mentally ill mothers in this study, as contrasted with well mothers, showed greater impairment both in selective attention, or the ability to disembed the simple figure from the background, as well as in sustained attention or concentration. The children of these mentally ill mothers also show greater impairment in both selective and sustained attention than the children of well mothers. Girls of mentally ill mothers appear particularly at risk for impairment in selective attention, while the boys of both mentally ill and of well mothers show some greater impairment than girls of either mentally ill or of well mothers in the ability to concentrate. There is little evidence that the children of mentally ill mothers are more impaired in their intellectual performance than children of well mothers.

The relationship between child care attitudes and childrens' ability to concentrate and to disembed the simple form from the background figure was much as expected. Particularly within the group of mentally ill mothers, and especially when considering attitudes regarding differentiation of her own needs from those of the child, mothers believing to a greater extent in fostering a sense of separateness have children who show greater psychological differentiation or more field-independent performance. This finding is consistent with Witkin's observations regarding the importance of the mother's sense of identity as a major determinant of the child's ability to develop psychological differentiation.

References

Anthony, E. The developmental precursions of adult schizophrenia. In D. Rosenthal & S. Kety (Eds.), *The Transmission of Schizophrenia*. New York: Pergamon Press, 1968, pp. 293–319.

Bee, H., Van Egeren, L., Streissguth, A., Nyman, G. & Leckie, M. Social class differences in maternal teaching strategies and speech patterns. *Developmental Psychology* (1969) *1*, 726–734.

Beisser, A., Glasser, M. & Grant, M. Psychosocial adjustment in the children of schizophrenic mothers. *Journal of Nervous and Mental Disease* (1967) *145*, 429–440.

Buhler, C. The reality principle. *American Journal of Psychotherapy* (1954) *8*, 626–647.

Byrne, D. Childrearing antecedents of repression-sensitization. *Child Development* (1964) *35*, 1033–1039.

Campbell, D., Dyer, F. & Boersma, F. Field dependency and picture recognition ability. *Perceptual and Motor Skills* (1967) *25*, 713–716.

Cohler, B. Psychoanalysis, adaptation and education: I. Reality and its appraisal. *Psychological Reports* (1972) *30*, 698–718.

Cohler, B. Psychoanalysis, adaptation and education: II. The development of thinking. *Psychological Reports* (1972) *30*, 719–740.

Cohler, B., Weiss, J., Woolsey, S. & Grunebaum, H. Childbearing attitudes among mothers volunteering and revolunteering for a psychological study. *Psychological Reports* (1968) *23*, 603–612.

Cohler, B., Weiss, J. & Grunebaum, H. Child-care attitudes and emotional disturbance among mothers of young children. *Genetic Psychology Monographs* (1970) *82*, 3–47.

Cohler, B., Grunebaum, H., Weiss, J., Gallant, D. & Hartman, C. Child-care attitudes, social role performance, stress and psychopathology among formerly hospitalized and nonhospitalized mothers. Unpublished manuscript, Committee on Human Development, University of Chicago, 1973.

Corah, N. Differentiation in children and their parents. *Journal of Personality* (1965) *33*, 300–308.

Crandall, V. & Sinkeldam, C. Children's dependent and achievement behaviors in social situations and their perceptual field dependence. *Journal of Personality* (1964) *32*, 1–22.

Dreyer, A., Nebelkopf, E. & Dreyer, C. Note concerning stability of cognitive style measures in young children. *Perceptual and Motor Skills* (1969) *28*, 933–934.

Dyk, R. & Witkin, H. Family experiences related to the development of differentiation in children. *Child Development* (1965) *36*, 21–55.

Fish, B. The maturation of arousal and attention in the first months of life: A study of variations in ego development. *Journal of the American Academy of Child Psychiatry* (1963) *2*, 253–270

Fish, B. & Alpert, M. Abnormal states of consciousness and muscle tone in infants born to schizophrenic mothers. *American Journal of Psychiatry* (1962) *119*, 439–445.

Fish, B. & Alpert, M. Patterns of neurological development in infants born to schizophrenic mothers. In J. Wortis (Ed.), *Recent Advances in Biological Psychiatry*. New York: Plenum Press, 1963, Vol. 5, pp. 24–27.

Ferenczi, S. States in the development of the sense of reality (1913). In S.

Ferenczi (Ed.), *Sex in Psychoanalysis.* New York: Dover Books, 1956, pp. 181–203.

Freud, S. Formulations on the two principles of mental functioning (1911). In *Standard Edition of the Complete Psychological Works*, Vol. XI. London: Hogarth Press, 1958, pp. 218–226.

Freud, S. Recommendations to physicians practicing psychoanalysis (1912). In *Standard Edition of the Complete Psychological Works*, Vol. XII. London: Hogarth Press, 1958, pp. 109–120.

Gallant, D. Attention deficit in young children of psychotic mothers. Paper presented at the 80th Annual Convention, American Psychological Association, 1972a.

Gallant, D. Selective and sustained attention in young children of psychotic mothers. Unpublished doctoral dissertation, Boston University, 1972b.

Gardner, R. Cognitive controls in adaptation: Research and measurement. In S. Messick & J. Ross (Eds.), *Measurement in Personality and Cognition.* New York: Wiley, 1962, pp. 183–198.

Galle, A. & Lynn, R. A developmental study of attention. *British Journal of Educational Psychology* (1972) *42*, 260–266.

Goldstein, H. & Peck, R. Maternal differentiation, father absence, and cognitive differentiation in children. *Archives of General Psychiatry* (1973) *29*, 370–373.

Goodenough, D. & Eagle, C. J. A modification of the embedded-figures test for use with young children. *The Journal of Genetic Psychology* (1963) *103*, 67–74.

Grunebaum, H., Weiss, J., Gallant, D., Cohler, B. & Hartman, C. Mentally ill mothers in the hospital and at home. In G. Abroms & N. Greenfield (Eds.), *The New Hospital Psychiatry.* New York: Academic Press, 1971, pp. 159–174.

Hartman, C., Cohler, B., Gallant, D., Grunebaum, H. & Weiss, J. Toward the prevention of psychopathology: Evaluation of aftercare for psychotic mothers. Panel No. 143, Annual Meetings, American Orthopsychiatric Association, New York, 1973.

Hartmann, H. Notes on the reality principle. *Psychoanalytic Study of the Child* (1955) *10*, 9–29.

Hess, R. & Shipman, V. Early experience and the socialization of cognitive modes in children. *Child Development* (1965) *36*, 869–886.

Heston, L. Psychiatric disorders in foster home reared children of schizophrenic mothers. *British Journal of Psychiatry* (1966) *112*, 819–825.

Higgins, J. Effects of child-rearing by schizophrenic mothers. *Journal of Psychiatric Research* (1966) *4*, 153–167.

Kagan, J. & Kogan, N. Individual variation in cognitive processes. In P. Mussen (Ed.), *Carmichael's Manual of Child Psychology,* 3rd edition. New York: Wiley, 1970, pp. 1273–1365.

Karp, S. Field dependence and overcoming embeddedness. *Journal of Consulting Psychology* (1963) *27*, 294–302.

Katz, D. & Stotland, E. A preliminary statement to a theory of attitude change. In S. Koch (Ed.), *Psychology: The Study of a Science*, Vol. 3. New York: McGraw-Hill, 1959.

Klein, G. Cognitive control and motivation. In G. Lindzey (Ed.), *Assessment of Human Motives.* New York: Holt, Rinehart and Winston, 1958, pp. 87–118.

Levy, D. *Maternal Overprotection.* New York: Columbia University Press, 1943.

Lidz, T., Fleck, S. & Cornelison, A. *Schizophrenia and the Family*. New York: International Universities Press, 1965.

Lynn, D. Sex role and parental identification. *Child Development* (1962) *33*, 555–564.

Maccoby, E. (Ed.) *The Development of Sex Differences* Palo Alto, Calif.: Stanford University Press, 1966.

Maccoby, E., Dowley, E., Hagen, J. & Degerman, R. Activity level and intellectual functioning in normal preschool children. *Child Development* (1965) *36*, 761–770.

Mahler, M. *On Human Symbiosis and Individuation*. Vol. I New York: International Universities Press, 1968.

Marcus, L. Studies of attention in children vulnerable to psychopathology. Unpublished doctoral dissertation, University of Minnesota, 1972.

Meissner, W. W. Notes on identification: The concept of identification. *Psychoanalytic Quarterly* (1972) *41*, 224–260.

Mumbauer, C. & Miller, J. Socioeconomic background and cognitive functioning in preschool children. *Child Development* (1970) *41*, 461–470.

McClellan, S. & Pugh, F. Childhood development following maternal mental illness. Paper presented at Annual Meeting, American Public Health Association, Miami, Florida, 1962.

McClelland, D. *Personality*. New York: Dryden Press, 1951.

Mednick, S. & Schlusinger, F. Some premorbid characteristics related to breakdown in children with schizophrenic mothers. In D. Rosenthal & S. Kety (Eds.), *The Transmission of Schizophrenia*. New York: The Pergamon Press, 1968, pp. 267–291.

Miller, A. (with Cohler, B.). Identification and ego-development. *Bulletin of the Chicago Society for Adolescent Psychiatry* (1971) *1*, 1–9.

Minturn, L. & Lambert, W. *Mothers of Six Cultures: Antecedents of Child-Rearing*. New York: Wiley, 1964.

Orzack, M. & Kornetsky, C. Environmental and familial predictors of attention behavior in chronic schizophrenics. *Journal of Psychiatric Research* (1971) *9*, 21–29.

Orzack, M. & Kornetsky, C. Attention dysfunction in schizophrenia. *Archives of General Psychiatry* (1966) *14*, 323–326.

Rapaport, D., Gill, M. & Schafer, R. *Diagnostic Psychological Testing* (1945). Rev. ed., R. R. Holt, (Ed.) New York: International Universities Press, 1968.

Reisby, N. Psychoses in children of schizophrenic mothers. *Acta Psychiatrica Scandinavica* (1967) *43*, 8–20.

Rolf, J. Social and academic competence of children vulnerable to schizophrenia and other behavior pathologies. *Journal of Abnormal Psychology* (1972) *80*, 225–243.

Rosenthal, D. The offspring of schizophrenic couples. *Journal of Psychiatric Research* (1966) *4*, 169–188.

Rosenthal, D. *Genetics of Psychopathology*. New York: McGraw-Hill, 1971.

Rosvold, H. E., Mirsky, A., Sarason, I., Bransome, E. & Beck, L. A continuous performance test of brain damage. *Journal of Consulting Psychology* (1956) *20*, 343–350.

Sander, L. Issues in early mother-child interaction. *Journal of the American Academy of Child Psychiatry* (1962) *2*, 141–166.

Sander, L. Adaptative relationships in early mother-child interaction.

Journal of the American Academy of Child Psychiatry (1964) *3*, 221–263.

Sander, L. The longitudinal course of early mother-child interaction: Cross-case comparison in a sample of mother-child pairs. In B. Foss (Ed.), *Determinants of Infant Behavior*. London: Methuen, 1969, pp. 189–228.

Sarnoff, I. Psychoanalytic theory and social attitudes. *Public Opinion Quarterly* (1960) *24*, 251–279.

Santostefano, S. Cognitive controls versus cognitive styles: An approach to diagnosing and treating cognitive disabilities in children. *Seminars in Psychiatry* (1969) *1*, 291–317.

Scallon, R. & Herron, W. Field articulation of enuretic boys and their mothers. *Perceptual and Motor Skills* (1969) *28*, 407–413.

Schachtel, E. The development of focal attention and the emergence of reality. *Psychiatry* (1954) *17*, 309–324.

Schachtel, E. On attention, selective inattention, and experience: An inquiry into attention as an attitude. In E. Wittenberg (Ed.), *Interpersonal Explorations in Psychoanalysis. New Directions in Theory and Practice.* New York: Basic Books, 1973.

Seder, J. The origin of differences in extent of independence in children: Developmental factors in perceptual field dependence. Unpublished bachelor's thesis, Radcliffe College, Cambridge, Massachusetts, 1957.

Shakow, D. Segmental set: A theory of the formal psychological deficit in schizophrenia. *Archives of General Psychiatry* (1962) *6*, 1–17.

Shakow, D. Psychological deficit in schizophrenia. *Behavioral Science* (1963) *8*, 275–305.

Silverman, J. The problem of attention. *Psychological Review* (1964) *71*, 352–379.

Singer, M. & Wynne, L. Thought disorder and family relations of schizophrenics: III. Methodology using projective techniques. *Archives of General Psychiatry* (1965) *12*, 187–200.

Singer, M. & Wynne, L. Thought disorder and family relations of schizophrenics: IV. Results and implications. *Archives of General Psychiatry* (1965) *12*, 201–212.

Singer, M. & Wynne, L. Principles for scoring communication deficits and deviances in parents of normals, neurotics, and schizophrenics. *Psychiatry* (1966) *29*, 260–288.

Smith, M. B., Bruner, J. & White, R. *Opinions and Personality*. New York: Wiley, 1956.

Vernon, P. The distinctiveness of field independence. *Journal of Personality* (1972) *40*, 366–391.

Wachtel, P. Conceptions of broad and narrow attention. *Psychological Bulletin* (1967) *68*, 417–429.

Wachtel, P. Style and capacity in analytic functioning. *Journal of Personality* (1968) *36*, 202–212.

Wachtel, P. Field dependence and psychological differentiation: Reexamination. *Perceptual and Motor Skills* (1972a) *35*, 179–189.

Wachtel, P. Cognitive style and style of adaptation. *Perceptual and Motor Skills* (1972b) *35*, 779–785.

Wechsler, D. *Manual for the Wechsler Preschool and Primary Scale of Intelligence*. New York: The Psychological Corporation, 1963.

White, R. Ego and reality in psychoanalytic theory. *Psychological Issues* (1963) *11*.

Witkin, H. Individual differences in ease of perception of embedded figures. *Journal of Personality* (1950) *19*, 1–15.

Witkin, H. Psychological differentiation and forms of pathology. *Journal of Abnormal Psychology* (1965) *70*, 317–336.

Witkin, H. A cognitive style approach to cross-cultural research. *International Journal of Psychology* (1967) *2*, 233–250.

Witkin, H., Dyk, R., Faterson, H., Goodenough, D. & Karp, S. *Psychological differentiation.* New York: Wiley, 1962.

Witkin, H., Oltman, P., Raskin, E. & Karp, S. *A manual for the embedded figures tests.* Palo Alto, Calif.: Consulting Psychologists Press, 1971.

Wynne, L. & Singer, M. Thought disorder and family relations of schizophrenics: I. A research strategy. *Archives of General Psychiatry* (1963) *9*, 191–198.

Wynne, L. & Singer, M. Thought disorder and family relations of schizophrenics:II. A classification of forms of thinking. *Archives of General Psychiatry* (1963) *9*, 199–206.

Zigler, E. A measure in search of a theory? *Contemporary Psychology* (1963) *8*, 133–315.

Notes

[1]This research was supported in part by the National Institute of Mental Health, Grant MH-13,946, and by a faculty grant to the first author from the Social Science Research Committee, University of Chicago.

[2]It has been suggested that intergenerational correlations for sustained and, particularly, selective attention may be confounded with intergenerational correlations in intelligence (Wachtel, 1972a). Partial correlations between maternal and child sustained and selective attention, controlling for intelligence, did not change the magnitude of the Pearsonian correlations reported in Table 4.

[3]Within the group of hospitalized mothers there was little correlation between verbal intelligence and either errors of omission ($r = -.10$) or errors of commission ($r = .22$). However, verbal intelligence was related to both measures of selective attention. The correlations with time to correct response ($r = -.34$) and number of failures ($r = -.32$) are significant at less than the .05 level. Within the controls sustained attention is not correlated with verbal intelligence for either errors of omission ($r = .13$) or errors of commission ($r = .17$). Both of the selective attention measures—time to correct response ($r = -.46$) and number of failures ($r = -.49$)—were significantly related to verbal intelligence at less than the .01 level.

CHAPTER NINE

The Modality Concept: Including a Statement of the Perceptual and Conceptual Levels of Learning

Joseph M. Wepman

> "The intellectual life of man consists almost wholly in his substitution of a conceptual order for the perceptual order in which his experience originally comes."
>
> William James
> *Essays on Radical Empiricism*

In a recent newsletter from a suburban Chicago special education group the lead article dealt with learning disabilities and mental retardation. A plea was made that the schools recognize that "maturational lags or temporarily arrested development not be confused with low potential." The article continued with the statement that ". . . of every thousand American school age children, 150 will have learning problems, 30 will be mentally retarded, and 5 will have learning disabilities and mental retardation." (1) Whether the incidence figures quoted are correct or not, we are all concerned about such children, es-

Reprinted with the permission of J. M. Wepman and the International Reading Association from H. K. Smith (Ed.) *Perception and Reading*, Newark, Delaware: IRA, 1968.

pecially those with normal intellectual potential who are underachievers.

Learning theories and learning theorists, whether biologically or environmentally oriented, have most often failed in their treatment of this issue. They have described the learning process as they see it, but have failed to describe the child who must do the learning. They have rarely provided data on the evolution of individual differences in learning abilities of children. Literally, they have never given us reasons why, according to their theories, the underachiever underachieves.

Figure 1.

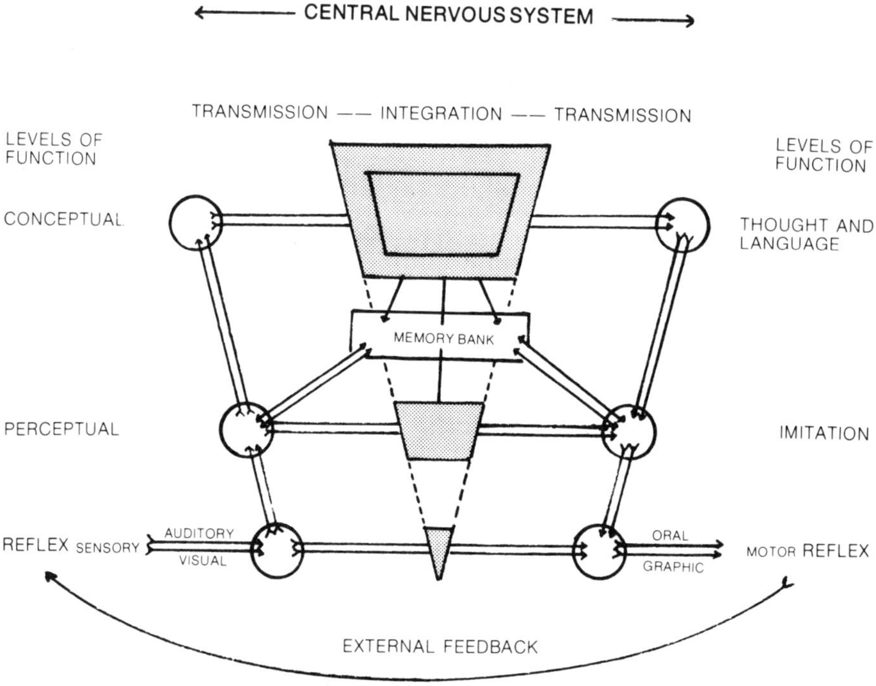

AN OPERATIONAL DIAGRAM OF THE LEVELS OF FUNCTION IN THE CNS

The present paper is an attempt to rectify, at least in part, this neglect of a crucial aspect of learning. While it is not the statement of yet another learning theory, it does provide a modus operandi for learning, e.g., how it is achieved and, therefore, why some children do not achieve when it seems as though they should. It also serves as a partial explanation of individual differences in the manner of learning. Through the approach advocated, it is hoped we can gain some greater insights into the problems of the 15 percent of all schoolchildren who are said to be underachieving.

The present paper deals with the initial stages of learning, especially the early steps taken by children as they develop the capacity to utilize their maturing neurological system. It is not intended as a criticism or as a support of any of the well-publicized theories of learning. It is in fact compatible with any or all of them.

The hypothetical model presented as Fig. 9-1 stresses two features of the structural base underlying the learning act. First, it emphasizes the unique modality-bound nature of all sensory input signals and all motor output patterns. Second, it elaborates the hierarchical yet interrelated nature of the maturation and development of the neural system. In this regard it parallels what is known of the physiological maturation of the central nervous system.*

Fig. 1 is designed to illustrate both the modality-bound nature of the input and output signals and the increasing levels of complexity of function as the individual matures. The modality-bound nature of children's learning behavior was initially recognized in the clinically observed fact that many children with learning problems appeared to have greater facility using one input pathway rather than another and—an observation of equal importance—they had considerably less facility along other pathways. This was seen most easily in children with known impairments of neurological structure such as localized brain tumors or accidents affecting, for example, the transmission of auditory signals, but not visual or tactual signals. Similar behavior, however, was seen in some children who had no demonstrable neurological impairment. The learning behavior of this group of children was so similar to the earlier group that even today they are sometimes—erroneously, I believe—said to have minimal brain impairment. As more children were studied from this modality viewpoint, it became apparent that a predilection for one sensory input

*In the present context the word *maturation* is used to describe the establishment of the neurological components necessary for sensory transmission, integration, and motor transmission of signals within the nervous system. The term *development* is reserved for the functional adaptation of an established neural pathway.

channel over the others could be observed, regardless of whether a suspicion of organic impairment or pathology was present. This seemed in keeping with the concept first suggested by Charcot and reported by Freud (2), that each person has a particular modality of choice in learning, a typology of "audile," "visile," and "tactile" learners.

Phenomenological data for the division of people into learning types seems to abound in life around us. Toscanini is said to have *heard* every note of music he read. Picasso, on the other hand, is said to have *seen* in his own unique way even the sounds of animals in the field. People select occupations based upon their predilection for auditory stimuli (musicians), while others pursue the graphic arts (painting) because of their visile-ness.

Clinical data from the handicapped learner or underachiever is equally omnipresent, if one is alerted to it. Some children have been known to be so deficient in auditory processing of signals that for most environmental situations they are functionally deaf, even though their hearing acuity is quite normal. One such child was incapable of recalling a telephone number or a single item from a list of ten items read to him. Another could not distinguish the letters of the alphabet at 12 years of age, yet suffered no loss of visual acuity. Studies of adult brain-injured subjects showed with clarity residual ability that was modality-bound as they processed verbal stimuli. A factor-analytic study of the responses of 168 adult aphasic patients to visual and auditory stimuli on the Language Modalities Test for Aphasia showed ". . . for all analyses [a single factor] was best defined by all items demanding oral response to visual stimuli . . . while the oral response to auditory stimuli appeared as a separate factor" (3) Still furthur evidence has been collected from the behavior of a variety of populations, which will be reported in some detail during the course of this chapter.

It should be sufficient to say at this time that the concept of differential use of the separate input pathways is no longer purely theoretical but is assuming the proportions of an acceptable fact about children and their learning.

The differential modality distinction appears to be related more closely to the innate capacity of a child than to any determinable environmental factor. No specific deprivation of stimulation could be found in the home or play environments of children with poor auditory, poor visual, or poor tactile-kinesthetic learning. In fact, within the populations studied clinically such children have been found to come from all types of homes, including the highly verbal university setting as well as the almost nonverbal disadvantaged environments. They came from homes where they were the only child and from homes where they were the eldest or youngest of multiple sibling groups.

For most children the two major modalities seemed to reach a stage of equalization of function by the time they reached their ninth birthday—whatever lags in development were present seemed to be overcome by that time. Usually, however, the modality showing the most rapid development indicated the child's predilection. Perhaps from this it might be said that a modality matures due to some innate neurological tendency—for the audile child, the auditory pathway matures soonest; for the visile child, the visual pathway. With maturation there is an accompanying developmental sequence—again, the earliest to mature nominates the earlier development of function. The audile child, then, not only matures earliest in an auditory sense, but develops his more mature pathway with the greater ease. Here, use of the pathway assists with its development. It comes to complete function and use at an early age. Practically, this would mean that both perceptual and conceptual function would develop early, with consequent early and accurate acquisition and use of speech. The visual function of such an "audile" child could be either rapid or slow in its development. If it is rapid, reading would be accomplished easily, but if it is slow, reading might be delayed somewhat by the need for compensation to assist the auditory pathway. If the visual were very slow indeed, then reading might present a real block, since only the auditory percepts would be available, and while reading is more than a visual skill, it does require vision.

The visile child would pose quite a different problem. If he is average in auditory learning, his reading might be slightly affected in the early school years. If he is markedly slow in auditory perceptual development, however, only high intelligence that provided almost automatic compensation would be helpful—or the services of an alert and patient therapist.

To understand the effect of modality preference on such skills as reading, speech, and spelling, one must be able not only to isolate the preferred modality, but to assess the level of achievement and the potential for training of whatever modality is delayed in its development.

While the emphasis here has been the development of visual and auditory pathways, the visuo-motor and moto-kinesthetic pathways need equal attention. In some ways they are perhaps the better attested of the developmentally related modality functions, as Frostig (4) and others have demonstrated.

Attempts to reduce the effect of a lag in developmental progression in any one of the modalities have been somewhat equivocal. Auditory training for children with slow development of such processes as discrimination, memory, and sequencing along that modality has produced good results in some children but failed to produce results in others. These are clinical data, however, and should be studied under the more rigorous analyses of research. For what it is worth, however, those children with poor auditory discrimination who showed what was believed to be causally related speech articulatory inaccuracy failed to improve in auditory discrimination with directed training. On the other hand, children with inadequate auditory discrimination who had difficulty learning to read, again with supposed causal relationships, did indeed improve in discrimination with training.

The major importance of the modality distinction lies in the direction that it may give for assisting the underachiever. Too often the remedial reading teacher follows the same pattern in remedial work that the classroom teacher follows in general instruction. We have long assumed that a particular method or pattern for teaching or remediating the art or skill of reading was appropriate—whatever that method might be. The concept of differential modality proclivity would argue for tailoring the instruction and the remediation, especially the latter, to the capacity of the indididual child. When this is not done, problems arise. Consider the child who has an inadequate auditory perceptual ability as demonstrated by his incapacity to differentiate the sounds of the language, retain and recall them, sequence them properly, or associate them with previously learned visual or tactual-kinesthetic clues, when he is faced by an instructional or remedial program based on the learning of phonics. Consider, on the other hand, the child who demonstrates a slower progression of his visual skills than is expected of him, who is faced by a school system that fosters sight training. In either instance the failure to recognize the differential modality distinctions for these children almost foredooms them to failure in achievement of reading. While this may affect in a major sense only a minimum of the children who are underachievers, it may be partially at the base of a wide variety of other problems engendered by the original failure. Perhaps the entire thesis of the argument for considering the modality distinction can be most succinctly stated as providing a way of understanding underachievers. If they can be seen as children who are underachieving because of some real modality distinction, then programs can—and, I believe, will—be developed that will be of assistance to them.

To this date attempts to predict reading problems from results on prior perceptual testing have been less than rewarding. While it is true that a greater number of children with poor reading achievement showed poor visual discrimination and memory as well as poor auditory discrimination and memory, the number of false positives has made the prediction an unlikely one. However, at the time when poor reading achievement can be identified, the presence of poor visual or auditory perception can point the way to directed remediation.

The second important aspect of the model presented as Fig. 1 is the time-bound progression of the neural system, as it builds each succeeding layer upon previously developed layers, in the sense of both maturation and development. The infant begins life with a mature and well-developed reflex system that soon differentiates into a bridge permitting the flow of environmentally induced signals that proceed from input through integration to output. At this stage, psychologically, only recognition is achieved, not comprehension. At this level of behavior children learn to imitate and echo their environment. They learn to discriminate the sounds of the language they hear and later to differentiate the letters and other forms that they see. Finally, they develop their highest level of neural behavior—they receive, integrate, and express signals from a variety of modalities with comprehension of the input, they synthesize and associate the interpreted signal with previous learning, and they formulate an output signal with intent to communicate.

Two kinds of learning, then, are evident—the perceptual, prelinguistic, preoperational learning described most completely by Piaget and his followers as *sensory-motor learning,* and the more complex, conceptualizing type of learning with comprehension and intent. Attention in this chapter is directed to the former, not because this is the more important of the two, but because it seems that there has been overemphasis on the latter for beginning learners of any skill. This overemphasis has led to a tendency to focus on the child's attack on new learning at the conceptual level, frequently before the child has established a proper perceptual base for that learning. Werner and Kaplan (6), in their study of symbol formation, pointed out that ". . . a fuller psychological insight into all representation, including linguistic, will be obtained only by operating on the assumption that linguistic representation emerges from and is rooted in non-linguistic forms of representation."

Children having difficulty learning to read, it is here argued, may well be started at too high a level for them if comprehension is demanded before they have mastered the preverbal perceptual distinctions necessary for phonic interpolations. The development of the maturing perceptual level can be seen in the progressive achievement of such skills as discrimination, retention and recall of sounds and letters, sequential ordering of phonemes and graphemes, and the ability to interrelate one with the other.

To illustrate what it is the child must learn and be able to use at this precomprehension level of behavior, let us explore in some detail the act of auditory discrimination. This auditory perceptual function is the ability to differentiate each sound of the language from every other sound of the language; at its grossest level, for example, it is the ability to separate vowels from consonants, then vowels from other vowels, and finally consonants from other consonants. Vowel discriminations are, for the most part, well accomplished by all but a handful of children by the end of the third year, yet all of us experience some difficulty discriminating certain vowels from others, when spoken—did he say /pen/ or /pin/? is a common adult question, when the context does not provide a satisfactory clue. The difference between the /e/ and /i/ when used medially in a single-syllable word is a minimal contrast of considerable difficulty. The distinctions between some consonants is equally difficult—for example, /p/ and /b/ cannot be considered as within the differential speaking armamentarium of children until they can listen to word pairs like /pat/ and /bat/ and /pin/ and /bin/ and recognize them as being different. The linguistic term for this recognition of difference is called the method of "minimal contrasts" (7). A growing body of research now points to the fact that this ability to form minimal contrasts is a developing process that goes on quite normally in children through their eighth year of life. Some children develop the ability early in life—their speech efforts reflect this early development. They speak accurately almost from the onset. They have the "ear" to guide their speech attempts. Other children develop this discriminatory ability more slowly, and their speech accuracy often mirrors their development. Some children have difficulty with auditory discrimination throughout their lives, learning to speak with accuracy only by compensatory means.

Turning back to what has been said about Charcot's concept of learning typology mentioned earlier, the child with good intelligence but slow in development of auditory discrimination ability would undoubtedly need to be thought of as a "visile" child, or perhaps "tactile" in his learning, while the child who speaks early and accurately, but later shows some difficulty acquiring the distinctions necessary for differentiating visual forms, would most probably be "audile" or "tactile." Some children, of course, will be found who are slow at developing any of their perceptual skills, regardless of the modality involved. These would need to be classified as mentally retarded, since they would have no avenue open to them for learning—and after all, that is what we mean by mental retardation, the inability to learn.

Stress needs to be placed in initial stages of learning, on this perceptual level, or the later learning at the conceptual level may be faulty and without a basic structure upon which the child can develop his linguistic skills. Where a lag in the developmental process along any of the modalities can be determined, the remedial task seems most properly directed at that modality—yet if success cannot be achieved through such a direct approach, the teacher should not hesitate to turn to the other modalities, since reading—like speech or writing or spelling—cannot be considered the product of any single modality but rather a confluence of them all. It is believed that this generalized attack through parallel alphabets is the source of the success achieved with such teaching approaches as the Initial Teaching Alphabet (8), which takes advantage of a common alphabet of sounds and letters. Similarly, the Illinois Test of Psycholinguistic Abilities (9) develops with considerable acumen the modality differential in language acquisition, especially at the conceptual level.

No brief is held here for or against any specific teaching method. Any method can be adapted to the purposes of modality distinctions or reduced to the level of perceptual function, if that is needed. Every teacher and therapist whose unlikely task it is to make every child literate must, at this time at least, be ingenious enough to provide the materials necessary for such teaching. Unless my estimate of the commercial adjuncts to reading is in error, however, and unless the proposed approach to underachievement turns out to be totally unsuccessful, materials will be produced in great abundance.

The paper stresses two factors—the difference among children in their use of specific modalities for learning, and the necessary establishment of perceptual bases for conceptual learning. It is hoped that at least for the child in need of remediation, education can take on the nature of a child-centered program and shift away from our ready acceptance of automatization and conformity. While we speak of education in the mass sense, it is the individual child who must learn. It is for his good that the ideas here proposed have been formulated.

References

1. Peppard, D. West Subarban Association for the Other Child. Monthly Newsletter. February, 1967.

2. Charcot, J. M. New Lectures, 1886, in Freud, S., *On Aphasia.* New York: International Universities Press, 1953.

3. Jones, L. V. & Wepman, J. M. Dimensions of language performance in aphasia. *J. Speech Hear. Res.*, 1961, *4*, 220–232.

4. Frostig, Marianne. Corrective reading in the classroom. *The Reading Teacher*, 1965, *18*, 573–577.

5. Flavell, J. H. *The Developmental Psychology of Jean Piaget.* Princeton: Van Nostrand, 1963.

6. Werner, H. & Kaplan, B. *Symbol Formation.* New York, Wiley, 1963.

7. Jakobson, R., Fant. C. G. M. & Halle, M. *Preliminaries to Speech Analysis.* Cambridge: M. I. T. Press, 1961.

8. Mazurkiewicz, A. The Initial Teaching Alphabet (i/t/a). In J. Money (Ed.), *The Disabled Reader.* Baltimore: Johns Hopkins Press, 1966.

9. McCarthy, J. J. & Kirk, S. *Illinois Test of Psychlinguistic Abilities.* Institute for Research in Exceptional Children, Urbana, 1961.

CHAPTER TEN

Infants' Effects upon Their Mothers' Teaching Strategies

Kenneth Kaye

Jerome Bruner sees skills as developing from the new combination of previously mastered subroutines. Three features distinguish Bruner's theory. First, the "intention" that guides action also guides learning; the adaptive use of old means for new ends enables even the young infant to accommodate his skills to environmental needs, without waiting for the gradual selective effects of reinforcement. Second, the integration and coordination of simpler skills for higher-order, specialized purposes cannot proceed until the necessary subroutines or "modules" are sufficiently practiced on their own, so as to free attention for the additional task of coordinating them. Third, some of the constituents that are to be combined in new skills develop in the infant autonomously, due neither to reinforcement nor to adaptation but to behavioral maturation "preadapted" in the evolution of the human species. (Bruner, 1971, 1972, 1973; Bruner & Bruner, 1968)

What implications does such a theory have for instruction or for facilitating the development of skill? The importance of intention would suggest that an instructor ought to take account of the learner's intrinsic motivations. The problem of modularization would suggest that instruction must be sensitive to the hierarchical structure of the skills that are to be taught. And both modularization and preadaptation imply that the instructor must take into account where the learner is, with respect to the skills and subskills involved in a given task.

Thus stated, the guidelines for instruction are reminiscent of a wide range of learning theories. Whether one is searching with Tolman for the appropriate goal object or with Hull for the appropriate reinforcer, and whether one analyzes task and learner to find the relevant habits, associations, operants, subroutines, or schemas, it makes common sense that one analyzes the learner's goals and abilities along with the task's structure and requirements, and tries to increase the fit between the two. In Skinner's (1954) terms:

> What behavior is to be set up? What reinforcers are at hand? What responses are available in embarking upon a program of progressive approximation which will lead to the final form of the behavior? (p. 93)

Bruner himself, long before he turned his attention to the skills of infants, organized *The Process of Education* (1960) around four themes, of which three were the structure of the subject matter, intellectual readiness, and the motives of the learner.

Although there is agreement and substantial research supporting the principle that instruction *ought to* take account of the learner's motivation, the structure of the task or subject matter, and the developmental fit between learner and task, there remains the question whether, under normal circumstances, human instructors do take account of these factors in selecting from among alternative strategies. And if they do so, how do they themselves acquire these teaching skills?

In the literature on skills from which the recent work of Bruner and his students derives most of its theoretical nourishment, we find strong arguments favoring an analysis of interaction in dyads or groups. Argyle and Kendon (1967), for example, discuss the model of skill that also underlies Bruner's theory—a programmatic system using feedback to realize intentions. They argue that groups of two or more persons with shared intentions can be system-analyzed in much the same fashion as a single organism. Communication between the partners will appear to be a matter of feedback loops. Dozens of studies support the hypothesis that interaction requires individuals to accommodate their posture, distance, attentional orientation, gestures, language, and various activity cycles to one another. Argyle and Kendon also review evidence that what Goffman (1961) calls *focussed interaction*, in which people converse or cooperate in a task, differs in the above aspects from casual or unfocussed interaction. But as of 1967, and still as of the present writing, there were no studies in the skill literature that looked at the development of goal-attainment capabilities in teams, or at the goal-attainment strategies of children in social contexts, or at interaction where one partner is the instructor and the other the learner.

There is plenty of evidence that the characteristics of learners and instructional treatments interact in the statistical sense, though these interactions are rarely disordinal; that is, rarely has one type of instruction been shown to be better for some learners and another type better for others (Bracht, 1970). There is also growing literature on processes of behavioral interaction (Blurton-Jones, 1972; Lewis & Rosenblum, 1974). Our object was to combine the analysis of both kinds of interaction with the model of sensorimotor skill, and to investigate instructional strategies.

METHOD

Subjects

Almost any age group could have been used for this study so long as an appropriate task was available. The author had completed a study with Jerome Bruner and Karlen Lyons (Bruner, 1971) in which infants attempted to reach around a barrier to grasp a wooden cube. The six-month-old infants in that study, seated in their mothers' laps, were unable to solve the problem on their own. Since many of their mothers expressed frustration at not being able to help, the task and the six-month-old age group seemed appropriate for the following investigation.

Subjects were recruited from among the pool of mothers volunteering for studies at the Center for Cognitive Studies at Harvard University. Extra efforts were made to advertise among working-class families, so as to balance the large number of graduate student and professional families. Since we were interested in social class as a possible independent variable, the experimenter wished to remain ignorant, so far as possible, of the social class background of each subject until after the session was over. Furthermore, we did not want to call the subjects' attention to education or social class as a variable

Table 1
Design of the Study (Number of Subjects)

Experimental Condition	*Sex of Infant*	*MOTHER'S EDUCATION LEVEL* (1) *High School Only*	(2) *Some College*	(3) *College Grad*	(4) *Beyond College*	*Total*
Screen on left	Male	7	3	5	6	21
	Female	6	6	7	5	24
Screen on right	Male	7	4	4	6	21
	Female	6	6	7	6	25
Total		26	19	23	23	91

likely to affect their behavior, so no questions at all were asked of them until the end. This meant that it was not possible to assign subjects to cells of the design until we had already observed them. Therefore, we ran as many subjects as necessary for us to end up with at least 25 mothers who had no education beyond high school and at least 25 who had graduated from college. The total number of subjects turned out to be 91. Table 1 shows the design.

Subjects came to the Center for Cognitive Studies for only one visit, which lasted from 30 to 45 minutes. At the end of the session we asked questions regarding the parents' education, the number of siblings, the precise age of the baby, and the number of weeks it had been breastfed. The infants were all between 26 and 31 weeks old.

Apparatus

The detour reaching apparatus consisted of a large wooden box 18 inches high by 36 inches wide by 24 inches deep, as shown in Fig. 1. Across the front of the box the lower 5. inches were open, revealing a brightly lit white interior. The exterior of the box was painted gray, and there was no other source of illumination in the room outside the

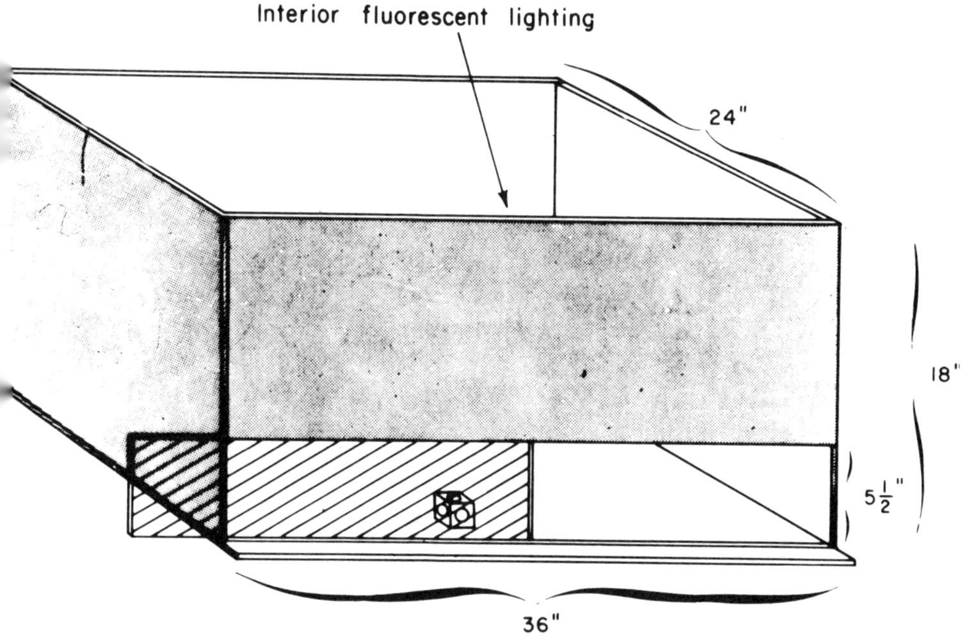

Fig. 1. Detour reaching apparatus.

box. The infants were seated in their mothers' lap in front of the box, with their eyes just above the level of the opening; together with the fact that the illumination came from inside, this meant that the infants saw no reflection in the plexiglass barrier that was mounted in the opening. The barrier extended from the infant's midline all the way across either the left or the right half of the box (See Table 1). The toy was placed in the apparatus through the open top, at a position just inside the edge of the barrier as shown in Fig. 1.

The recording apparatus was one designed by Lentz (Lentz & Haith, 1969) for continuous recording of binary information in up to 32 categories. Onset and offset of the behavioral events to be described below were coded "live" by two observers and stored as a continuous electronic signal on magnetic tape. This tape was subsequently processed on a PDP-9T computer, which produced a printed transcript of each session and extracted summary statistics so that cross-subject comparisons could be made using the Harvard DATA-TEXT system on an IBM 7094 computer.

Procedure

The session consisted of a pretest, a teaching period, a posttest, and a transfer test. The length of the teaching period was entirely left to the mother's discretion. The other three periods were a little over two minutes in length. They were terminated when one of the following criteria was reached: (a) 30 consecutive seconds without progress toward a reach; (b) heavy crying that could not be ignored; (c) three successful retrievals of the toy from behind the barrier; or (d) two and one-half minutes. The mean length of the pretest was 123.8 seconds, with no systematic differences across any of the cells of the design. (Posttest and transfer were shorter, rarely reaching criterion d.)

When a mother entered the experimental room, she was offered an armchair a few feet away from the apparatus. We handed her infant the wooden cube (containing a bell). Nearly all babies reached for this toy and grasped it immediately; a few were so shy of the experimenter that they would only take the block from their mothers. Even something so apparently trivial as the fact that the baby was interested in the toy seemed to ease our rapport with the mothers as we began:

> We've done a rather large study in which babies were to solve this problem. The problem is simply to get this toy out from behind this screen. It looks easy but it isn't. One of the things we learned was that babies around six or seven months old couldn't

> figure out how to solve this problem without any help. What we want to find out now is whether they can learn the task when they have the help of an adult. But the first thing we have to do is to check that (COGNITA) can't solve the problem on her own—occasionally we get a baby who can reach around the screen at this age, in a clumsy sort of way. I don't expect that will happen, though. If you'll just sit in this chair and hold her so that her middle is about here, we'll watch her for about two minutes. Then we'll give her a rest. You should hold her loosely so she's free to reach around if she can, but sit back a bit so as not to give her any hints.

At the end of the pretest mother and baby returned to a more comfortable chair. Note that the mother had not yet been told who was going to be doing the training. When the child was calm and cheerful, the session resumed:

> Well, as we expected she didn't get the toy (*or*, she surprised us by getting the toy but there's still room for improvement in speed and smoothness). Now we want to find out if babies this young can learn to get the toy when they have the help of an adult. I've tried teaching them myself but that doesn't work very well: I think the best way is to try and have their mothers teach them. Since we don't know what the best method of teaching the solution is, we won't give you any advice; we'll be interested in seeing what works. You'll be completely on your own. Now she is one of our younger babies, but she might be solving the problem beautifully by the time you're through. Take as long as you like, and just tell us when she's either mastered it or gotten fed up with it. You can do anything at all that you think might help; you can even stand her on her head if that seems to work. When you tell us you're through, we'll just have her try it without any help, like we did before. When we test to see if she's learned it, she'll be sitting here and the toy will be right here, like before. You can try anything you like that you think might work. Any questions?

Needless to say, these instructions varied somewhat in response to the mothers' apparent reactions.

Behavioral coding proceeded in three stages. The first consisted of live continuous recording of six maternal behavior categories and six infant behavior categories. Mother and baby were observed independently by the two experimenters. Each observer had six small finger buttons which could be held down so long as an event was "on."

The six categories observed in the mothers were: RESETTING, or putting the toy back in its position behind the screen; MODELING the detour reach for the child; TEMPTING, by pointing at or shaking the cube; SIMPLIFYING the task by moving the toy to the open side of the apparatus; TUGGING the baby's hand or arm; and moving the BABY bodily in her lap. No attempt was made to interpret the mother's intent in any of these instances; for example, MODELING was scored every time the mother reached for the toy.

The other observer coded the baby as follows: POINTING at the toy through the screen; REACHING around the screen toward the toy; TOUCHING the toy inside the box; PLAYING with the toy outside the box; looking AWAY from the task; and DISTRESS indicated by crying or screaming. (These behaviors were also recorded in the pretest, posttest, and transfer test.)

Several factors constrained the choice of categories; they had to be few enough so that all possible combinations could be recorded as they occurred; they had to be discrete categories so that there was no ambiguity about classifying any event; and they had to exhaust all of the salient behavior that seemed relevant to the task.

Our measure of reliability was the proportion of discrete events coded, in the same sequence, by two pairs of observers from a videotape. The actual observers had trained the two additional teams using videotapes made during pilot sessions. Reliability was based upon the first codings of an additional 10-minute videotape the observers were seeing for the first time. There were 160 events on this tape, of which 153 were coded by both sets of observers in exactly the same sequence. Thus, reliability was estimated at 96 percent; it was about the same for the observers of the infant as for the observers of the mother. This videotape was randomly selected from among tapes we made of our first ten sessions. We assume that some sessions were coded less, and some perhaps more, reliably. The method of estimating reliability is conservative in that (a) we use discrete events rather than units of time for comparison between the two teams; (b) we used the total number of events known to be visible on the videotape as our denominator rather than the total number coded by either team; and (c) we used interobserver reliability *between* observers whom we trained, which can be assumed to be lower than the reliability *within* the experienced observers who actually saw all 91 subjects.

However, it should be pointed out that our highly satisfactory reliability estimate refers to the sequence and frequencies of events, not to their latencies and durations. Although the vast majority of differences in response latency between the two sets of observers were less than 2 seconds, we did not measure the reliability of our response latencies. The latencies of interest for the paper would be those of only 1 to 2 seconds, and therefore we will report no results dealing with latencies.

In the second stage of analysis the computer reconstructed meaningful acts from the sequences of discrete categories. For example, MODEL-TEMPT-RESET meant that the mother's purpose had been to demonstrate the skill, while MODEL-SIMPLIFY, though counted as an opportunity for the baby to observe the detour reach, was considered from the mother's point of view to be an attempt at breaking down the task.

The twelve behavioral categories were not all treated alike at this stage of processing. For example, the category BABY was used primarily as a flag to indicate how other events were to be interpreted. If the mother moved the baby bodily at any time between the start of a reach and the point at which the baby touched the toy, even if the baby then took the toy out of the box, this was not scored as a success. If the categories of BABY and AWAY continued simultaneously for more than a few seconds, this indicated that the mother had removed the baby from the task to console it. All such signal combinations were established by the observers during practice sessions and became routine, so that they could be interpreted unambiguously.

The sequence RESET-REACH-TOUCH-PLAY meant that the infant scored what we arbitrarily called a success, unless HAND-TUGGING, BABY, or SIMPLIFYING had been coded between the onset of REACHING and the onset of TOUCHING.

The final stage of processing, after obtaining transcripts and summary statistics of each session but before analyzing the results, was a rating of the mother's predominant teaching strategy. Pilot studies had led us to expect three basic types of strategy—one based on MODEL-TEMPT-RESET, one based on SIMPLIFYING, and one based on HAND-TUGGING. In fact, it was fairly easy to sort the subjects into three groups using the following criteria, listed in the order with which we weighted them: (a) repetition of an action pattern, such as MODEL-TEMPT-RESET or MODEL-SIMPLIFY, throughout the session (75 subjects were classified unambiguously on this basis alone); (b) supporting evidence of the mother's intention, such as RESETTING the toy behind the screen after a series of SIMPLIFYINGS; and (c) the behavior that predominated earlier rather than later in the session. Using these criteria there was independent agreement between two raters on 90 of the 91 subjects.

RESULTS

The three principal teaching strategies came to be known as *showing, shaping,* and *shoving.* The most important thing we can say about these strategies is that most of the mothers used all three. Of the 37 whom we characterized as relying principally on a demonstration or *showing* strategy, most tugged the infant's hand at least once and most simplified at least once. Hand-tugging and demonstration also tended to be used by the 25 *shaping* mothers (whose major strategy was to begin with a direct reach and gradually build up to the detour reach). Most of the 29 mothers who relied mainly on *shoving* the infant around the screen also simplified and demonstrated the task one or more times. It was not our purpose to typologize mothers as different kinds of teachers, though independent maternal variables did predict teaching strategies to some extent. The real reason for grouping our subjects in this way was our hypothesis that the predominant teaching methods would depend upon behavioral differences in the infants, and would in turn have different degrees of success.

The first set of results to be considered involves the immediate context of the mother's teaching behavior, the teaching period itself. We will then consider the pretest as predictor of the mothers' strategies in teaching; then the background variables that accounted for some of the variance in both infant and maternal variables; and finally the question of which strategies led to success as measured on the posttest and transfer test.

Teaching Period

Although we were able to categorize our subjects according to the principal teaching strategy that seemed to dominate their sessions, we are more concerned with the objectively coded acts within sessions. We did test the hypothesis that basic teaching strategy would affect the infants' success in the task, and those results will be discussed below. For the most part, however, results for the three basic strategy groups simply confirmed our findings based upon frequencies of different maternal acts across the sample as a whole; we regard the latter type of findings as more meaningful.

The sequence MODEL-TEMPT-RESET (MTR) occurred 636 times, or an average of seven times in each teaching session. This meant that the mother reached around the barrier for the toy, took it out and shook it without giving it to her infant, and placed it back behind the barrier. Ten mothers never did this; in the other 81 sessions it occurred between 1 and 30 times. The context in which it occurred was very consistent; almost never when the infant was actively reaching toward the toy, most often when the infant had looked away from the task and back to it again. Table 2 does not reveal the fact that the most common infant sequence before *pointing* was also looking away and looking back to the task. And although we do not have a category in Table 2 for "looking back," we can report that 75 percent of the infants in the upper-right-hand cell of that table had already looked back to the task when their mothers modeled, or looked back *as she reached* for the toy. So the typical pattern of behavior is represented in Fig. 2.

This conclusion from the quantitative data is confirmed by observation of any of our live sessions or videotapes (see appendix). Furthermore, we know that it takes many repetitions of the sequence before an infant imitates the mother's reaching around the barrier. Only 8 percent of the MTRs were followed immediately by the infants' reaching, and these reaches were often thwarted when the infants knocked the toy away, failed to grasp it, or withdrew their arm after banging their wrist on the edge of the barrier. Of course there were also some successful and unsuccessful reaches that did not immediately follow an MTR. The general picture was that the infant gradually accommodated to the spatial requirements imposed by the barrier, improving over many trials which alternated with demonstrations by the mother. Although we will report below that the success rate of learning by these infants was far from impressive, a more important result was that the cases that conformed to this idealized "typical" pattern of gradual accommodation over trials also conformed to the idealized "typical" pattern of looking away, looking back, MTR, try again.

The fact that MTR did not always lead to imitation would be ac-

Table 2
Infants' Activity Just Before, During, and After Mothers' MODEL-TEMPT-RESET Sequences (Percent of 636 MTR Sequences Across all Subjects)

Infant Act	*Passive Looking*	*Pointing*	*Reaching*	*Looking Away*
Immediately preceding	21[a]	35	7	37
During MTR	62	23	4	11
Immediately following	28[b]	40	8	24

[a]Continuously since previous RESET by mother.
[b]Continuing until next intervention by mother.

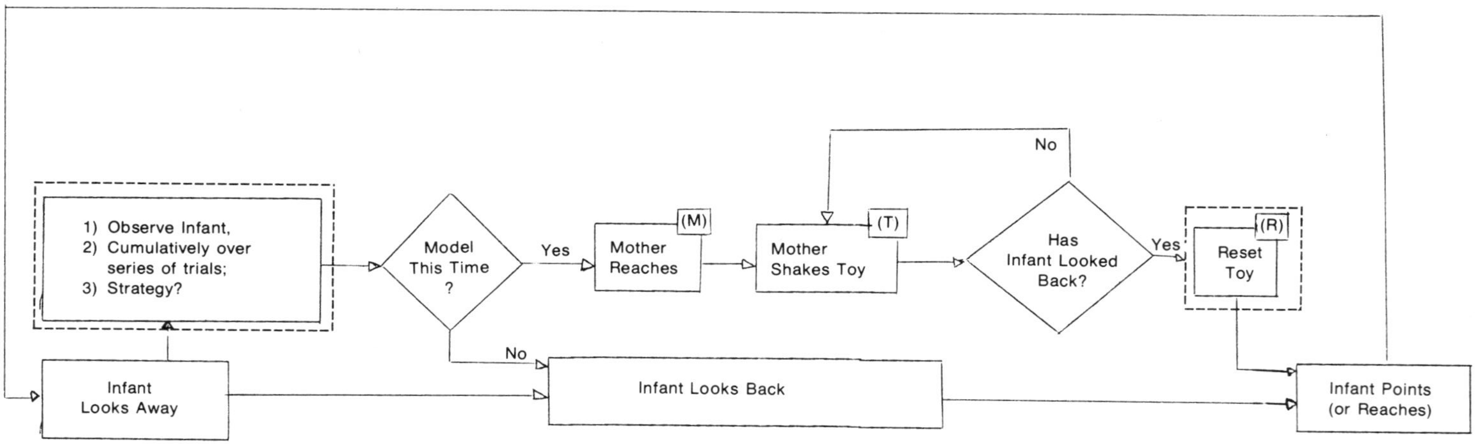

Fig. 2. Model representing temporal relation between infant sequence AWAY-BACK-ATTEMPT and mother sequence MODEL-TEMPT-RESET.

counted for in part by our finding that 25 percent of the models occurred when the infant was still looking away. This is probably an indication that the mothers were reaching for the toy so as to shake it and ring the bell, thus hoping to attract the infants' attention back to the task. But of course in such instances the infants would not have had an opportunity to observe the mother's reaching.

When we ignored the time before each infant first looked away, which was often 15 seconds or more, and the time after he last looked away, which was sometimes prolonged distress, we found that the cycle *look away-look back-look away again* occurred between 7 and 10 times per minute, and this was no diferent during the teaching period than during pretest, posttest, and transfer periods. So the mother's intervention cannot be said to have been responsible for bringing the infant back to the task. Gaze aversion was consistently self-terminating even on the pretest. Although in the teaching period it did elicit a maternal response, which was typically followed by the infant's looking back to the task, the *looking back* could not be said to be contingent upon maternal intervention.

Since MODEL meant only that a mother reached for the toy, a high rate of MODELS did not necessarily mean a high rate of MTRs or, in other words, a *showing* strategy. Sometimes the sequence was AWAY-MODEL-SIMPLIFY; the infant's gaze aversion still triggered an intervention by his mother, but for the purpose of simplifying the task. It is of interest that this maternal response, when it occurred, did so at the same point in the sequence where an MTR might have occurred. The dotted line around the "RESET" step in Fig. 2 indicates that we wonder why the mother sometimes SIMPLIFIES instead. Apparently the behavior categories we used were not subtle enough to allow us to detect the immediate elicitors of SIMPLIFY as opposed to MTR; in fact, there might not have been any such immediate elicitors. When we looked at the rate of simplifying over the whole teaching period, however, we found that it was predicted by aspects of the infant's pretest behavior (this will be discussed in the following section).

HAND-TUGGING did not typically occur at the same point in a sequence where MTR or MODEL-SIMPLIFY might have occurred. Instead, mothers who attempted to pull or push their infants' hands around the barrier did so when the infants were looking at the toy and resting their hands either on the plexiglass (POINTING) or on the ledge at the front of the apparatus. The infants' responses to these attempts were highly consistent, and our experience with other infants as well as children of other ages suggests that it is a fairly universal response: increased tonus, flexion of the arm, resistance to passive movement, and gaze aversion. In addition, some infants cry when their mothers persist with such a strategy; curiously, others do not cry and may even lessen their reluctance over the course of the session, suggesting that the infants might be reinforced by the effectiveness of this strategy at obtaining the toy for them.

There is reason to suppose that the subjects who fell into our *shoving* group did so because the babies allowed themselves to be tugged; it cannot be simply a matter of the mothers' inclinations. At any rate it did not turn out that the *shoving* strategy led to crying. Despite the fact that the infant's negative reaction to passive extension of his arm and hand is so universal and so marked that we almost expect him to cry or scream when his mother persists, our data suggest that mothers relied heavily on HAND-TUGGING primarily when their infants were already crying. This is best demonstrated by the analysis of pretest determinants in the following section. It should be mentioned here, however, that how *early* in the teaching period an infant began to cry correlated .32 with HAND-TUGGING ($p<.025$ two tailed; $N = 37$ babies who cried). In other words, instead of a pattern in which mothers would try HAND-TUGGING and then abandon it in the face of their infants' distress, it was more often the case that mothers began and/or persisted in HAND-TUGGING *after* their infants had become upset.

In order to give a more vivid account of the interaction of our subjects during the teaching session, we have included in an appendix (in prose translation) our coded observations of one pair.

Pretest Determinants

The two ways in which mothers deviated from the MODEL-TEMPT-RESET strategy were in SIMPLIFYING and in HAND-TUGGING. We divided the number of times each of these responses occurred by the length of the teaching period. We could then ask how the rate of SIMPLIFYING and the rate of HAND-TUGGING were affected by the principal ways in which infants differed on the pretest. Table 3 presents the multiple regression coefficients for each of these dependent variables.

SIMPLIFYING was predicted mainly by the infant's failure to respond to the task on the pretest; none of the 17 mothers whose infants succeeded at all on the pretest fell into the *shaping* strategy group, and few of them even simplified the task once. This suggests merely that the mothers were satisfied that the task was not too difficult for their babies. More interestingly, mothers tended to SIMPLIFY if their infants had looked AWAY a great deal on the pretest, thereby not even POINTING very much. Recall that in the teaching period SIMPLIFYING (when it occurred) typically followed gaze aversion, though gaze aversion did not most typically lead to SIMPLIFYING.

In the case of HAND-TUGGING distress on the pretest was the major predictor, and as we reported above, the sooner an infant began to cry during training, the more his mother tended to resort to TUGGING. Furthermore, 8 of the 29 babies in the *shoving* group had succeeded on the pretest, and most of the others in all groups, like Lise (appendix), had shown some sign of being close to success, either in the pretest or in the teaching period itself, before their mothers first attempted HAND-TUGGING.

None of the pretest variables predicted the rate of MODELING. This is understandable, since MODELING was coded every time the mother reached for the toy, regardless of purpose. However, the pretest behavior of subjects in our *showing* group was just what should be expected in the light of Table 2: some successes (9 of 37 subjects), less crying than the *shoving* group (NS), and less looking away than the *shaping* group ($p<.025$ two-tailed). Differences among the three basic strategy groups are reported in Table 4. Note that a variable that predicts maternal behavior in the sample as a whole, such as pretest crying, does not necessarily discriminate significantly among the three groups. The result presented earlier, that crying correlated with HAND-TUGGING, was true of all three strategy groups. Each group merely represents one end of a distribution, arbitrarily divided.

Background Variables

The design of the study allowed an analysis of variance with three

Table 3
Standardized Regression Coefficients,
Mothers' Training Techniques, on Infants' Pretest Behavior

Pretest Variable	*Rate of Simplifying (87 d.f.)*[a]	*Rate of Tugging (87 d.f.)*[a]
Number of successes	−.30**	−.0[a]
Crying (% time)	.0[a]	.46***
Away (% time)	.17*[b]	−.16
Point (% time)	−.09	−.05
(Multiple correlation squared	(.17)***	(.25)***

[a]Stepwise regression halted when r^2 increased less than .01.

[b]Significant at .05 level when entered with successes, but drops below significance when pointing is entered.

*p < .05

**p < .01

***p < .001

Table 4
Background, Pretest, and Teaching Variables, by Basic Strategy Group

	Shove (29)	*Shape (25)*	*Show (37)*	*Total (91)*	*Significance*
Sex (boys/girls)	15/14	9/16	18/19	42/49	NS
Screen side (L/R)	14/15	12/13	19/18	46/45	NS
Mother's education level (see Table 1)	2.4	3.0	2.2	2.5	Shape > Show** (60 *d.f.*, *t*=2.81) F(2,88)=3.77*
Pretest successes (mean number)	0.4	0.0	0.5	0.3	Shove > Shape* (52 *d.f.*, *t*=2.65) Show > Shape* (60 *d.f.*, *t*=2.27) F(2,88)=2.89*
Percent of pretest time:					
pointing	38	31	32	34	NS
away	24	31	24	26	Shape > Shove* (52*d.f.*, t=2.11) F(2,88)=2.47
crying	1	0	0	1	NS
Mother's rate/minute, in teaching period:					
hand-tugging	2.9	0.7	0.9	1.5	F(2,88)=35.59***
simplifying	0.8	2.5	0.8	1.3	F(2,88)=33.15***
modeling	1.4	2.0	3.1	2.3	F(2,88)=17.66***

*$p < .05$
**$p < .01$
***p .001

Table 5

F Values from Analyses of Variance (See Text)

	d.f.	Pretest Success	Pretest Pointing	pretest Away	pretest Crying	Rate of Simplify	Rate of Tugging	Posttest Success
Sex	1	0.93	10.25**	3.06[a]	0.21	1.77	0.07	0.39
Screen	1	2.88[a]	0.83	1.05	0.30	0.80	0.63	0.97
Education	3	1.74	0.75	0.66	0.46	0.85	0.48	0.17
Sex × screen	1	0.84	0.74	3.64[a]	1.17	2.45	0.42	0.37
Sex × educ	3	0.69	0.64	2.63[a]	0.92	0.39	0.44	0.56
Screen × educ	3	1.37	0.88	1.49	0.92	4.29	0.23	1.58
Sex × scr × ed	3	0.13	3.43*	0.13	0.91	0.23	1.10	0.55

[a] $.05 < p < .10$
**$p < .01$
*$p < .05$

independent variables; sex of infant, mother's educational level, and screen side. Recall that half the subjects were trained with the screen on the left (right hand appropriate) and half with the screen on the right (left hand appropriate). Although hand preference is far from being established in six-month-old infants, the study by Kaye, Bruner, and Lyons (Bruner, 1971) found slight superiority of learning when the screen was on the left. In addition, the fact that dominant right-handedness was certain to be found in our sample of mothers led us to control for the variable of screen side.

Table 5 presents F values for the seven dependent variables: number of successes on pretest; proportions of time POINTING, CRYING, and looking AWAY on pretest; rates of SIMPLIFYING and HAND-TUGGING during teaching; and success or failure on the posttest. The full ANOVA tables are condensed here in view of the paucity of significant effects. The marginal superiority of the right hand, on the pretest, was confirmed. The Screen X Education interaction effect upon rate of SIMPLIFYING was curious; with the screen on the left (right hand used) SIMPLIFYING increased linearly with

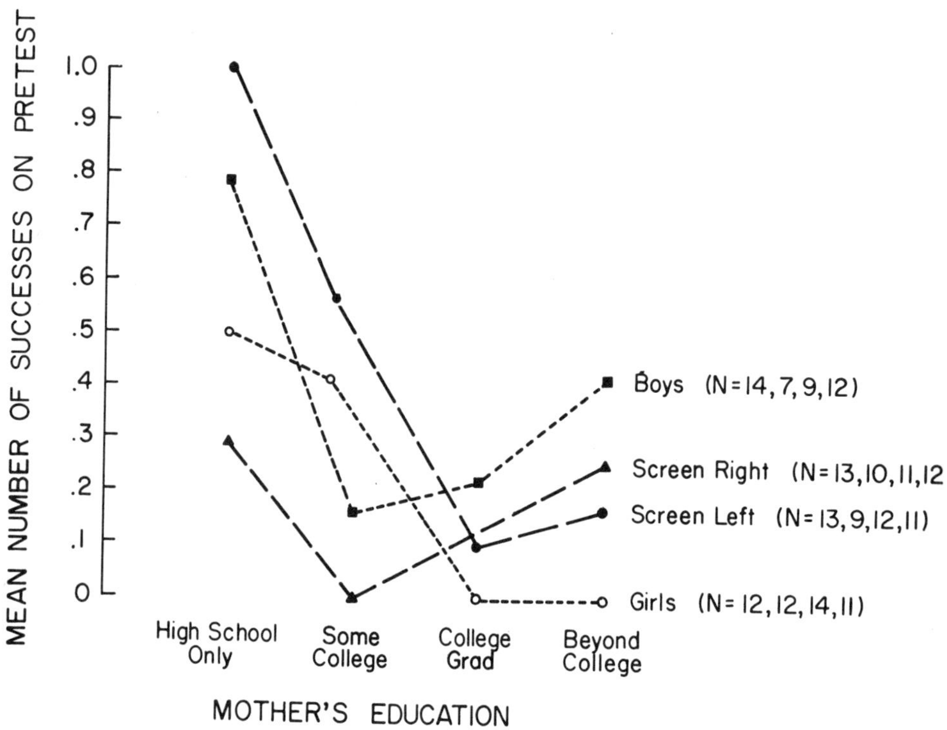

Fig. 3. Pretest success as a function of social class, sex, and screen side.

mothers' educational levels, whereas with the screen on the right it decreased linearly. We regard this as uninterpretable. There are two direct effects, however, that might be important. First, boys tended to do more POINTING and less looking AWAY than girls; the two variables, obviously, were intercorrelated (r = −.44). Second, the infants of more educated mothers were less successful on the pretest. This fell short of significance because the effect was not completely linear; but a glance at Fig. 3 shows that the infants in the lower social class were clearly superior in pretest performance.

Either of these two background variables, sex and education, might have been indirectly responsible for the relations between pretest behavior and maternal teaching techniques. The fact that the latter correlations were higher than those between education or sex and the pretest behaviors suggests, however, that the background variables were less important.

This was tested by multiple regression (Table 6). In the path analysis diagram of Fig. 4 the arrows on the left side of the diagram are labeled with standardized coefficients obtained by regressing each

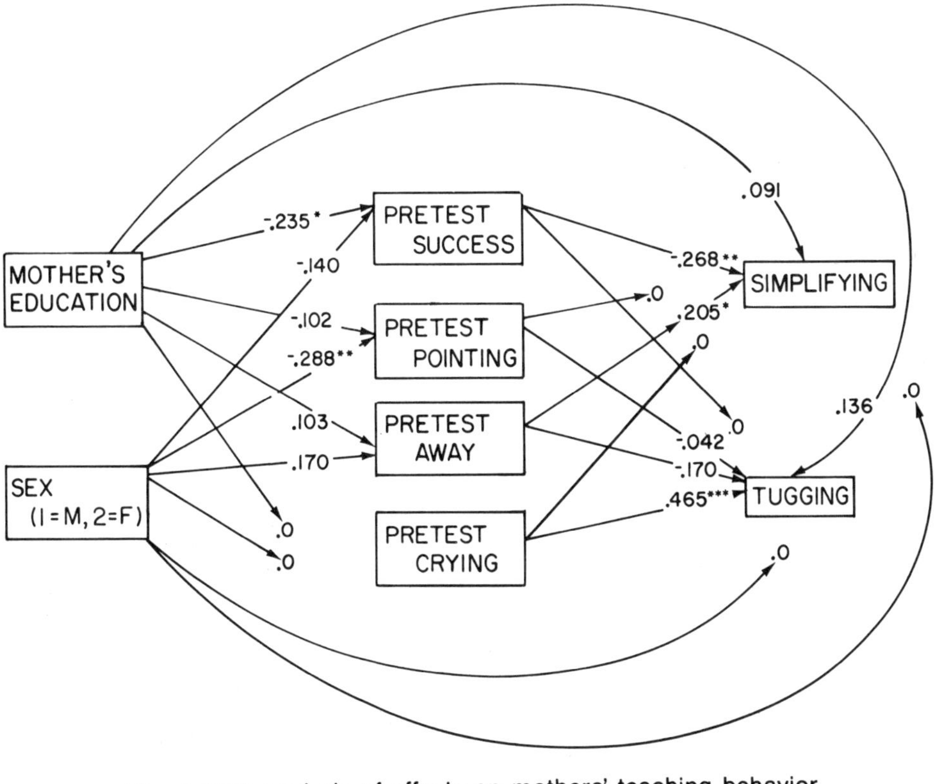

Fig. 4. Path analysis of effects on mothers' teaching behavior.

of the pretest variables on education and sex. The arrows extending to the right-hand side of the diagram are labeled with the standardized coefficients from Table 6, which were obtained by regressing each of the teaching variables on all six prior variables.[2] In summary, the mothers were influenced more by their infants' actual behavior in our task than by either their own educational level (social class) or the infant's sex. And entering these two variables, which receive by far the most attention in the literature as probable influences upon maternal behavior, accounted for no additional variance as compared with Table 3.

Table 6
Standardized Regression Coefficients, Mothers' Training Techniques, on Pretest and Background Variables

Prior Variables	*Rate of Simplifying (87 d.f.)*[a]	*Rate of Tugging (86 d.f.)*[a]
Sex of baby	.0 a	.0 a
Mother's education	.09	.14
Pretest successes (#)	−.27**	.0 a
Pretest pointing (%)	.0 a	−.04
Pretest away (%)	.21*b	−.17
Pretest crying (%)	.0 a	.47***
(Mult. correln squared)	(.17)***	(.27)***

[a]Stepwise regression halted when r^2 increased less than .01.

[b]Significant at .05 level when entered with successes, but drops below significance when education is entered.

*p < .05

**p < .01

***p < .001

Success on the Posttest

Of the 74 babies who failed the pretest, 17, or 23 percent, succeeded on the posttest. Only one variable predicted success on the posttest: number of successes on the pretest. This is indicated in Tables 5 and 7. Multiple regression analysis revealed that neither the maternal teaching variables, nor any other pretest variable, nor the background variables (also tested by ANOVA in Table 4) predicted posttest success.

Success in the teaching period predicted posttest success no better (r−.46) than did pretest success (r−.46) perhaps the most telling result was that for infants whose first success came during the teaching period, the chances were still 3 to 2 *against* success on the posttest. This is shown in italics in the left-hand column of Table 7.

Table 7
Success in Training as Related to Pretest and Posttest Success

	Succeed in Training	*Fail in Training*	*Total*
Succeed on pretest	12	5	17
Succeed on posttest	12	2	14
Fail on posttest	0	3	3
Fail pretest	40	34	74
Succeed on posttest	*16*	1	17
Fail on posttest	*24*	33	47
Total succeed on posttest	28	3	31
Total fail posttest	24	36	60

Did a mother's basic teaching strategy affect her infant's success in the task? Fig. 5 suggests that it did so in only one sense: the initial inferiority of babies in the *shaped* group was eliminated, apparently as a result of the shaping strategy their mothers employed. But we can hardly call this instruction successful, since half the infants who had "learned" by this method subsequently failed the posttest.

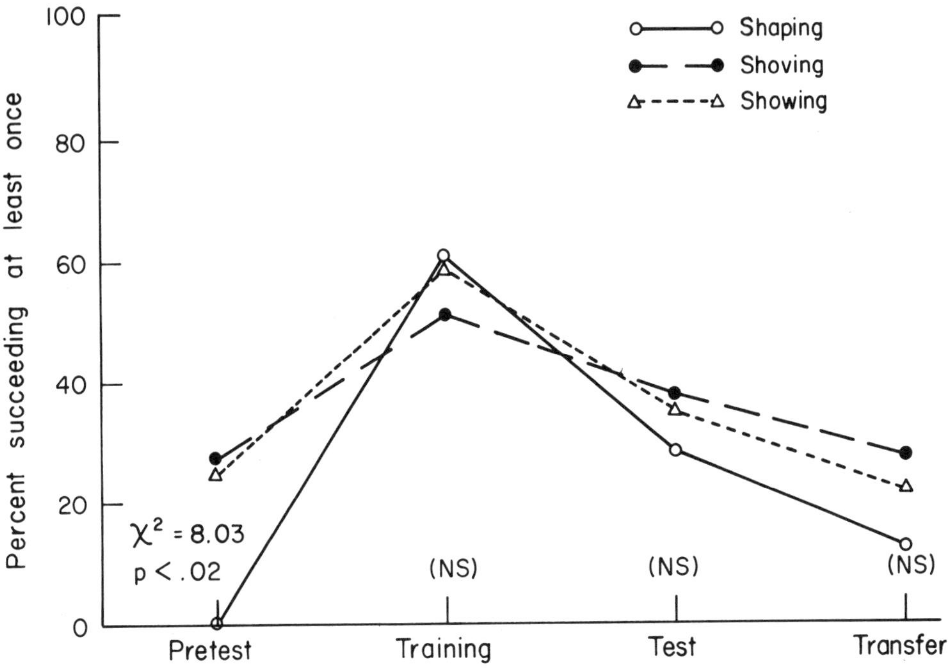

Fig. 5. Success (at least once) on each of the four parts of the session, for the three basic strategy groups.

Infants' Effects

Transfer

In cases of successful learning where I served as the model, we have consistently found positive transfer effects when the screen was switched to the other side, or a new toy substituted, or both (Kaye, 1970). In one case the new skill transferred to the other hand even though we waited several days between posttest and transfer test. However, normally we have not done this, since we had no way of controlling the mother's interventions during the interim. In all of our studies to date success on the transfer test has been less than that on the posttest but better than on the pretest. In the study reported here, however, as indicated in Fig. 5, the transfer success was not impressive and was apparently unaffected by mothers' basic strategies. Nonetheless, when infants who succeeded on the pretest were omitted from the analysis, transfer of the detour reaching skill to the opposite hand was statistically significant beyond the .05 level (Table 8, chi square−5.97).

Table 8
Effect of Initial Learning on Transfer
(74 Infants Who Failed Pretest)

	Succeed on Transfer	*Fail Transfer*	
Succeed on posttest	6	11	17
Fail posttest	6	51	57
	12	62	74

Further details of the infants' behavior on the transfer test help to shed some light on the nature of what is learned in the detour reaching task. The majority of the infants appeared no different on the transfer test than on the pretest; indeed, for those who had not succeeded in learning with one hand we could say that this was simply a pretest for the other hand. (Thus, it is not surprising to find a sex difference on the transfer test, as shown in Fig. 6.) But 28 of the 91 infants did behave in a noticeably different way on the transfer test. They favored either the left or the right hand to the exclusion of the other hand, at least for the first half-minute, a time period during which they would normally, on a pretest, have switched back and forth between the two hands several times for pointing, exploring the edge of the barrier, and reaching into the open side of the apparatus. This was so noticeable that we were able to rate these infants (only when both observers agreed) as transferring either negatively or positively. Negative

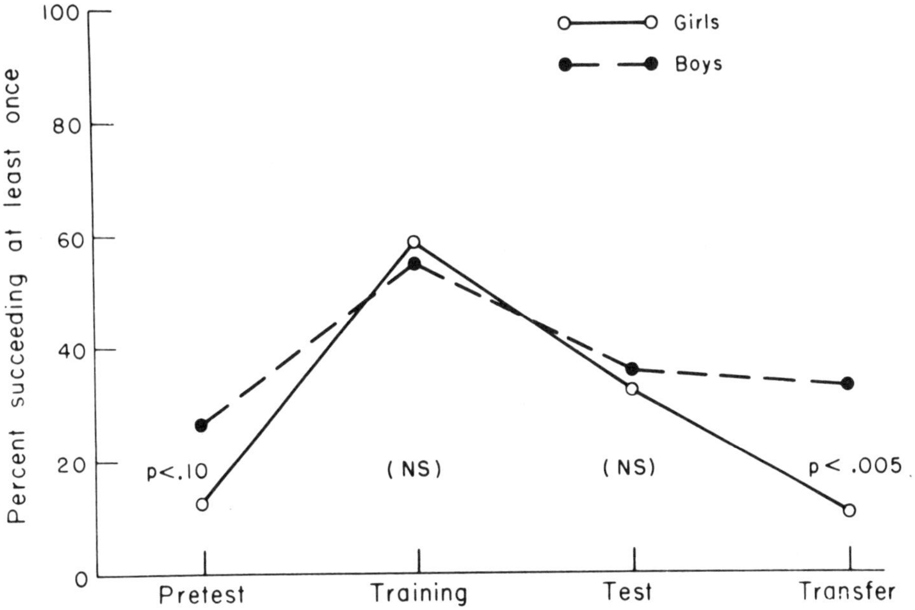

Fig. 6. Success (at least once) on each of the four parts of the session, by sex of infant.

transfer was scored when the infant favored the hand that had been appropriate during training, but was now blocked by the barrier; positive transfer was scored when the infant favored the hand that was now appropriate. These ratings were made regardless of the infants' history of success. The results are shown in Table 9. The numbers italicized in the left side of the table indicate that success on the posttest significantly predicted either negative or positive transfer, as opposed to no transfer at all (chi square=25.46, $p<.001$). Figures in the right-hand column indicate that while only 6 percent of the infants showing no asymmetry of approach to the transfer test succeeded in

Table 9
Hand Preference Noted by Experimenters During Transfer Test

	Fail Posttest	*Succeed Posttest*	*Total*	*Succeed on Transfer Test*
No asymmetry noted	52	*11*	63	4 (6% of 63)
Positive transfer (open side)	*5*	*10*	15	12 (80% of 15)
Negative transfer (Barrier side)	*3*	*10*	13	3 (23% of 13)
Total subjects	60	31	91	19 (21% of 91)

getting the toy, 23 percent of the negative transfer group and 80 percent of the positive transfer group did so (chi square=39.83, p1.001). Even the advantage of those showing negative transfer (that is, initial transfer to the wrong hand) over those showing no transfer at all is almost significant (Fisher's exact p=.078.)

In summary, the detour solution as learned with one hand did not simply transfer immediately to the other hand, as though there were some sort of mirror transformation of a cognitive map. Nor was it the case that the infants behaved like split-brain preparations. Infants who had been taught to reach around the barrier on one side were able, despite exhaustion and cumulative frustration, to learn the solution on the other side without help. Although this statement accurately describes only a minority of our subjects, we feel it can be inferred that what they learned was *how to solve* a detour problem, rather than merely a set of hand movements.

DISCUSSION

We have tried to describe a composite image of what we regard as the "typical" responses of mother-infant pairs to the detour task, as well as to convey our results indicating that differences in teaching behavior across mothers can be explained to a large extent by differences among their infants. Both the generalities and the individual differences are important for an understanding of early cognitive development.

The basic strategy adopted by mothers in Cambridge—and no doubt, with variations, by mothers everywhere—consists of demonstrating the detour reach over and over again, alternating with pauses in which the infants could make their own attempts. Mothers typically combined their demonstrations with pointing and shaking the toy, to maintain the infants' orientation and arousal, and with the use of their own voice (not studied here) to soothe and encourage as well as to arouse the babies. The two most important things we can report with a great deal of certainty about this strategy are: (1) it is the infant who controls the timing of the mother's demonstrations, their frequency, onset, duration; and (2) the *showing* strategy is often effective. Although posttest performance in this study was no better than pretest performance, a high proportion of the mothers did succeed in the teaching period to do what they were asked to do—get their infants to reach around the barrier and retrieve the toy.

I regard the "typical" picture referred to earlier as more meaningful in this context than the pretest-posttest scores for the various groups. From the point of view of traditional theories of learning, and even from Piaget's account of the sensorimotor period, it is surprising that *any* infants were able to accommodate their detour reach under the "typical" *showing* condition purely by imitation without extrinsic reinforcement. Under a strict behaviorist learning theory this sort of learning could not be explained even for adults (though it is obviously our fundamental way of developing skills); even if we postulate the necessary intervening cognitive processes to mediate the learning, these processes have not usually been attributed to six-month-old infants. Furthermore, by using the *showing* strategy as we saw it employed by a few of our most graceful and relaxed subjects, we have been able to teach 60 to 80 percent of six-month-olds to reach around the detour; we have been able to elicit certain phoneme sequences from eight-month-olds and random sequences of tone or typewriter-key sequences from four-year-olds (Kaye, 1971). The method requires an adult to be willing to keep repeating the desired pattern dozens of times, ignoring (not reinforcing or commenting upon or making an accommodation to) the child's attempts, but allowing the children to signal when they are ready for the next presentation of the model. This signal may take the form, for example, of dropping their hands, as speakers do when yielding the floor (Duncan, 1972); of averting their eyes from the task, as in the present study; or of returning their eyes to contact with the adult (Stern, 1974). We find that it normally takes six-month-old infants sitting in their mother's lap facing the experimenter only one or two trials to realize that the experimenter's "Ba-ba-ba-ba" is under the control of their own eye movements. Operant learning, of course, accounts for this—head and eye movements being the most easily conditioned of infant operants—but it does not account for the fact that many of these infants after twenty minutes or so are saying "Ba-ba-ba-ba" themselves.

For those who wish to try this method, it is the same as the "typical" mother's pattern in this study: let the infants signal their readiness for an MTR, show them slowly, then wait for their own attempts, which will improve gradually over trials (Kaye, 1971).

In the present study the analysis of gaze aversion from the task highlighted the importance of cyclic alternation in the responses of infant and mother. The "turn-taking", or rhythmic attention and withdrawal, has emerged as a pervasive pattern in interaction beginning at birth, an example of the "preadaptation" referred to by Bruner. Kaye and Brazelton (1971) found origins of mother-infant reciprocity in the burst-pause patterns of neonatal sucking, and Brazelton, Koslowski, and Main (1974) studied rhythms of about the same order of magnitude (5 to 10 seconds) in the face-to-face interaction of mothers and infants between one and five months. There is a direct comparison between what we have found in the burst-pause pattern of neonatal sucking (Kaye, 1972; Kaye, in press) and what we find in the present study. During feeding, an infant's pause elicits jiggling or stroking by the mother, which in turn is typically followed by a resumption of sucking. However, while the mother's jiggling is contingent upon the infant's pause, a resumption of sucking is not contingent upon jiggling. In the case of modeling the detour reach at six months, as in the case of jiggling in the first month of life, mothers express a belief that their behavior is instrumental in their infant's resumption of the task; but this conviction is not supported statistically. The infants would look back to the task anyway. It is easy to see sequellae of these early forms of turn-taking in such studies as Bruner and Sherwood's (1974) of the game of peekaboo at one year of age, and in the vast numbers of studies of language acquisition in which the mother-child dialogue is the inevitable unit of analysis.

In all such studies one is impressed by the extent to which infants control their mothers' intervention. In the detour reaching study, as well as in the study by Brazelton et al., the movement by the baby that was most likely to elicit a change in maternal behavior was gaze aversion. In our study, when the infants *first* looked away from the task during the training period, the median latency of their mothers' responses was under 2.5 seconds, with the majority of these responses being MODEL-TEMPT-RESET. Face-to-face interaction, and particularly gaze aversion, have been subject to much study during the first few months of life, primarily because of an ethological interest in the face's innate releasing properties (e.g., Robson, 1967; Freedman, 1974) and a psychoanalytic interest in mirroring as a process in ego formation (Kohut, 1971). Our present concern with gaze aversion, however, is merely one instance of a class of infant responses that signal the appropriateness of adult intervention, and thus at least partly control the instructor.

Yet that control is not so simple that the mother responds every time her infant looks away. As the problematic box at the upper left of Figure 2 indicates (surrounded by a dotted line to suggest a cloud), the mother must be responding to more than just the momentary event. By analyzing differences among our subjects, we found that the teaching session as a whole could also be regarded as under the control of the infants. In the response to gaze aversion, for example, Fig. 7 illustrates the way mothers were apparently integrating two different types of information from their infants: the signal as to when to intervene and the evidence from the pretest (as well as from the rest of the session), which apparently guided the choice of how to intervene. When the infants averted their gaze, their mothers modeled a detour reach if the babies' pretest behavior had indicated the task was within their range of learning, but simplified the task if their pretest had seemed completely hopeless.

Other factors external to the session, such as the mother's education or her infant's sex, must of course also be taken into account in explaining differences among our subjects. But we have tried to show that such factors are often predictive without being causal. It might be noted that Goldberg and Lewis (1969) found differences in maternal treatment of boys and girls at six months, which they regarded as causing or contributing to the development of sex differences in the infants over the course of the next year. Yet the present study and others show that the differences in maternal treatment are themselves based on sex differences already established in the infants. The original discriminatory treatment presumed to cause sex differences might be pursued all the way back to birth or even earlier, but to do so would be to miss the real subtlety and complexity of interactive processes.

What implications do these findings have for a theory of instruction and for Bruner's theory of early skill development with which we began? If we conceptualize the development of a skill as involving the putting together of constituents (Bruner 1971, 1972, 1973), there are a number of functions that a tutor might serve:

Motivating. The tutor can present a problem and provide incentives in the form of encouragement or threats. Presenting the problem may take the form of a verbal or gestural challenge—"Can you do this?" "Can you achieve this result?"—or of physically forcing the learner into a situation where learning is the only escape route. As a child I was told that the American Indians used to throw their children

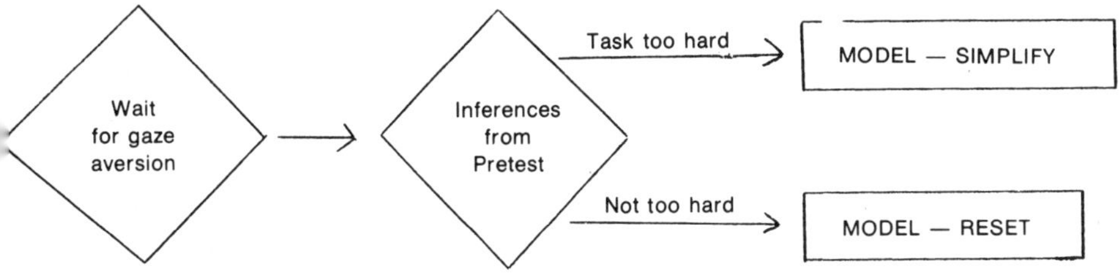

Fig. 7. Process model representing mothers' decisions to simplify or demonstrate the detour reaching task.

into a lake and that those who did not drown learned to swim. (Whether or not this was true the story motivated me to learn to swim.)

Breaking down. The tutor can help break the task down into its constituents. The learner must select from his repertoire of skills those that can be recombined in the new routine. Sometimes the process of recognizing a schema in one's repertoire requires a kind of minipractice, confirming the adequacy of a constituent just by trying it in the absence of competing responses. This is as true of an adult learning to play squash after tennis as it is of an infant learning to pronounce sounds. Often the constituent proves insufficiently mastered. Separate constituents need to be practiced and smoothed, because even though they will have to be reshaped somewhat in integration with each other, each of them must be able to be executed relatively free of attentional monitoring and control, so that attentional capacity can be focussed on the integration of the whole and on the end to be reached. Bruner (1971) has called this perfection of the individual constituents *modularization.*

The selection of constituents can be facilitated by tutors who make them salient, either exaggerating the segments of their own modeled acts or structuring the task so as to elicit separate segments in the learner. By reducing the degrees of freedom in a task they can enable components to be executed singly. And they can maintain an appropriate balance between providing opportunity for practice of the components and pushing for solution of the new problem.

Ordering. Once the constituents are accessible, the learner has to see or hear how to put them together. This is the function served by a model. However, we would not suggest that the modeling wait until the constituents have been identified and perfected. Normally the learner cannot select the right skills from his repertoire until he has a sense of the whole in which they are to be embedded. What he needs from the model, apparently, is a chance to analyze the task by synthesis of recognized parts (Neisser, 1967), and this often means that modeling the new skill is the best means of breaking it down for a learner as well as of ordering the constituents in time. In the development of sensorimotor skills, as in conceptual development, it helps to have "advance organizers" (Ausubel, 1968) that let the system know what it is going to be doing with the information it is storing.

These three types of intervention in the acquisition process can be illustrated in terms of the basic teaching strategies we observed in all of our mothers when they were asked to "help in any way you can." If each mother seemed to be emphasizing one of the three strategies more than the others, it may have been that her infant was in a stage of acquisition, with respect to the particular task given, which made that strategy more appropriate.

The mothers who used primarily a *shaping* strategy, letting their infants work on the constituents of reaching into the open side of the box and grasping the toy, were those whose infants had shown no sign of being able to solve the problem on the pretest. In fact, they had spent a significantly higher proportion of the pretest averting their eyes from the apparatus. Many of the mothers told us they concluded the task was too difficult; the infants needed to have it broken down into simpler steps, and they also needed to be reinforced and shaped up to the more difficult task. In short, these mothers were concentrating on the *motivating* and *breaking-down* tutorial functions.

Those who depended extensively on *shoving* could also be seen as attempting both to provide encouragement and to emphasize a critical constituent of the task. Considering the influential pretest as a very short history, one can argue that a mother who chose *shoving* as opposed to *shaping* was probably reflecting her relationship with the infant over the preceding six months. This suggests hypotheses for future work, involving bidirectional effects.

Although lacking data about the history of interaction of subjects in this study, we did discover some situational determinants of strategy. If the shoving mothers were trying to make salient a constituent of the task, it was a different constituent from those made salient by the shaping strategy. Instead of simplifying the task, the mothers in this group pushed the babies forward, in time as well as space, so that they could get past the "appropriate hand" and "open side" hurdles so as to work on the "behind screen" constituent. Several mothers told us afterward that they felt that if their babies could only see their hands behind the screen, they would realize that they could get the toy. Thus, making the infants see that the task was within their capabilities was very much part of the motivating process. Mothers tended to use hand-tugging as a last resort after their infants had been frustrated by the task to the point of crying. Their subconscious assumption may have been that it was too late to build up the task step by step, but that getting the baby closer to the solution might still save the day.

As for those who relied upon *showing*, it must be said that they were doing much more than simply presenting a challenge, on the one hand, or modeling an ordered sequence of constituent acts on the other. The whole manner with which mothers modeled the detour reach was clearly slowed down and exaggerated to give saliency to the hand, the trajectory of movement, the open side of the box, the edge of the screen, and the grasping of the toy.

The 91 mothers in our study were implicitly asking themselves questions about the presence of certain relevant skills or parts of the detour reaching skill in their infants' repertoires. An unpublished study by Greenfield and Childs (reported in Bruner, 1969) made use of a completely different task—the embedding of a series of nested plastic cups within one another—with Zinacanteco Indian mothers of children in the second year of life. They found striking confirmation of our general findings: task simplification for children who were at the lowest level, demonstration for those who had used a more intermediate strategy, and physical interference with the children who had already performed the crucial embedding component of the task. "This sensitivity to the child's level is amazing when one considers that it occurs without any sort of task analysis, in reference to a task that is alien to the culture" (Bruner, 1969, p. 25).

Although our mothers' success as instructors was not impressive under the stressful conditions of our laboratory, a prima facie argument has been made that their instructional strategies were highly adaptive. Furthermore, we believe that these mothers had spent the preceding six months not just picking up knowledge about what their babies could and could not do, but more importantly learning to respond to subtle signals in interactive situations of various kinds—feeding, bathing, playing, and teaching. Their infants, too, had been learning to respond to signals as well as to give them. The two together, mother and infant, form an interaction system that undergoes its own development. Our current work attempts to trace the adaptation of such signal systems in a longitudinal sample, with attention both to the "typical" and to the individual patterns of interaction.

References

Argyle, M. & Kendon, A. The experimental analysis of social performance. In L. Berkowitz (Ed.), *Advances in Experimental Social Psychology.* New York: Academic Press, 1967, Vol. 3, pp. 55–98.

Ausubel, D. *Educational Psychology: A Cognitive View.* New York: Holt, Rinehart and Winston, 1968.

Blurton-Jones, N. *Ethological Studies of Child Behavior.* Cambridge, England: Cambridge University Press, 1972.

Bracht, G. H. Experimental factors related to aptitude-treatment interactions. *Review of Educational Research,* 1970, *40,* 627–645.

Brazelton, T. B., Koslowski, B. & Main, M. Origins of reciprocity. In M.

Lewis & L. Rosenblum (Eds.), *The Effect of the Infant on its Caregiver.* New York: Wiley, 1974, Vol. 1, pp. 49–76.

Bruner, J. S. *The Process of Education.* Cambridge: Harvard University Press, 1960.

Bruner, J. S. Ninth annual report. Center for Cognitive Studies, Harvard University, 1969.

Bruner, J. S. The growth and structure of skill. In K. Connolly (Ed.), *Mechanisms of Motor Skill in Development.* New York: Academic Press, 1971.

Bruner, J. S. The nature and uses of immaturity. *American Psychologist,* 1972, *27*, 688–704.

Bruner, J. S. The organization of early skilled action. *Child Development,* 1973, *44*, 1–11.

Bruner, J. S. & Bruner, B. On voluntary action and its hierarchical structure. *International Journal of Psychology,* 1968, *3*, 239–255.

Bruner, J. S. & Sherwood, V. The game of peekaboo. Manuscript, Oxford, 1974.

Duncan, S. Some signals and rules for taking speaking turns in conversation. *Journal of Personality and Social Psychology,* 1972, *23*, 283–292.

Freedman, D. G. *Human Infancy: An Evolutionary Perspective.* New Jersey: Lawrence Erlbaum Associates, 1974.

Goffman, E. *Encounters.* Indianapolis: Bobbs-Merrill, 1961.

Goldberg, S. & Lewis, M. Play behavior in the year-old infant: Early sex differences. *Child Development* 1969, *40*, 21–31.

Kaye, K. Maternal participation in infants' acquisition of a skill. Unpublished Ph.D. dissertation, Harvard University, 1970.

Kaye, K. Learning by imitation in infants and young children. Presented to the Society for Research and Child Development, Minneapolis, April 2, 1971.

Kaye, K. Milk pressure as a determinant of the burst-pause pattern in neonatal sucking. *Proceedings,* The American Psychological Association, 1972, *80*, 83–84.

Kaye, K. Toward the origin of dialogue. In H. R. Schaffer (Ed.), *Interactions in Infancy: The Loch Lomond Symposium.* New York and London: Academic Press, (in press).

Kaye, K. & Brazelton, T. B. Mother-infant interaction in the organization of sucking. Presented to the Society for Research in Child Development, Minneapolis, April 1, 1971.

Kohut, H. *The Analysis of the Self.* New York: International Universities Press, 1971.

Lentz, R. & Haith, M. Audio tape storage of experimental data. *Behavior Research Methods and Instrumentation,* 1969, *1*, 272–275.

Lewis, M. & Rosenblum, L. *The Effect of the Infant on its Caregiver.* New York: Wiley, 1974.

Neisser, U. *Cognitive Psychology.* New York: Appleton-Century-Crofts, 1967.

Robson, K. The role of eye-to-eye contact in maternal-infant attachment. *Journal of Child Psychology and Psychiatry,* 1967, *8*, 13–27.

Skinner, B. F. The science of learning and the art of teaching. *Harvard Educational Review,* 1954, *24*, 86–97.

Stern, D. Mother and infant at play: the dyadic interaction involving facial, vocal, and gaze behaviors. In M. Lewis & L. Rosenblum (Eds.), *The Effect of the Infant on Its Caregiver.* New York: Wiley, 1974, pp. 187–214.

APPENDIX

This pair of subjects is no more "typical" than any other, but it is a good illustration of how easy it is for us to differentiate repetitive sequences in the stream of behavior. We are helped in this account by having a filmed record that provides a few details not normally a part of our observations.

Lise is the firstborn daughter of parents who both have master's degrees. Her father is a pharmacist and her mother had been a teacher. On the pretest Lise spends about 30% of the time POINTING and 46% AWAY; she looks away 14 times, averaging 4.4 seconds each. She never REACHES around the edge of the barrier, which is on the right side of her midline.

The mother begins the training period by SIMPLIFYING, placing the toy so that it is only partly blocked by the barrier. Lise immediately REACHES for it, bumping the screen but groping to the left of it and getting the toy (TOUCH, PLAY). Her mother RESETS it behind the screen, and Lise looks AWAY. As she looks back, her mother MODELS, shakes the toy (TEMPTS), and puts it back in the SIMPLIFIED position, where Lise gets it immediately (RTP). Her mother puts it behind the screen (RESET) but then slides it out to the open area again (SIMPLIFIES) without waiting for an attempt by Lise. At the simplified position Lise reaches and gets the toy (RTP). It is put back, only partly protruding around the edge of the screen (SIMPLIFIED). She gets it easily (RTP). Then the mother RESETS the block behind the barrier, and Lise POINTS and then looks AWAY. The mother MODELS, shakes the toy, and RESETS it (MTR). Lise POINTS, then REACHES and TOUCHES the toy, but withdraws her hand and POINTS.

After another MTR her mother TUGS at Lise's hand for one second; the infant reacts with flexion and looking AWAY. Her mother MODELS, shakes the toy (TEMPTS), and SIMPLIFIES. Lise REACHES, grasps, and retrieves the toy (RTP). It is RESET behind the screen, and Lise looks AWAY. When she looks back and POINTS, her mother takes her hand and guides it around the screen (TUGGING), releasing it as Lise continues the REACH, grasps and retrieves the toy (RTP). Another RESET leads to a look AWAY, during which the mother MODELS, TEMPTS, and RESETS. Lise looks back, POINTS, looks AWAY, looks back, POINTS, and then REACHES and succeeds (RTP). Again the mother SIMPLIFIES so that the toy is only partly behind the barrier; Lise POINTS, REACHES, and takes it out.

So repetitive are interaction patterns within a mother-child dyad that the following paragraph must be read twice, exactly as one would repeat a passage of music:

‖: The toy is RESET by the mother, who waits less than two seconds before MODELING, TEMPTING, and RESETTING again. Lise looks AWAY. Another MTR, this time followed by a POINT and then a look AWAY. Lise looks back, her mother MODELS, TEMPTS, and RESETS the toy, Lise POINTS, then looks AWAY and back, her mother MTRs again, Lise POINTS, looks AWAY, looks back, and her mother MODELS again. This time she SIMPLIFIES, and Lise POINTS, REACHES, grasps, takes the toy out (RTP), and looks AWAY while playing with it. :‖

After the second time through this sequence, the mother RESETS the toy and waits while Lise POINTS. She then takes the baby's hand (TUGS), but Lise resists, looks AWAY, and the hand is released. Lise looks back, POINTS, then succeeds (RTP). When the toy is RESET, she looks AWAY and back, then again POINTS and succeeds (RTP). For the next 100 seconds, however, she will not reach around the screen; six MTRs lead to POINTING and then looking AWAY. Finally her mother SIMPLIFIES, but Lise does not REACH, and when she looks AWAY for four seconds, training ends, at 352 seconds.

Both the posttest and the transfer test are very much like the pretest. On the posttest Lise POINTS 6 percent of the time and is AWAY 39 percent; on transfer she POINTS 16 percent and is AWAY 48 percent.

Note that while Lise got the toy out of the apparatus 12 times, her mother had SIMPLIFIED for eight of these and TUGGED her hand around the edge for one more. So she actually succeeded only three times, and for some reason did not succeed on the posttest or transfer test. This was fairly typical, as the results in figure 5 and 6 will show. (This subject, incidentally, was classified in the *shaping* group.)

Notes

This study was conducted with the able assistance of Susan Wise, and was supported in part by National Institute of Mental Health grant HD-03049 to Jerome S. Bruner and by the Milton Fund of Harvard University. The author is indebted to Jerome S. Bruner, Martin Richards, and Sheldon White for guidance through all phases of the work, and to his colleagues Fred Lighthall and Jack Glidewell for critical readings.

[2]A path analysis diagram is merely a way of visualizing the results of multiple regression. The six arrows converging on SIMPLIFYING, for example, represent six independent variables that competed with one another to ac-

count for the variance in mothers' rates of simplifying the task. Pretest success (or failure) accounted for the largest share of this variance (albeit only $.268^2$, or 7 percent); time looking away during the pretest accounted for about 4 percent additional variance after partialling out pretest success; and error variance, or other variables not measured in the experiment, accounted for the remaining variance.

CHAPTER ELEVEN

Helping Subsystems

John C. Glidewell

In all sorts of societies and cultures there is an old, honorable, and traditional method for dealing with an individual (child or adult) who responds to the demands of the society by acting so badly or strangely that he upsets the system: isolation. Continued social isolation is an experience with which few persons can cope. If *simple* isolation doesn't work, the difficult individual is subjected to a more *complex* detachment. He is temporarily relieved of his usual responsibilities and assigned to a helping dyad—a temporary relationship with a person of special status who is to help him. Sometimes the one-to-one interaction in the dyad is training, sometimes tutoring, sometimes consultation, sometimes treatment, sometimes rehabilitation, sometimes confession, sometimes exorcizing evil spirits, and sometimes it is therapy.

A dyad is the simplest of social systems. In a dyad the nature of the interaction can be most clear and explicit to the two actors. Consider the socialization process in a dyad. Socialization may be defined as a process that begins with learning the likelihood of receiving rewards and punishments from others in response to alternative ways of behaving in a social system. Nowhere are such likelihoods more clear and explicit than in the one-to-one interaction of a dyad.

Reprinted with the permission of the Goodyear Publishing Co. from A Social Psychology of Mental Health in S. E. Golann & C. Eisdorfer (Eds.), *Handbook of Community Mental Health*, New York: Appleton-Century-Crofts, 1972, pp. 230-246.

Helping Subsystems

The helper in the dyad is some person of special status and power based on age, knowledge, skill, or magic. The high-power helper is almost always constrained by social sanction not to abuse his power over his client, to act in his client's best interests, and to try to restore him quickly to his usual responsibilities in the larger system. The deviant client, often in distress, is constrained to cooperate, which usually means trying hard to follow the instructions of the helper.

Characteristic of the helping dyad is some form of privileged communication. The deviant client is expected to expose his personal problems—or personal devils—in his interaction with the helper, but he is protected from a more general exposure and thereby from the social sanctions that would accompany a more general exposure. The privileged communication reduces the costs of errors in behavioral experiments. Connected with this privilege are very close limits on system linkage by interaction—limits on the interchange of ideas and feelings between the subsystem unit and the suprasystem. Even with all the bureaucratic supervision in complex societies, the professional practitioner in the helping professions is very rarely directly observed in the process of interaction with his client or patient. System linkage is confined to overlapping roles (see Merton's conception of the social mechanisms for the articulation of roles in the "role set," 1957).

Under such freedom from observation and limitations on linkage with the larger system, the helper is given license to decide just what the best interests of his client really are (see, for example the work of Blau and Scott, 1962, on professional bureaucracies). This license gives the helper a considerable power over the client and creates a power imbalance. Such power imbalances have at least a slight tendency to change in the direction of balance. This social force interacts with the system constraints on the amount of time available for the helping process. An extended time may, on the one hand, keep the client subservient to the helper to the point of exploitation. It may, on the other hand, limit the power of the helper and increase the power of the client in ways that have been subjected to analysis by several investigators.

Homans has put forth the proposition (1950) that continued interaction between any two persons will increase the dependency of each of the persons on the rewards supplied by the other. The trend of such increased dependencies is toward a balance of power. The helping dyad is a *temporary* system, limiting the balance of power that would accrue from continued interaction. The limitation of the time available is one of the safeguards the larger system places on the tendency for such subsystems to stabilize and become rigid. The doctor must not extend his patient's illness; the lawyer must not prolong litigation indefinitely; the welfare worker must not perpetuate his client's poverty—such rules are made to counteract the tendency for a powerful person to maintain his power.

The opposite social force is not so widely recognized. The continuation may limit rather than increase the power of the helper. If the welfare worker becomes dependent on his client's continued poverty, the client may develop as much power over the worker as the worker has over the client. Thibaut and Kelley (1959) have proposed that if the client (in the low power position) can lengthen his time perspective far enough into the future, he can devaluate the assistance of the helper (in the high power position), reflect question on the skill of the helper, and thereby make the helper dependent on him for the demonstration of his competence. Sometimes children discover how their achievement reflects credit or discredit on a teacher and begin to act on the power that this discovery gives them. (Personal communication, 1968, from Dan Lortie suggests that his interviews with teachers show that children are the primary source of reward for teachers.) Such a dependency creates a balance of power.

Given the limitations on power equalization placed by the larger system on the life of the dyad, one might expect other power-balancing forces to be generated. Following Emerson (1962) and Secord and Backman (1964), one would expect that a prime effort of the deviant client toward a power balance would be an assignment of increasing value to the assistance of the helper. Such increasing value would tend to justify the power the client awards to the helper. He is "getting" valuable help in return for the power he "gives" the helper. Two findings are related to this phenomenon. Thibaut and Kelley (1959) found that the more powerful person in a dyad is a better able to keep the values with which he enters the relationship; the less powerful is more likely to change them. If, in addition, the client entered the dyad by choice—and many deviants do ask for help in their distress—he often tries to decrease the tension generated by perceiving the chosen alternative (the help received) to be increasingly more valuable. Brehm's (1956) experiment demonstrated this tendency to increase the value assigned to a chosen alternative. A prime norm of almost all systems is that power is obtained in exchange for instrumental help (Blau, 1954). Under such an arrangement a common sequence of events ensues. Clients receive valuable help, become more acceptable to the larger system, are relieved of assignment to the helping dyad, and are returned to their usual responsibilities in the larger system. The cause of the change in the behavior would be attributed to the acts of the more powerful helper, as had been shown by Thibaut and Riecken (1955 a & b). The operation of such social forces probably accounts for much of the long and honorable tradition—and effectiveness—of the helping dyad in so many societies.

There are conditions, however, under which the client does not assign much value to the assistance of the helper, and the failure of reciprocity persists. Following Emerson again, one would expect the client to attempt to withdraw from the dyad—against the helper's professional advice. It is from just such forces that many helping dyads are terminated while they are still in process.

Withdrawal is often difficult. Sanctions from the larger system often make withdrawal more costly to the client than continued interaction in the helping dyad, as costly as it may be. Under such conditions one might expect the client to begin to ration his positive responses to the helper—gratitude, approval, conformity, esteem—and thereby achieve some control over the rewards available to the helper. A number of students have observed this phenomenon (Newcomb, 1961; Thibaut & Kelley, 1959; Emerson, 1962). To the extent that the helper becomes dependent on his client for such status-reinforcing rewards, the client will have achieved greater power in the dyad. In order to limit the dependency of the helper on his client for positive evaluation, most systems are designed to provide primary status-reinforcing rewards to the helper from the larger system.

Within the time and reward-control limits set by the larger system, there are still other psychosocial forces that act to bring the power in the helping dyad into balance. The client may extend the power network as described by Emerson (1962). If he can establish relationships with other legitimate helpers, he has options about whose instructions to follow. Inherent in the helping dyad there is one set of forces that generates a very common extension of the power network. Helpers, being persons of special status committed to the best interests of the client, find themselves identifying with the client. His costs and benefits become their costs and benefits. Such expressive ties often come into conflict with the instrumental requirements of the helper's role. To confront the client with his distortions of reality is to cause him pain and distress. To cause the client pain and distress is also to cause the helper pain and distress. The helper finds himself in the typical conflict of the person who undertakes to perform both instrumental and expressive roles in the same interaction. This conflict motivates both members of the dyad to seek a third role. These are the forces that lead to the formation of a helping *triad.*

John C. Glidewell

THE HELPING TRIAD

It may be that if one examined the informal as well as the formal helping systems, the helping functions are always performed by a triad. Even where the dyad is the formally established structure, one may well find a third person functioning informally in a high-status expressive role, complementing the high-status instrumental role of the formally designated helper. Roethlisberger and Dickson (1939) noted such triads in the Hawthorne Plant; Homans (1950) observed them in Firth's (1936) reports of socialization among the Tikopia; Blau (1955) found such triads in the informal organization of a government bureau. Freilich (1964) has made a discerning analysis of natural triads in both simple kinship systems and more complex social systems. Although Freilich was interested in a more general phenomenon, by following his lead one may explicate some powerful psychosocial forces influencing helping functions in social systems. Following is an attempt at such an explication.

The proposition is that the upsetting tensions that are induced by failures of socialization are often managed by a natural triad. The triad always includes a high-status instrumental figure responsible for the success of the socialization or rehabilitation process, a high-status expressive figure responsible for expressive support and tension relief, and a low-status subordinate (the deviant client) whose behavior is not satisfactory—his bad or strange behavior is upsetting the people in the system. Freilich was interested in the typical tensions induced by the usual socialization process and the use of the triad to manage those tensions. Here the interest is in the more intense tensions, induced by inequities of social control or support producing bad or strange behavior. The functions of the triad should become even more clear and explicit under such conditions.

The roots of the social forces leading to the formation of helping triads may be found in the wide prevalence of this basic form. Benne and Sheats (1948), Carter (1954), Bales and Slater (1955), Slater (1965), and others have observed that in the development of small groups, the "task" leadership role, supplying instrumental inputs, is regularly complemented by a second central role supplying expressive inputs. The functions of this very common role differentiation have been described as (a) reduction of conflict in the instrumental leader by relieving him of demands for expressive inputs, (b) management of the tensions induced in the group by the necessary demands for control from the instrumental, task-oriented role, and (c) modifying and extending the power structure of the group.

Studies of more primitive societies have also revealed the wide prevalence of the basic form of the helping triad. In patrilineal societies the triad is formed the father, the mother's brother, and the son. In an analysis of the reports of Firth (1936) Homans clearly described the expressive input and the tension management connected with the role of the mother's brother in Tikopia. "In all the great occasions of life . . . the mother's brother acts as an older friend . . . and helps him [the son] over the rough places . . . Emotionally the relationship between them is friendly, free, and easy . . ."

It should be clear by now that the mother's brother is a practical and emotional necessity to a Tikopia man (Homans, 1950, p. 218). Freilich (1964) describes the general from of the triad in patrilineal societies as follows:

> The father has jural authority over ego: he has the right to give orders and ego has the obligation to obey them. This relation, between a superior and an inferior, is often marked by formality and considerable restraint, while relations between ego and his mother's brother are characterized by ease and freedom. The mother's brother, though superior in status to ego, frequently plays the role of intimate friend, adviser, and helper. The . . . triad . . . exists in many societies including Batak, Gilyak, Karadjeri, Lakher, Lhota, Lovedu, Mbundu, Mende, Murngin, Sema, Venda, Wik-Munkan and Tikopia. (p. 530)

The triad also appears in matrilineal societies, but there it is the mother's brother who has jural authority over the child while the father performs the expressive role of friend, confidant, and supporter. Such matrilineal triads are found, according to Freilich, among the Trobriand Islanders, the Haida, the Tlinget, and the Pende.

Zelditch (1955) studied the family structures of 56 societies and found that in 46 of them a clear differentiation between the instrumental and expressive role occurred. Bernard (1942), Parsons and Bales (1955), and Bronfenbrenner (1961) differ about whether the mother or the father is more likely to perform the instrumental or expressive role in the American family, but all agree that this particular differentiation in parent-parent-child triads is widely prevalent. Where the differentiation is absent, role conflict and incompatibility are more common.

A triad of the same structure can be found in most bureaucracies. There is a high-status figure who ensures compliance with rules, but the low-status worker confronted with a knotty problem will consult a friendly colleague—high in the informal power structure—before he takes the risk of exposing his difficulties to the person in the high-status instrumental role. Such triads have been found in government agencies (Blau, 1955); in prisons where the warden, the chaplain, and the prisoner form the triad; it is indicated in hospitals where the physician, the nurse, and the patient take the three roles; in high schools where the principal, the counselor, and the student are the actors (Stringer, 1959); and in mental health centers where the psychiatrist, the social worker, and the patient form the triad.

It seems reasonable to conclude that any consideration of the helping functions of a social system should take account of the triadic structures within the system, even if it is necessary to look closely into the informal interactions within the system.

Given that the helping triad has evolved as a psychosocial structure for coping with the tensions of inequities between social support and social control, one may turn to an analysis of the nature of the psychosocial forces that are generated to produce the helping function in the triad.

The helping triad aids in mitigating the power problems of the dyad. Extending the network to the high-status supporter offers alternative benefits to the client, but because the supporter is expressive and supportive only, he does not offer a competitive substitute for the instrumental helper. It becomes harder to withdraw from the triad than the dyad, because it is harder to find more attractive and equally supportive alternative arrangements. It is particularly effective in providing positive affection and friendship while avoiding the undermining of the helper's power by making him subject to demands from the client based on duties to supply friendship or affectional support.

The triad is particularly adaptable to power balancing based on coalition formation. Beginning with the observations of Simmel (1950), a long line of research has substantiated the tendency of triads to form into coalitions of two persons exerting influence on the third (Mills, 1954; Caplow, 1956; Vinacke & Arkoff, 1957; Gamson, 1961).

If one assumes a norm of reciprocity (Gouldner, 1960) that maintains the change in output from an actor equal to the changes in input, one may deduce the impact of the social forces generated when a helping triad is created as an open system.

The environment isolates the deviant and thereby the environment reduces both instrumental and expressive output to the deviant. The other aspect of the isolation lies in the fact that the deviant reduces both instrumental and expressive output to the environment. The deviant and the environment thus create a vacuous reciprocity; or, as is more often the case, any existing violations of reciprocity are temporarily suspended by the cessation of interchanges.

The instrumental helper must increase his instrumental output to the deviant. This increased output of instrumental resources by the helper must be balanced by a reduced instrumental output to either the supporter or the environment. Because the system does not relieve the helper of his usual responsibilities, he cannot reduce his output to the environment without failing in those responsibilities. The reduction must be in his instrumental output to the supporter.

The expressive supporter must increase his expressive output to the deviant. He, too, must maintain his responsibilities in the suprasystem. The increased output of expressive resources by the supporter is counterbalanced by a reduction in expressive acts toward the helper. The changes discussed thus far leave the helper relatively deprived of expressive resources; the supporter relatively deprived of instrumental resources; and the deviant relatively well supplied with both instrumental and expressive resources. Forces thus exist to reduce the "privileged" position of the deviant and reduce the costs to the helper and supporter. If rehabilitation of the deviant is rapid, the triad can tolerate such a violation of reciprocity, concentrating its resources on the "treatment" of the deviant, and no further changes may appear until the triad and system are rewarded by conformity from the deviant—and the triad is dissolved. The added responsibilities (outputs) of the helper and supporter and the lack of linkage with the suprasystem are compensated for by the rewards from the system for quick return of the deviant to the system.

If the rehabilitation requires a more extended time, however, the helper and supporter are motivated to improve the equity of their positions in the triad, and the suprasystem seeks linkages to maintain surveillance and to prevent prolongation of the isolation of the triad. Typically, interchange with the deviant is avoided, and the system seeks some additional interchange with the helper and the supporter. Considering that the instrumental resources of the helper are already taxed, he tends to add an expressive output usually by entering into an expressive, supportive role with a person outside the triad. This additional output must be compensated for, and the tendency is to reduce the privileged position of the deviant by decreasing the helper's expressive output to him. In a similar manner the expressive supporter is constrained to enter an instrumental role with a person outside the triad and reduce his instrumental output to the deviant. These actions also (a) make both the instrumental and expressive roles more nearly "pure," and (b) establish a linking extension of the network of power and sentiment.

To review the analysis in quantitative form, assuming an open system, the changes occurring in the triad of helper, supporter, and deviant are as follows: (1) En (environment) decreases both I (instrumental) and E (expressive) output to D (deviant). (2) D reduces both I and E output to En. (3) H (helper) increases I output to D. (4) H reduced I output to S (supporter). (5) S increases E output to D. (6) S reduces E output to H. If rehabilitation takes more time, these additional steps occur. (7) H increases E output to En. (8) H reduces E output to D. (9) S increases I output to En. (10) S reduces I output to D.

Restating this process in algebraic terms (subscripts designate steps in the sequence above):

$$
\begin{array}{llll}
-H(+I_3-I_4+E_7-E_8) & +S(-I_4 \qquad) & +D(+I_3-E_8) & +En(+E_7 \qquad)=0. \\
+H(-E_6 \qquad) & -S(+E_5-E_6+I_9-I_{10}) & +D(+E_5-I_{10}) & +En(+I_9 \qquad)=0. \\
+H(\qquad) & +S(\qquad) & -D(-I_2-E_2) & +En(-I_2-E_2)=0. \\
+H(\qquad) & +S(\qquad) & +D(-I_1-E_1) & -En(-I_1-E_1)=0.
\end{array}
$$

These equations are identities. Each shows that the total change in output from the actors (H,S,D, and En) is equal to the total change in input from each actor to the others. The algebraic additions, although not included here, can by performed for each column of this set of equations and represent the reciprocity existing after the changes are induced by creation of the helping triad.

These changes leave the deviant in balance, but the helper and the supporter are not (see Fig. 11-1). The helper is still deprived of expressive resources, and the supporter is still deprived of instrumental resources because of the uncompensated reduced output from each other. The same resources are oversupplied to the environment. If such resources are forthcoming from any source—deviant, environment, or each other—the triad will reach a balanced state within itself and with its environment and it will continue beyond its appointed time. Such balanced states occur when the suprasystem is rewarded by the continued isolation of the deviant, as with psychotic persons and retardates. For the triad to serve its purposes as a temporary system, the reduced interaction and deprivation of the helper and the supporter must be tolerated until the triad is terminated, with or without successfully inducing an accommodation between the deviant and the system. (This analysis has been greatly influenced by the quantitative formulations of Herbst, 1954, 1957. The reader may want to compare these with Herbst's algebraic forms.) The following sections contain further elaborations of the actions of these social forces.

The usual constraints obtain in the triad. The high-status figures, instrumental or expressive, are not to abuse their power. They are to act in the client's best interests, according to their judgments of his best interests and they are to try hard to restore him quickly to his usual responsibilities or duties in the larger system. The client is constrained to seek the instructions of the instrumental figure and to seek support and understanding from the expressive figure. The privileged communication is extended to the third role, and in fact, some communications between the client and the expressive supporter are not available to the instrumental helper. Most typically the client may express his hostility toward the instrumental helper only in communication with the expressive supporter—and in confidence—to avoid the sanctions that the larger system expects its agent, the instrumental helper, to invoke, Conversely, communication with the instrumental helper may be repeated to the expressive supporter without concern, because the original communication was usually carefully selected by

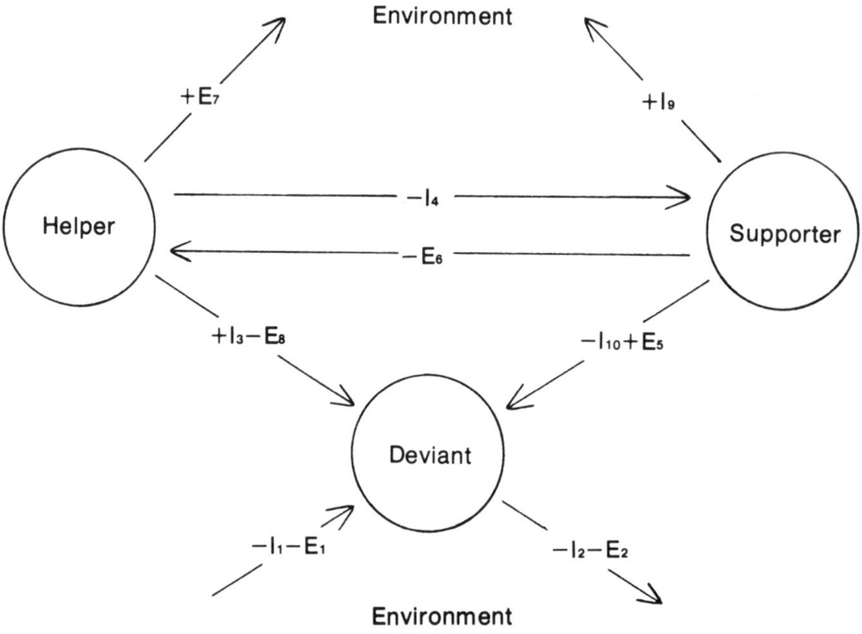

Fig. 1. A graphic representation of the changes generated by establishing a helpful triad. ("I" represents instrumental outputs. "E" represents expressive outputs. Subscripts designate steps in the sequence of creating the subsystem.)

the client, and because the expressive helper is not under constraint from the larger system to invoke sanctions.

As has been proposed by a number of students (e.g., Homans, 1950), the high-status expressive role acts as a check on the possible exploitation of the power of the high-status instrumental role. Should the actor in the high-status instrumental role become corrupt and use his power to extract resources (objects, ideas, or sentiments) from his client, the high-status expressive actor would become aware of the corruption. Through his linkage to the larger system and his status in it, the supporter could invoke sanctions against the instrumental actor to end his exploitation.

A second psychosocial force induced in the triad is generated by the tension incident to the demands made by the instrumental helper. If the instrumental helper is to correct the bad or strange behavior of his client, he must necessarily place his client in positions in which the client must suppress his urges to act in socially disapproved ways. Accordingly, he must induce tensions in his client. In Freilich's terms he feeds tensions into the system. Ordinarily, the tensions are generated in the helper when the low-status person experiments with new or unusual modes of behavior in seeking an adaptation between himself and the system. The client, feeling his urges frustrated by the demands of the helper, experiences negative feelings toward the helper. No matter how carefully the helper is trained to accept and work with such negative feelings from clients, the larger system, of which the helper is an agent, disapproves of them. The client, like all low-power persons, screens his communications to the high-power helper. The client finds it easier and less guilt-producing to express his negative feelings about the helper to the supporter, who is not a control agent of the larger system and need not invoke sanctions. Thus, the tensions in the individuals, induced by the system, are relieved.

The analysis of tension reduction thus far has not included the interaction between the high-status helper and the high-status supporter. The helper is acting as an agent of the larger system to help in the socialization of a client who behaves badly or strangely. His role requires that the helper restrain some of the urges that come naturally to him—to seek gratitude from the client, or to coerce compliance from the client, to moderate unusual experiments, or to temper demands on the client. He must absorb some of the tension his actions generate. Coordinately, the supporter also must restrain some of his natural urges—to criticize the instrumental helper, to express negative feelings toward the client, or to invoke sanctions on the client. He, too, absorbs some of the tensions generated in the system. The internal tension management acts mainly to change the deviant to fit the system. There is potential, however, to change the system to accommodate to the deviant.

In the basic analysis the point was made that the relief of the deviant's usual responsibilities to the system means a reduction of output from the triad to the system. As was indicated, such reduction is often compensated for by an increase in the output of expressive resources from the instrumental helper and an increase in the output of instrumental resources from the expressive helper. These forces lead to tension management by system linkage. To the extent that the helper feels some tension due to his interchange with his client, his tensions can be relieved by performing the expressive supporter role vis-a-vis another client. Similarly, the supporter may perform the instrumental helper vis-a-vis another client. The tension-management network is thus extended into the larger system, and the possibilities for complementary and reciprocal interchanges of tension induction and tension relief are multiplied.

It is the extension of the network—the subsystem linkages—that gives the helping triad its major potential as an agency for social change induction in the suprasystem. First, extension of the network manages tensions induced in both helper and supporter by any markedly unusual or innovative experiments mounted by the deviant client in trying to find an accommodation to the suprasystem. For example, a former member of an illicit gang may substitute social service to the deprived for open rebellion. Such a substitution may make the helper nervous about his client's good intentions. If, however, he is offering expressive support to another client's experiments, he must resolve the dissonance between withholding trust from the first client's experiment while supporting that of another client. *One possible* resolution is a change of perception about what sorts of experimental behavior are acceptable and trustworthy—the beginning of a change of expectation and eventually a change of norms. The linkage also provides a channel for diffusion for successful accommodation-producing experiments.

The helping triad also generates forces in the direction of what Heider (1958) and his students have called "congruence of sentiment" (see especially the summary in Berger et al., 1962). Considering first the internal exchange (Heider analyzes a closed system), where socialization has not been effective and the individual behaves badly or strangely, the relationship between him and the instrumental helper to whom he is assigned is expected to be negative. Further, the relationship between the client and the expressive supporter is expected to be positive. According to Heider's theory, the relationship between the helper and the supporter should be negative—unless the the two high-status figures remain out of contact with one another and thus achieve a vacuous balance. Under conditions of regular contact the helper and supporter would experience a negative relationship. The helper would resent the positive expressions to the supporter by the deviant client, and the supporter would resent the demands made on the client by the instrumental helper.

To reduce the negative feelings, the supporter is constrained to advise the client of the wisdom and competence of the instrumental helper. While he expresses sympathy for and understanding of the distress of the client, he also reaffirms the value that the distress is a necessary condition to achieve the accommodation of the deviant to the system. Within itself, the helping triad is not an instrument of social change. It evolved to change the individual to fit the society, not the society to accommodate the individual.

When mothers have taken on the role of supporter of a child in psychotherapy, the outcome frequently is that the mother resents the therapist and the therapist resents the mother. Under some conditions social workers in clinics have taken on the supporter role in complementation to the psychiatrist's instrumental role, and the negative relationship emerging between the two has presented a problem in staff relationships, often resulting in reduced or overly formal interactions to achieve a vacuous balance.

On the other hand, returning to the position that the triad is an open system, interaction between the helper and the supporter in other subsystems often leads to positive relationships between them. Again, according to Heider's theory, if the positive relationship is to continue, some change in the relationship of each with the client must take place. Either the helper-client relationship must become positive, yielding the balance of all positive relationships, or the supporter-client relationship must become negative.

The first case occurs when the deviant's behavior changes to conform to the norms of the total system, at which point the deviant resumes his usual responsibilities and the triad is dissolved. The second case occurs when the client's deviancy becomes so great that there is a cessation of interaction with him (as in the observations of Festinger, Schachter, & Back, 1950; Schachter, 1951; Emerson, 19 54). Again, the triad is dissolved as a helping subsystem.

The foregoing analysis indicates a balance of forces in the helping triad that tends to keep the deviant (1) isolated from the larger system, (2) under stress to modify his behavior to fit the norms of the larger system, in a position to experiment with new accommodations with the two high-status figures, and (3) supported in the distress due to the tensions he feels. The two high-status figures are induced to (1) reduce the rate of interaction with each other, (2) tolerate negative sentiments between them, and (3) seek to reduce those negative sentiments by achieving an accommodation between the deviant and the instrumental helper and thus return the deviant to his usual responsibilities in the larger system.

HELPING SUBSYSTEMS AND SOCIAL CHANGE

Increasing size, complexity, and density of modern societies has engendered forces of social change and has provided a setting highly conducive to the extension of the helping networks of the natural triad. It became more necessary to return the deviant to the society in some condition more adaptive than the *status quo ante.* There appeared in all sorts of creeds and movements a call for prevention of new deviancies and for contributing to "growth." Nowhere was the call more strong and clear than in the child guidance movement.

The child guidance clinic: An expansion of the triad.

The early orthopsychiatric interest in children was developed in the context of urbanization, increasing size and complexity, but decreasing facility of subsystem linkage, especially the linkage between the health institution, the educational institution, and the neighborhood. It began in the 1920s and grew fastest in the post World War II 1940s and 1950s. (The growth of ideology and practice can be traced in the collection of papers published in the *American Journal of Orthopsychiatry* between 1930 and 1957, edited by Tulchin, 1964.) The child guidance clinic was developed as an innovation within the health institution, perhaps as much to induce social change in child-rearing practices as to treat disorders of children. It called itself "orthopsychiatric" because it proposed to straighten the bent twig so that the tree might grow straight. While it concentrated upon the treatment of children, such treatment was believed to prevent mental illnesses in adults. Furthermore, the leaders of the movement thought the family was the most appropriate treatment unit and took the position that family treatment could prevent illnesses in the healthy children belonging to the same family as the treated ill children (Stevenson & Smith, 1934; Lowrey, 1957). The extension of the traditional doctor-patient dyad to a team-patient-family network had all the potential linkages for an extended, social-change-inducing network—but the linkages were potential only.

The child guidance clinic was manned by a team of both medical and nonmedical specialists, but the codes of medical practice were carefully followed—codes for helping *dyads*. In the eyes of the community medical practice was clearly the legitimized practice. Psychologists and social workers—explicitly or implicitly—found it easier to establish the legitimacy of their professional services when they associated themselves with "the doctor" and followed his dyadic codes and customs in "taking care of the patient." During the 1930s, to the patient who was ill and in distress, the doctor's codes and customs were appropriate. The practice of medicine had an excellent reputation for relieving distress and curing illnesses (Stevenson & Smith, 1934; Ackerman, 1945).

However, there were complications. The social role of the child who had the measles was quite clear to the family and the neighborhood. He was relieved of his usual responsibilities at school and at home. He was kept in bed, and he was expected to do the best he could to get well and resume his responsibilities as soon as possible. Getting well as soon as possible meant following the doctor's orders, and his parents were the agents of the doctor. They sympathized with the child's distress at having to stay in bed and take the foul-tasting medicine, but they assured the child of the doctor's wisdom and saw to it that the doctor's orders were followed. (This view of the social role of the ill person was much influenced by the conceptions of Parsons, 1951, 1958.) In helping a child recover from an infectious disease, the classic helping triad was altogether effective and rewarding for both the actors and the suprasystem. No extensions were mounted. Social change was unnecessary.

When a child had a phobia, however, his social role was not so clear as it was when he had the measles. He was rarely taken out of school, and when he was, the act was often considered to be illegitimate. He had to stay out of bed and discharge his usual responsibilities, no matter how crippling his phobic distress might be.

When a child had the measles, he had done enough when he followed the doctor's orders, but in the child guidance clinic the child was often told that relief from his distress depended as much on his own efforts as upon the doctor's—but there were very few clear-cut doctor's orders (Allen, 1934). The instrumental nature of the doctor's role was blurred. To complicate matters further, his parents were by no means the doctor's expressive agents. They were patients, too. The traditional helping triad was disrupted. The roles were confused, and the expected relationships were denied by the doctor.

Parents, however, often insisted on continuing what had worked so well in the past. They did not accept the role of the patient. They did not perceive themselves to be ill—nor did the family or neighborhood. In an effort to meet their responsibilities in the traditional triadic subsystem they took the role of the doctor's expressive agents, in spite of the clinic's advice, and tried sympathetically to implement what they inferred to be the doctor's advice—and added more confusion. Sometimes, in a traditional attempt to extend the power network, the parents told the teacher of the doctor's advice, and often found that the teacher confirmed their view that the doctor's advice was rather hard to understand and difficult to follow (see, for example, the report of Lowrey, 1934).

The role of the parent in the helping triad, altogether complementary and reciprocal in treating a child for an acute infectious disease, was vague, overlapping, inequitable, and confused when used in treating a family for a chronic, noninfectious distress that might not be a disease at all. As the contact of the clinic with the family grew, so did the tensions.

At the point at which the school referred a child to the clinic still further complications arose. In addition to the parents the teacher was involved. It was not often explicit whether the teacher, too, was a patient, but it was often implied, in the interchange between the teacher and the clinic team (such as it was), that the teacher's behavior in the classroom probably aggravated, if it did not induce, the child's distress. Furthermore, it was often explicitly stated that the teacher *could* become a therapeutic agent—an agent of the doctor—if only she could develop the proper relationship with the child—and the proper "therapeutic skills"—if she could just be more like a clinician (Tri-state Conference, 1962).

Analyses of the sources of tension in these attempts at system linkage have been widely reported from Crestwood Heights (Seeley, Sim & Loosley, 1956), from the Wellesley group (Elizabeth Lindemann, 1957), from New York City (New York City Board of Education, 1955), from St. Louis County (Glidewell & Stringer, 1967), from Sumter County, South Carolina (Newton & Brown, 1967), and from various reports of school psychologists (Tri-state Conference, 1962; Cutts, 1955).

The interdisciplinary child guidance clinic, however, had enough staff to provide a differentiated expressive, supporting role—often through a social worker. The tensions inherent in the helping triad, however, could not be readily managed. The production of negative sentiments between doctor and social worker became apparent. It was not as easy to reduce the rate of interaction between doctor and social worker on the same staff as between doctor and mother. (The reduction did sometimes occur, however, and the isolation was often attributed to personality conflicts.) Roles were rather fixed, and it was not as easy to reverse roles in extended relationships with other deviants in the larger systems.

Enter community mental health.

It is not surprising that a more extensive system linkage began to develop in other directions. Community mental health, as conceived in the 1950s, required of the practitioner more role flexibility in the interchanges between the clinic and the community. Much has been written of the demands of community mental health, but for the purposes of this analysis the relevant demands were (a) that instrumental roles be differentiated from expressive roles, (b) that the instrumental practitioner add some expressive roles to his repertoire when he entered the community, and (c) that the professional practitioner share some of his instrumental and expressive roles with nonprofessional community agents—both policy making and policy implementing.

Community boards, first formed to be expressive and supportive adjuncts to the doctors, became instrumental in influencing intake policies, fees for services, and even professional roles. Alternation of instrumental and expressive roles with respect to patients, parents, and teachers evolved.

The voluntary mental health association was often formed to support the clinic and reduce the tension between the clinic, the family, and the school. It was, however, expected to take minimum initiative, to support "the professionals," and develop community goodwill largely through mass media—all in all, to take the expressive supporting role. Community opinion leaders were often sought as leaders of the association in an effort to extend the power network upward—to link to powerful, high-status supportive roles—but to support doctors as well as, or even more than, patients. Such support directly opposed the social forces "naturally" generated in the helping triad.

The later development of the indigenous mental health worker was another attempt to extend the power network, but this time downward. The indigenous worker could speak the language of the family and provide for a successful interchange in what had been a blocked one. Whether the role is to remain only expressive and supportive is in question, but it represents the nearest parallel to the former parental supportive role in the triad subsystem—and it provides extensive linkages to many families in a neighborhood. Accordingly, indigenous workers may introduce a social change potential not before available, especially if they develop both instrumental and expressive roles—instrumental with one family, expressive with another.

In summary, perhaps the great promise of community mental health is that it is breaking up the static, social order maintenance function of the traditional helping triad. It is experimenting with a variety of extensions and linkages of helping subsystems and community institutions. The evolution is still in progress, but if the foregoing analysis has validity, it is through just such extensions—both upward into powerful resource-allocating groups and downward into resource-utilizing groups—that helping subsystems can give appropriate attention to modifying expectations, norms, and roles, in both subsystems and suprasystems, so that they may accommodate to wider variations in individual behavior.

A SUMMARY STATEMENT

The critical aspect of social order and social change as an influence on individual mental health lies in its effect on the accommodation between the individual and the systems of which he is a member. If, in the perception of the individual, the equity of the interchange of resources (motives, emotions, ideas, skills, objects) between him and the system is enhanced, mental health is enhanced; if the perceived equity is reduced, mental health is reduced.

There has evolved a powerful structure—the helping triad—for facilitating the "correction" or "treatment" of individuals whose behavior is so strange or bad or sick that they upset the system. The triad has a considerable effectiveness in managing the tensions of the helping process. It does not have, however, such effectiveness as an agent of social change except when the unit is linked with other such units in the suprasystem. Current innovations in helping structures developing in community mental health may be seen as attempts to create a helping system with extended linkages that will do as much to modify the system to accommodate to the individual as to modify the individual to accommodate to the system.

References

Ackerman, N. W. What constitutes intensive psychotherapy in a child guidance clinic. *American Journal of Orthopsychiatry*, 1945, *15*, 711–720.

Allen, F. H. Therapeutic work with children. *American Journal of Orthopsychiatry*, 1934, *4*, 193–202.

Bales, R. F. & Slater, P. E. Role differentiation in small decision-making groups. In T. Parsons & R. Bales (Eds.), *Family, Socialization, and Interaction Process*. Glencoe, Ill.: Free Press, 1955.

Benne, K. D. & Sheats, P. Functional roles of group members. *Journal of Social Issues*, 1948, *4* (2), 41–49.

Berger, J., Cohen, B. P., Snell, J. L., & Zelditch, M. *Types of Formalization in Small Group Research*. Boston: Houghton Mifflin, 1962.

Bernard, J. *American Family Behavior*. New York: Harper, 1942.

Blau, P. M. *The Dynamics of Bureaucracy*. Chicago: University of Chicago Press, 1955.

Blau, P. M. Patterns of interaction among a group of officials in a government agency. *Human Relations*, 1954, *7*, 337–348.

Blau, P. M. & Scott, W. R. *Formal Organizations: A Comparative Approach*. San Francisco: Chandler, 1962.

Brehm, J. Postdecision changes in the desirability of alternatives. *Journal of Abnormal and Social Psychology*, 1956, *52*, 384–389.

Bronfenbrenner, U. Toward a theoretical model for the analysis of parent-child relationships in a social context. In J. Glidewell (Ed.), *Parental Attitudes and Child Behavior*. Springfield, Ill.: Charles C. Thomas, 1961.

Caplow, T. A theory of coalitions in the triad. *American Sociological Review*, 1956, *21*, 489–493.

Carter, L. Evaluating the performance of individuals as members of small groups. *Personnel Psychology*, 1954, *7*, 477–484.

Cutts, N. E. (Ed.) *School Psychologist at Mid-Century*. Washington, D. C.: American Psychological Association, 1955.

Emerson, R. M. Deviation and rejection: An experimental replication. *American Sociological Review*, 1954, *19*, 688–693.

Emerson, R. M. Power-dependence relations. *American Sociological Review*, 1962, *27*, 31–41.

Festinger, L., Schachter, S. & Back, K. *Social Pressures in Informal Groups*. New York: Harper, 1950.

Firth, R. *We, the Tikopia*. London: George Allen & Unwin, 1936.

Freilich, M. The Natural Triad in Kinship and Complex Systems. *American Sociological Review*, 1964, *29*, 529–540.

Gamson, W. A. A theory of coalition formation. *American Sociological Review*, 1961, *26*, 373–382.

Glidewell, J. C. & Stringer, L. A. The educational institution and the health institution. In E. M. Bower & W. G. Hollister (Eds.), *Behavioral Science Frontiers in Education*. New York: Wiley, 1967.

Gouldner, A. W. The norm of reciprocity: A preliminary statement. *American Sociological Review*, 1960, *25*, 161–178.

Heider, F. *The Psychology of Interpersonal Relations*. New York: Wiley, 1958.

Herbst, P. G. An analysis of social flow systems. *Human Relations*, 1954, *7*, 327–336.

Herbst, P. G. Measurement of behavior structures by means of input-output data. *Human Relations*, 1957, *10*, 335–346.

Homans, G. C. *The Human Group*. New York: Harcourt, Brace, 1950.

Lindemann, E. Mental health in the classroom: The Wellesley experience. Paper presented at the annual meeting of the American Psychological Association, New York, September 1957.

Lowrey, L. G. Orthopsychiatry and prevention: Historical perspective. *American Journal of Orthopsychiatry*, 1957, *27*, 223–225.

Lowrey, L. G. Treatment of behavior problems. *American Journal of Orthopsychiatry*, 1934, *4*, 120–137.

Merton, R. K. *Social Theory and Social Structure*. Glencoe, Ill.: Free Press, 1957.

Mills, T. M. The coalition pattern in three-person groups. *American Sociological Review*, 1954, *19*, 657–667.

Newcomb, T. M. *The Acquaintance Process*. New York: Holt, Rinehart and Winston, 1961.

Newton, R. & Brown, R. A preventive approach to developmental problems in children. In E. M. Bower & W. G. Hollister (Eds.), *Behavioral Science Frontiers in Education*. New York: Wiley, 1967.

New York City Board of Education. *The Bureau of Child Guidance in the New York City Schools*. New York: Board of Education, 1955.

Parsons, T. Definition of health and illness in the light of American values and social structure. In E. G. Jaco (Ed.), *Patients, Physicians, and Illnesses*. Glencoe, Ill.: Free Press, 1958.

Parsons, T. *The Social System*. Glencoe, Ill.: Free Press, 1951.

Parsons, T. & Bales, R. F. *Family Socialization and Interaction Process*. Glencoe, Ill.: Free Press, 1955.

Roethlisberger, F. J. & Dickson, W. J. *Management and the Worker*. Cambridge, Mass.: Harvard University Press, 1939.

Schachter, S. Deviation, rejection and communication. *Journal of Abnormal and Social Psychology*, 1951, *46*, 190–207.

Secord, P. F. & Backman, C. W. *Social Psychology*. New York: McGraw-Hill, 1964.

Seeley, J., Sim, R. & Loosely, E. *Crestwood Heights*. New York: Basic Books, 1956.

Simmel, G. *The Sociology of Georg Simmel*. (Trans. & ed. by K. H. Wolff) Glencoe, Ill.: Free Press, 1950.

Slater, P. E. Role differentiation in small Groups. In A. Hare, E. Borgatta & R. Bales (Eds.), *Small Groups: Studies in Social Interaction*. New York: Knopf, 1965.

Stevenson, G. S. & Smith, G. *Child Guidance Clinics*. New York: Commonwealth Fund, 1934.

Stringer, L. A. Problems in the administration of school mental health programs. In Proceedings of the Regional Conference on the Health of School

Age Children, Chapel Hill, North Carolina. Washington, D.C.: Children's Bureau, United States Department of Health, Education, and Welfare, 1959.

Thibaut, J. W. & Kelley, H. H. *The Social Psychology of Groups*. New York: Wiley, 1959.

Thibaut, J. W. & Riecken, H. W. Authoritarianism, status, and the communication of aggression. *Human Relations*, 1955, *8*, 95–120. (a)

Thibaut, J. W. & Riecken, H. W. Some determinants and consequences of the perception of social causality. *Journal of Personality*, 1955, *24*, 113–133. (b)

Tri-state Conference on School Psychology, *Proceedings*, 1962.

Tulchin, S. H. (Ed.) *Child Guidance*. New York: American Orthopsychiatric Association, 1964.

Vinacke, W. E. & Arkoff, A. An experimental study of coalitions in the triad. *American Sociological Review*, 1957, *22*, 406–414.

Zelditch, M. Role differentiation in the nuclear family: A comparative study. In T. Parsons & R. F. Bales (Eds.), *Family Socialization and Interaction Process*. Glencoe, Ill.: Free Press, 1955.

Name Index

Name Index

A

B

C

D

Name Index

Subject Index

Subject Index

Subject Index